SHORT-TERM COUNSELING: A PSYCHOANALYTIC APPROACH

SHORT-TERM COUNSELING: A PSYCHOANALYTIC APPROACH

Barbara W. Tilley, M.S.W.

INTERNATIONAL UNIVERSITIES PRESS, INC.
New York New York

Library of Congress Cataloging in Publication Data

Tilley, Barbara W.
Short-term counseling.

Bibliography: p.
Includes index.
1. Short-term counseling. I. Title. [DNLM: 1. Counseling—methods. 2. Psychotherapy, Brief. WM 420 T576s]
BF637.C6T55 1984 616.89′14 84-9008
ISBN 0-8236-6072-9

Manufactured in the United States of America

Contents

Acknowledgments

Those who have enriched, inspired and given of themselves in fostering my professional growth and clinical competence over the years deserve my special appreciation for their contributions to this volume. First are the patients in my clinic and private practice from whom I gained respect for the human spirit as I grew and developed insights along with them. I dedicate this book to them and to two teachers and colleagues, Katherine W. Dunlap, M.S.W., whose wisdom, clinical acuity and humanity have left an imprint which is reflected throughout these pages; and Melvin Bornstein, M.D., for his stimulating guidance in weekly consultations over many years. I recall with pleasure our discussions ranging widely over theory, clinical techniques, the changing social climate affecting the nature and symptomatology of our clients, and not least his sensitive and acute comments on my cases, quickly picking up my errors and omissions and setting me on the right path. I want to express my warm appreciation to Mrs. Dunlap and Dr. Bornstein for their recent careful reading and criticism of my manuscript.

To Lyle E. Ward, M.S.W., I offer special thanks for his many years of loyalty and support as a friend and colleague, and for his helpful suggestions in preparing this volume. I am deeply grateful to Martha Gizynski, Ph.D., who generously spared time from work on her own forthcoming book on clinical theory, to read and comment on my manuscript and suggest clinical additions and references, and to Sidney H. Grossberg, Ph.D., for reading and criticizing an early version of the manuscript and encouraging me to pursue the project.

Kathleen Keegan, M.S.W., has been associated with me from the beginning in reviewing my writing, devoting many hours to our informal discussions about cases and clinical and theoretical issues, and finally rereading and criticizing most of the final draft. My daughter, Suzy T. Lincoln, M.S.W., has lived with this project from its inception and has been my sternest critic, offering valuable insights from the viewpoint of a relatively recent student and practitioner. She has also served as grammarian and stylist and patiently put in countless hours proofreading the many revisions of the manuscript. I also wish to commend LaVerne Emlaw for her care and competence in preparing the manuscript and her unfailing cheerfulness and good nature in retyping and incorporating my frequent additions and alterations.

Foreword

Although it has been several decades since Heinz Hartmann's *Ego Psychology and the Problem of Adaptation*[1] was translated and published in the United States, it has been only in the last ten years or so that ego psychology has been widely used as a theoretical framework for understanding human behavior and change by clinicians and mental health workers. Since early in this century psychoanalysis, as both a personality theory and a theory of psychopathology, has been a sensitive and comprehensive approach to understanding the complexities of the human psyche. However, psychoanalysis as a treatment technique is too cumbersome, inflexible and costly to find wide acceptance in the mental health field, especially when it expanded so enormously in the middle sixties. Professionals in both public and private agencies have to cope with the converging pressures of increased acceptance of psychotherapy as a viable form of treatment, increased size of caseloads, sharply diminished financial support from government sources with concomitantly diminished staffs, and time limits on treatment imposed by the decree of insurance companies and other sources of

[1]Hartmann, H. (1958), *Ego Psychology and the Problem of Adaptation*. New York: International Universities Press.

third party payment. This general trend of increased demand and decreased resources of money, time and personnel, began as mental health laws about commitment to mental hospitals were changing, so that many patients who would have been judged sufficiently disturbed to have been committed twenty years ago, now are showing up in out-patient treatment caseloads.

All of these changes compelled psychiatry, clinical psychology, and social work to devise more effective short term modalities of treatment than classical psychoanalysis afforded. Ego psychology with its emphasis on the individual's psychological strengths and weaknesses, or the characteristic repertoire of coping strategies, has proven to be of great utility in assessment and treatment in short term counseling with clients. Without violating psychoanalytic concepts, ego psychology focuses on the ways in which an individual negotiates all the necessary transactions with his physical and social environment; how he protects himself from psychological dissolution by overwhelming or painful emotions; how he relates to both the important and the peripheral persons in his world; how purposefully he can set a goal and work toward it, delaying gratification and ignoring distractions; how appropriately he seeks gratification of his wishes without provoking punishment from the social environment or his own conscience; how he remembers, fantasizes, plans, makes decisions and judgments; how he experiences himself as having a real and integral identity that endures across time and space.

By understanding the normal development of ego functions and those circumstances that may distort normal development, the clinician is able to reach his client at effective and sensitively empathic levels. One of the great advantages of ego psychology theory is that assessment always involves appraisal of the client's individual strengths and skills, rather than focusing on his psychopathology or maladaptive behavior. By designing treatment interventions that speak to the client's strengths it is possible to engage the client as an effective and responsible partner in his own treatment. The client is not the passive or helpless recipient of treatment, but rather he is an active participant in a therapeutic alliance, during which he will come to understand the meanings of his behaviors and better ways of coping with his problems. The counselor's task is not to "heal" the client but help him strengthen existing coping skills and educate him in skills that are in deficit.

Barbara Tilley has used ego psychology in this text on short term dynamic counseling as a theoretical framework with which to organize her recommendations for assessment and treatment. But she has achieved much more than the mere utilization of a theory; there is a seamless synthesis of personality theory and the clinical process, between assessment and the interventions derived from assessment. There has long been a problem in the education of mental health professionals because the typical curriculum tends to fragment instruction into treatment methods and instruction in the theories of personality and psychopathology. It is pretty much left to the student to muddle through and integrate all the little islands of knowledge that he acquires in the classroom, in the agency, and at the hands of his clients. As a result students are often overwhelmed by an inchoate mass of data that tumbles forth from their anxious clients because they have no conceptual structure with which to understand and organize the clinical material, much less plan ways in which to initiate change. Understandably desperate, they grab at bits and pieces of technique without understanding the underlying rationale, and pray for the best. This book meets that need in the student-counselor in providing a way of understanding the complexities of human behavior and emotions, how to use this understanding to assess the client's coping skills (or lack of them) and finally, how to translate this knowledge into concrete and thoughtful interventions in the treatment hour.

Perhaps the greatest value of this work is that it represents the distillation of a lifetime of professional experience, not only in counseling clients but in the supervision of students in their counseling experiences as well. The author writes with great sensitivity and perspicacity about the dilemmas and anxieties of the young professional who is undertaking his first transactions with clients, and she obviously has a tender concern not only about the client's welfare, but the students' as well. Although the text is intended to instruct the student step by step in the treatment process, it can also serve as a model for any psychotherapy supervisor. There is genuine empathy for the beginner and his profound feelings of inadequacy and desperation to be told what to do. She fastidiously avoids pedagogical pomposity and professional jargon, surely one of the most seductive traps for any teacher in academia. Explanations are both cognizant of the complexity of the subject matter and lucid. What particularly sets this book apart from others of its genre is the generous use of illustrative case examples, instructive to both beginners and experienced professionals. The richness and diversity of these clinical vignettes illuminate the author's exposition of theory and clinical practice, and give the reader a very real sense of assessment and treatment process.

There is patient and detailed concern given in this book to the multitudinous issues that invariably arise in the treatment process, such as whether or not to take notes for process recording in the session, managing phone contacts, the client's presentation of gifts, and so on. One section that will be very useful to professionals in general is a thoughtful clarification of the meaning and use of ego support in treatment. "Supportive treatment" has been a carelessly used, even abused, phrase in the clinical literature. It has often been used to mean placating or encouraging moral support, roughly the psychological equivalent to patting someone on the head and telling them to buck up, things are going to get better. There is certainly a suggestion that it is anti-analytical, useless in eliciting profound therapeutic change, and so simple minded that it can be done by anyone with sufficiently good intentions. On the contrary, Mrs. Tilley makes it clear that ego supportive treatment is a disciplined intervention that requires accurate assessment of the client's ego structure and considered thought given to the choice of interventions that will be used to enhance the client's coping skills. The therapeutic aim is to help the client function better, not just feel better. For instance, many therapists now doing psychoanalytic psychotherapy feel that the sine que non of treatment is to analyze and diminish the client's defenses. However, if one were seeing an anxious borderline patient, with defenses that were already precarious and ineffective, then it would be appropriate to strengthen and support defensive functioning, rather than analyzing it. As we are seeing more and more clients with marginal adjustments, whatever their diagnoses, it seems important to develop treatment modalities that emphasize support and direction of existing ego skills. Often all that is needed to restore the equilibrium and coping skills of this kind of patient is the concern and understanding of a reality-focused, disciplined therapist.

In a profession beseiged by a profusion of therapeutic approaches, many of which prove to be evanescent and meretricious, this book is a welcome return to the importance of teaching students a thorough knowledge of personality theory, how to make an accurate psychosocial assessment, and how to establish a sensitive, flexible, and self-disciplined relationship with clients.

Martha N. Gizynski, Ph.D.
The University of Michigan
Ann Arbor, Michigan
May 1984.

Introduction

This book adapts the broad concepts of psychoanalytic personality theory to short-term counseling. It is soundly rooted in theory but is not a treatise on theory or an academic text. It is essentially a guide to clinical practice. In allying ego psychology theory to brief counseling, my purpose is to afford clinicians who are embarking on careers in mental health a dynamic model for attaining skills in understanding, diagnosing and treating emotionally troubled clients.

Since student interns and newly fledged professionals are assigned to offer direct service to clients in community mental health, crisis intervention and family agencies, they have an immediate need for techniques in helping adolescent and adult clients with the broad range of problems they present. Students read and discuss theory in their classrooms but often lament that it doesn't tell them what to do when they face their first clients in an interview. Professors of clinical theory and professionals who supervise counselors in their initial years of practice also remark on the dearth of manuals that apply dynamic theory to practice at introductory levels.

To fill this need, and in the conviction that psychoanalytic theory constitutes an essential framework for understanding human behavior, I have distilled from long practice in counseling, psychotherapy, supervision and training of graduate students the fundamentals of interviewing, evaluation and counseling techniques that apply these theoretical formulations to the brief counseling that is offered in community agencies. Short-term counseling may consist of as few as two or three often intensely experienced sessions; it may occasionally continue for as long as six months or even a year but is still considered "short-term" in its focus on problem solving and limitation of goals.

That the concepts of ego psychology can be successfully applied in brief counseling has been amply demonstrated in my years of practice. The clinical material presented reflects my own experience and the observations and innovative contributions of colleagues I was closely associated with for many years in a psychoanalytically-oriented mental health clinic, as we evolved effective and tested techniques for welding dynamic theory to our assessment and treatment of clients.

As a counseling approach, ego psychology is particularly pertinent and effective in meeting the needs of the typical clientele who currently seek help at community agencies. While literature on the subject abounds in its application to the practice of intensive psychotherapy, adaptation of this approach to short-term counseling has not received adequate attention. It offers distinct benefits to many clients. As they master current problems through self-understanding, a new sense of esteem, identity and control over their lives are often lasting by-products. The enhancement of ego strength may be achieved through the counselor's recognition and support of the individual's assets and healthy drives; through the dynamic client-counselor relationship which mobilizes the client's optimum engagement in self-help; through understanding the relationship between current feelings and past emotional experiences, by which the individual gains a fresh perspective on his problems, and finally, through the client's gratifying realization of his own capacity and potential to solve problems and to change.

Implicit in this approach to counseling, and a corollary thesis of this book, is to convey a humanistic point of view: that individuals are to be trusted, respected and accepted in all their manifestations of humanness and endless variety, and that treatment should enhance their uniqueness rather than endeavor to fit them into a preconceived or conventional mold through the use of coercive or manipulative tactics.

The question most often asked by students—how and why counseling helps clients—and seldom clarified in the literature, is the subject of the opening chapter on the analysis of the dynamic counseling process. The book continues with a detailed model for conducting initial interviews designed to help counselors develop skills in history-taking and forming evaluations based on ego assessment, focusing on healthy drives rather than on pathology. How to listen and respond to the underlying messages in clients' communications, to utilize the dynamic client-counselor alliance in stimulating their maximum participation in problem resolution, and simple and direct methods for managing client reactions that commonly occur in counseling are illustrated with many case examples. Strategies for identifying emergencies, especially potential suicide threats, are clearly spelled out.

Particular attention is devoted to helping counselors develop professionalism by cultivating objectivity and disciplined responses to their clients. Counselors' emotional reactions also receive special consideration, recognizing that they too need support and reassurance in allaying their own natural anxieties while working with troubled and often frightened clients.

Psychoanalytic theory has been reviewed where it seemed essential to counselors' understanding of ego development, personality structure and behavior, using nontechnical language as far as possible. I have purposely avoided the vocabularies of the various clinical disciplines and written in clear and direct language that will be understandable to all counselors, whatever their prior training or academic background. Noting a tendency to excessive use (and often misuse) of psychological terminology and labels by some new practitioners, I chose to restrict inclusion of technical vocabulary and have focused instead on understanding and response to human emotions and to feelings, which are the essence of counseling.

The terms "counselor" and "counseling" need explanation. While "counselor" is bland and unspecific (we have investment counselors, pastoral counselors, and counselors-at-law, and so on) and in spite of the fact that it carries an undesirable implication of advice giving, it seemed the best choice of available alternatives. The word "worker" used in social work is somewhat denigrating and graceless; I prefer "therapist," since any intervention that helps individuals resolve personal or emotional problems is therapeutic. However, the word "therapy" is objectionable to some agencies, as denoting more intensive treatment than their services provide. All disciplines tend to merge in community agencies, so counseling may be practiced by paraprofessionals, mental health specialists, psychiatric nurses, social workers, psychologists, guidance counselors, etc.

I have omitted extensive bibliographies of current literature, since these are abundantly available in students' academic reading lists and libraries, but have recommended a few reference books on theory and carefully selected significant early writings on psychoanalysis. I suggest these classic papers and books, which are rarely assigned to students, in the belief that practitioners should be familiar with important contributions to the development of the theories they will be applying.

Finally, the generic "he" is used throughout this volume in order to avoid the monotonous repetition of "he/she" or unwieldy circumlocutions. It should not be taken as implying an antifeminine bias.

CHAPTER 1

The Counselor and the Counseling Process

ANALYSIS OF THE DYNAMIC PROCESS

Men and women who choose a counseling career enter the field in a spirit of idealism and a sincere dedication to helping people. If questioned, however, most would admit to only a vague concept of the counseling process. With all their helpful intent they are apt to be hazy as to just how or why counseling helps people feel better. What happens? What dynamic process takes place when two people sit down together in a counseling interview? What skills and knowledge that the counselor possesses can enable a troubled individual to master or ameliorate his problems?

The natural starting point for a book on mental health counseling is to examine and dissect the counseling process: how it works, why it works and what part the counselor plays in the dynamic interaction in which he and his clients engage. As the elements of the counseling process are illuminated, this will lead to a clearer understanding of how the counselor's motivation can be forged into a professional stance so he can make optimum use of himself in treating emotionally troubled clients.

Mental health counseling is sometimes referred to as a "talking treatment." Talking? How can talking help a client to feel better about himself, to function more effectively and to improve his personal relationships?

Counselors, psychotherapists and psychoanalysts observe that many of their clients and patients gain a gratifying sense of well-being through talking. In psychoanalysis, patients are usually seen five times a week in intensive therapy aimed at profound changes in personality structure, resolution of early childhood conflicts and alteration of defenses. During the process repressed memories and feelings are brought into consciousness. Psychotherapy is less intensive; patients are seen at least two and often three times a week. Here the goal is modification of maladaptive defenses, insight into early conflicts and their relation to current behavior. The purpose of both therapies is to promote a freeing and expansion of the patient's ego so that he will experience more satisfying personal relationships, a fuller sense of self-esteem, productivity and control over his life. The only requirement of the patient is that he talk as honestly as possible about himself.

In counseling, clients are usually seen once a week and often on a time-limited basis. Its goals are less ambitious. Personality restructuring is not considered; nor is resolution of repressed conflicts. While the primary aim is symptom relief, the client is encouraged to recognize his conflictual feelings, to better understand his maladaptive behavior, to examine the way he perceives himself and others, and to seek realistic and more gratifying solutions to problems. The purpose, as with the other therapies, is enhancement of the client's sense of well-being as he participates in problem solving, that is, expansion and growth of his ego. This dynamic view of mental health counseling as a treatment for emotional problems distinguishes it from a primarily advice giving, directive or manipulative approach.

The Function of Talking

A beginning counselor may well ask how all this is accomplished through talking. Only after considerable experience do counselors accumulate evidence that many of their clients do change and feel better after a period of counseling. As proof, clients may report that they get along better with families or spouses, that school or job performance improves, and that they feel an enhancement of vitality and self-esteem.

How do these changes come about? Two elements in the counseling process foster a client's emotional growth: First, the act of talking itself; and second, the unique relationship with the counselor. The two are dynamically interrelated.

Talking is a highly organized activity of the rational ego as distinguished from mere emoting. A child gives vent to emotion by tears and temper tantrums when he is frustrated. However, when he reaches a verbal level of communication he calls on rational and intellectual resources as well, if asked to put his complaints into words. Usually a client who solicits help has been too closely and emotionally involved in his difficulties to view them objectively. Ruminating about his problems has been unproductive and distorted as he goes around the same old emotional circles, and he may feel helplessly confused. Talking to friends or family often leads to the same result as they are too intimately related to him to respond objectively, may take sides or offer biased advice.

The act of talking about his feelings to a concerned but impartial listener in the person of the counselor will help him to gain perspective and mobilize his rational resources, which may have been temporarily diminished under overwhelming stress. The counselor serves as a sounding board, enabling the client to hear himself as he cites his complaints. As he hears, judges and evaluates what he communicates, he is better able to perceive distortions and unrealities in his thinking. In permitting and encouraging free verbalization, the counselor fulfills a valuable service to his client even without further intervention.

By raising questions that lead the client to enlarge on his complaints and explore his situation in detail, the counselor helps him to carry the process of self-examination further. The client, in hearing himself, also begins to consider how his words must sound to the counselor. Has he simply been so badly treated, rejected, or unlucky, or does he begin to question whether he may have misjudged his situation or contributed to his difficulties by his own behavior? The talking thus shifts him from the realm of emotionalism to the level of reality testing and coherent thinking.

The Client-Counselor Relationship

The relationship with the counselor is crucial in this ongoing process. In using the counselor as a mirror to reflect his ideas back to him, the healthier part of the client's personality—his more mature ego—is called into play to observe the less healthy, disorganized or immature part that is giving him trouble.

As a client repeats, examines and adds new dimensions to his thoughts about himself over time, and ponders the counselor's questions and comments, he may gradually begin to view his situation in a different light. Old memories and forgotten events that have a bearing on his current problems may be recalled. In becoming aware of connections between past experiences and current behavior a client often gains insight and understanding, which helps him to make sense of the feelings and problems he is experiencing. With this new understanding of the source of his conflicting emotions he is able to feel more in control, less helpless and hopeless, and begins to appreciate that there are possible alternatives to be examined and solutions available. This is accomplished by repeatedly examining, dissecting and clarifying his feelings with an impartial listener.

But the counselor is a special kind of listener. Ideally, he asks nothing for himself, has no personal involvement, and no wish to influence the client to behave or change in a particular way. Comparably, the client does not need to please or appease the counselor or to seek his approval, and has no fear of rejection from him. The counselor by his interest and concern conveys that he accepts the client as he is and that he only wishes to help him find a solution or make a decision that is best for him.

No other relationship is quite as one-sided as that of counselor and client. Clients sometimes complain that there is no "real" relationship in the conventional sense and that they know nothing about the counselor while he knows all the intimate details of their lives. There is a good reason for this. It is only because the counselor maintains a degree of anonymity and separateness that he can continue to be objective and effective. Thus, in the dynamic interaction between client and counselor, interviews are structured to maintain a level of tension that distinguishes a counseling session from the casual give and take of a friendly conversation. This tension is produced by the counselor's relative silence and inactivity, and his expectation that the client talk, as well as by the emotionally charged subject matter. Under this stimulus and pressure the client is drawn into optimum participation in the counseling process. Unlike the medical model of patient-physician consultations, in which the doctor is the sole arbiter, in counseling the responsibility falls on the client to examine himself and provide answers.

Were the counseling interviews allowed to lapse into mere "visits" the client would not feel forced to examine painful feelings and might gloss over uncomfortable material or divert the conversation into more superficial channels. The same difficulty would arise if the counselor assumed a friendly role outside the counseling relationship. The client would then need to seek his approval, possibly fear rejection, and tend to close off communications that he felt might offend or lose the counselor's respect. However, these remarks in no way imply that a counselor should withhold warmth, responsiveness and empathy for the client, or be cold or distant, but rather that his demeanor should be disciplined and treatment goals kept in focus.

There is a further dynamic aspect to the client-counselor relationship. Clients often tend to attribute special and even omnipotent qualities to their counselors even though they may not be consciously aware, or only dimly aware, of this. They may see the counselor realistically as an expert who can help them, but also as a powerful parent figure on whom they wish to become dependent and attached. They may bask in the counselor's strength and identify with it. This has both advantages and disadvantages.

On the positive side, identification with the counselor's perceived strength allows the client to borrow, in a sense, some of the counselor's more mature ego and to incorporate it within his own ego. Just as a child identifies with a good parent in establishing controls and forming a self-image, so a client often uses a counselor as a model. To the extent that the client repeats and reactivates old relationships that he experienced toward his parents, it will yield insight into early conflicts. It will also be helpful in affording the client a corrective emotional experience, since he will observe that the counselor responds differently than his parents did. He may condone where parents criticized; encourage self-expression where parents inhibited it; be tolerant where parents exhibited prejudice, and be more trusting of the client's capacity to solve his own problems.

The counselor can permit, to a degree, the client's dual perception of him as a parent and as a real person, as long as it fosters a positive working relationship. He must be cautioned, however, that a client's excessive idealization of him may arouse negative reactions at times. This is to be anticipated because old attitudes toward parents, which are repeated in the relationship with the counselor, are characterized by ambivalence. Clients' overevaluation of the counselor may stir up old feelings of resentment of their helplessness and dependency, and disappointment that he cannot gratify all their wishes and fantasies. If the negative side of the ambivalence flares up in the form of resistance, the positive relationship will be impaired unless the counselor intervenes. Calling the client's attention to his reactions and examining them with him will usually be sufficient to restore the situation. It will induce the client to think about, recognize and correct his unrealistic expectations and fantasies by separating his distorted view of the counselor as a parent from the perception of him as a real person.

Resistance To Change: The Counselor As Catalyst

We now turn our attention to an unexpected obstacle that is met in counseling: client opposition to change. This phenomenon, called the repetition compulsion, is a central concept in psychodynamic theory and is at the nucleus of the counseling process. It would appear that given a client's wish to end his suffering and the counselor's encouragement to overcome his problems, the client would readily give up his maladaptive behavior and the desired results would be achieved. But a powerful dynamic force intervenes. This is the universal compulsion of all individuals to repeat old and familiar behavior patterns acquired early in life. These are deeply ingrained and clung to tenaciously.

Thus a client's desire to change, to establish more mature and rewarding modes of behavior, clashes with his unconscious tendency to perpetuate the old ways of reacting. Tension is produced by the struggle that ensues between these two opposing forces. The counselor with whom the client's healthy ego has formed an alliance then assumes the form of an adversary, pressuring the client to give up part of himself that he values. This arouses conflict and anxiety. As the client's expressed and conscious wish to change collides with his unwillingness to relinquish old ingrained habits, he may balk and become resistant. Resistances may not be voiced explicitly or even recognized consciously by the client, but may be covert, manifested in his rationalizations for perpetuating his old behavior, his hesitancy and fear to initiate change, the tension and anxiety he feels in interviews, the tendency to backslide after taking a forward step, and negative reactions implicit in the frequently heard complaints by clients that counseling is progressing too slowly or is not helping, and that the counselor is not providing hoped for answers.

With recognition of the concept of resistance, we now arrive at the conclusion that it is not just talking, but talking to a special individual in the person of the counselor, that is the essence of the counseling process. The relationship with the counselor becomes the catalyst, provoking the client to engage in battle with part of himself. As a client becomes temporarily attached to a counselor, trusts and values him, this alliance exerts a positive influence, activating the client to mobilize his healthy resources to oppose the maladaptive part of himself and shift from the old patterns to more gratifying modes. Because of this struggle the course of counseling does not always proceed evenly but may fluctuate, progressing harmoniously when the client's healthy ego is dominant, stalling at times when the negative forces assert themselves.

Due to the time limit in short-term counseling, it is always desirable to maintain and protect a positive working relationship with clients by promptly helping them to overcome any resistances. Fortunately, as counselors learn to recognize resistances and acquire skill in managing and resolving these temporary setbacks, they will find that positive relationships can usually be restored fairly quickly. Counselors should not be alarmed at the prospect of encountering occasional resistance in their clients, but need to be aware that it will occur at times and prepared to deal with it. (Clinical management of resistance is fully reviewed in Chapter 5.)

In conclusion, it is through the gratification a client derives from mastering his problems that he gains self-esteem and ego strength. In exchanging old destructive reaction patterns for more satisfying and productive behavior, his newly acquired confidence provides further impetus to change and grow. If instead of active participation that is fostered in psychodynamic counseling, a client were directed, advised or coerced, his self-trust would be diminished and further helplessness and dependency induced. Only in the rare instances when a client is too regressed or incapacitated to make a rational decision is it appropriate for a counselor to step in and be directive or assume responsibility for the client's welfare.

THE COUNSELOR

PERSONAL QUALITIES

The foregoing description of "talking" treatment has already shed considerable light on the attitudes, demeanor and personality qualities of counselors who undertake this type of approach. It has been assumed that any man or woman who chooses to do counseling, however lacking he may be in experience, is motivated by respect and human concern for the individual, has a capacity for warmth and empathy, is relatively free of prejudice and personal conflicts, and can maintain objectivity when faced with troubled, confused and often frightened clients.

Ideally a counselor should also possess the intellectual ability to understand complex psychological processes and be able to verbalize freely and fluently. Even more important is a kind of intelligence of the heart which enables a counselor to listen, to hear and to respond, not only to the words a client uses but to their underlying message and the feelings they communicate. "Listening with the third ear" is the apt phrase coined by Theodore Reik[1] to describe this quality of empathic listening.

These are optimum qualities and may sound daunting to an aspiring counselor who may not be at all sure he is so blessed. While rare individuals have a natural gift for counseling, for most others, and even those with special talent, forging a sincere motivation and desire to help into a true professionalism is a gradual

[1] Reik, T. (1948), *Listening with The Third Ear*. New York: Farrar, Straus and Co.

process. Patience, self-control and self-awareness, as well as technical ability, are acquired with time and experience as a counselor learns to use himself as an instrument in the counseling process. After working with a variety of clients he will in time come to recognize almost intuitively familiar behavior patterns, personality traits and symptomatology that he has encountered before and that will provide clues in sizing up new clients and their problems. For example, observations of defenses that a client exhibits—facades of bravado, denial of feelings, especially anger, projection of blame onto others, rationalizations, particular complaints, the manner of relating and certain combinations of characteristics—will set up echoes in the counselor's mind of psychological qualities he has encountered in the past, even though they will be manifested somewhat differently in each client. He may even recall past experiences when he misjudged or failed to see through similar defenses, enabling him to profit from earlier mistakes.

While we do not advocate that intuition be trusted entirely in the absence of clinical material and solid thinking to back it up, this "feel" for a client and his presentation of himself, which is only acquired with experience, gives an added and important dimension to a counselor's initial evaluations and subsequent work with clients.

Meeting the First Client

A counselor's first lesson in developing competence begins when he interviews his first client. No matter how adequate the training that has preceded it, his first contact with a real client is bound to cause some apprehension. He will be talking to an unknown client with an as yet undisclosed problem. He will be asking himself if he is capable of conducting the interview responsibly, of making the right assessment or decision, if one is called for, and of recognizing and meeting the client's needs, all without revealing his inexperience.

In anticipation and preparation for their first interview, student interns and inexperienced professionals will find it reassuring and tension-relieving if they recognize that it is also a "first time" for the client. An awareness that the client may be more apprehensive than the counselor as he ventures on unfamiliar ground, in strange surroundings, unsure what to expect or how he will be perceived, will shift the counselor's focus from himself to an appreciation of and response to the client's feelings. In setting the client at ease, the counselor's concern for his own performance can thus be diminished.

In addition, a counselor rarely needs to make a decision or take action during a first interview with a client. He can listen, try to size up the client and his problems, get as much relevant information as possible and then arrange for a follow-up interview. A suggestion to the client that the counselor would like to learn more about him and talk over his problems further before they make plans, will inform the client of his interest and concern. This will allow time in the interval for the counselor to discuss the client with his supervisor and to have help in evaluating the information he has acquired and planning the next step.

Cultivating Objectivity

The following is such an important key to the establishment of a professional stance that it merits considerable elaboration: A counselor must make a clear distinction between the client's problem and his own function as a counselor. If he fails to make this separation he will feel as helpless as the client. To guard against confusing the two—seeing the client's problem as his problem as he listens to the client's complaints—it will help to remind himself, "This is the client's problem under scrutiny. Only he can resolve it. My part is to hear and understand what he is communicating."

In their commitment and zeal to be helpful, inexperienced counselors are apt to feel pressured to come up with answers or solutions, and, in a sense, to take over the client's problems. Most counselors at times experience this urgency, especially with clients who seem to be helplessly enmeshed in troubling situations and easily elicit the counselor's sympathy and compassion.

To become very involved and identified with a client is not helpful to the client and places a burden on the counselor that limits his effectiveness. He becomes over-zealous and makes an impossible demand on himself. It may sound callous at first, but a counselor will be most helpful if he can detach himself somewhat while he listens to clients. By maintaining objectivity and distance, the counselor is free to listen as a client's story unfolds, examine the problem and how it came about, and explore the client's options with him. He can neither take over the client's troubles, even if he would wish to, nor resolve them. Counselors who are able to assure themselves during a difficult interview with a new client that they do not need to provide answers are relieved of pressure and tension and better able to devote themselves to what actually is their responsibility—to try to understand the client's feelings and to communicate this understanding to the client. It is rewarding and gratifying to clients to find that someone "understands" them. They often express this with surprise and pleasure. It may never have happened to them in the same way before. A counselor who truly recognizes this distinction between a client's problems and his own role has taken his first step in acquiring professionalism.

This brings us to a definition of the counselor's prime function. He is an attentive and empathic listener, sometimes a clarifier, as his client states and expands on his complaint in his effort to understand, explore and search for ways to mitigate or solve it. The counselor's role is to aid in stimulating the client to resolve his own difficulties.

Since the counselor is seen as an important ally, or even a lifeline in time of stress, a troubled client will be receptive to forming a positive working relationship with him. The counselor's first priority is to foster its development. This does not imply, of course, that he should be tempted to seduce the client by charm or flattery but that he should convey his concern and understanding of the client's feelings, while maintaining a disciplined professional manner that will inform the client of his competence and expertise.

Recognizing Role Limitations

Placing responsibility for problem-solving on his clients and thereby putting limitations on the counselor's function will tend to diminish any sense of power or control he may have wishfully perceived in this role. Along with the recognition that he cannot solve his clients' problems, a counselor must also accept that all clients cannot be helped or saved from their own destructive behavior, or even motivated to resolve their dilemmas despite the counselor's efforts. A counselor should not be discouraged or necessarily blame himself when some clients refuse an offer of service, fail to keep follow-up appointments or make demands that the counselor provide some impossible solution.

It is important, of course, to review such situations with a supervisor and to talk over and evaluate what may have gone wrong. If the counselor did make an error it will be a valuable learning experience and should be viewed accordingly. On the other hand, it must be recognized that there are individuals who have insufficient motivation to face self-examination or who are deriving so much gratification from their maladaptive behavior, however painful, that they resist any change.

The fact that certain individuals have applied to an agency for help indicates some discomfort but it may be too slight or transient for them to be willing to engage in counseling. Some who fail to continue may be dependent and immature persons seeking "magical" answers, shifting the entire burden on the counselor to take care of them. Still others demand that either circumstances in the environment or spouses or other individuals in their lives be changed to accommodate them. Such clients are apt to reproach the counselor for failing them and sometimes succeed in arousing defensiveness and guilt if the counselor already feels insecure or inadequate. While effort should be made to engage these clients and hope to instill motivation, occasional failures to do so must be accepted philosophically.

In summary, a new counselor will be most comfortable in approaching his clients if he is clear about his function and the limits of his ability and responsibility to help. If he listens as calmly as possible, assesses clients and their situations as objectively as he is able, and conveys a genuine respect for them, he will be offering the best service of which he is capable at the time. He can also console himself that any unease or anxiety he may feel at the beginning will gradually subside as he gains confidence and experience. Even if he makes an error it should not be viewed as a disaster. The most experienced professionals do make mistakes.

RECOMMENDED READING

Brenner, C. (1973), *An Elementary Textbook of Psychoanalysis*. New York: International Universities Press.

This is a good introductory book to familiarize counselors with basic psychoanalytic theory.

Freud, S. (1926), The Question of lay analysis. *Standard Edition*, 20:179–258. London: Hogarth Press, 1959.

In this slim volume addressed to the uninformed layman, Freud explains the concept of the unconscious and the basic discoveries of psychoanalysis. It is recommended as an introduction to Freud's writings.

CHAPTER 2

The Initial Interview

GATHERING INFORMATION

An individual who seeks help for the first time is venturing into unfamiliar territory. He is already apt to be anxious because of the problem that is troubling him and, in addition, to be wondering uneasily how an unknown person, the counselor, will respond and react to him. For the counselor who is expecting to meet a potential client, there is the necessity to learn a great deal about him in order to determine how to help and at the same time convey a reassuring attitude that will dispel the client's discomfort at being there.

Since the first contact is crucial in engaging the individual and insuring that he will indeed become a "client," the counselor must maintain sufficient objectivity to respond calmly, without losing his own composure or becoming infected by the client's anxiety.

ENLISTING THE CLIENT

Important as it is that the counselor acquire a solid body of data, both factual and subjective, about the client he is interviewing, his first objective is to enlist the client into the counseling process and lay the foundation for a mutually trusting alliance. As the counselor leads his client to talk about himself and his problems, his manner of acceptance and concern communicates that this is a new and special kind of relationship. The client begins to experience what counseling is like.

Fostering the client's participation in a positive working relationship or partnership is accomplished through a special kind of attentive and empathic listening by the counselor; the counselor's evident effort to understand what the client is communicating, implicit in his interest and questions; and finally, by a focus on feelings. How does the client *feel* about the events or situations he is describing, about relationships he discusses, about his past, even about his decision to seek counseling? As these questions are asked by the counselor, he is continually informing the client that feelings are important, that the counselor wants to hear about them, and that it's acceptable to talk about them. With this stimulus clients will feel free to talk about feelings they may never have shared with anyone before. Perhaps they have never before found anyone so willing to listen.

Some verbal expressions of understanding are appropriate within limits, although implied more often than spoken, by the counselor's responsive manner. Such comments by the counselor as "That must have been a disappointment to you," or "I can understand how painful your parents' divorce was," or "It's not surprising that you were angry," are supportive and will usually lead the client on to further exploration of his feelings.

Oversolicitousness and sympathy, on the other hand, are apt to sound insincere and patronizing. There is a difference between maintaining objectivity while *understanding* how a client feels and actually *sharing* a client's sense of helplessness and despair. In the latter instance, both client and counselor would be in the same dilemma. A calm manner and some professional distance on the part of the counselor will communicate to the client that here is someone he can rely on. As was pointed out in the previous chapter, professional distance never need suggest a lack of warmth or concern, and should not be confused with indifference or disinterest or any implication of superiority. It does say, "I am the expert here to help you and to look at your problem with you." By making clear his role the counselor can also forestall the efforts of some clients to tilt an interview into a friendly visit and thus to dilute its effectiveness.

Overcoming Negative Reactions

It has been taken for granted so far that clients will respond positively to counselors' well-intentioned overtures and enter willingly into a cooperative working relationship. Anticipating that rapport will be quickly established and that the first interview will proceed harmoniously, counselors may be dismayed when they sometimes encounter immediate negative reactions from clients. Such clients will resist their efforts and remain aloof, stubborn or antagonistic.

These reactions generally are not a reflection on the counselor's competence but a characteristic response of some individuals to an unfamiliar and threatening situation. Clients may feel humiliated in asking for help, fearing loss of control and independence, and may displace their resentment onto the agency or counselor. Intense negative feelings from the past toward parents, or authority figures as parent surrogates, may awaken resistance to what the clients experience as passive submission to the counselor, arousing anger at their consequent sense of helplessness. An attitude of belligerence may compensate for the injury to self-esteem.

While not necessarily openly voiced by clients, their opposition may be expressed by too bland replies, restiveness, evasions, aggressive questioning of the counselor, tendencies to minimize their problems, or resigned and negative statements that they don't expect the counselor to be able to help them. Some clients may be more overt in criticizing the agency, the way the appointment was made, or the inconvenient hour of the appointment, or even complain about difficulty in parking.

If a counselor senses antagonism and does not step in quickly to alleviate it he may encounter continued friction or lose the client entirely. Recognition of the client's feelings by commenting that it may have been difficult for him to apply for help, with its implied invitation for him to talk about any negative feelings, may be sufficient to overcome his hesitance. Whether or not the client goes on in detail to express his resentment, he is aware that the counselor understands his chagrin or anger. Some clients will find relief in discharging their hostility directly and, noting the counselor's acceptance of such feelings, will then be able to relate more comfortably.

Clients often warn a counselor at the start that they don't want to become dependent on him. They should be led to talk about such feelings, and might be told that although they may need the counselor's help temporarily his aim is to help them eventually to be more *in*dependent. This is reassuring, as is a statement that the counselor won't be telling the client what to do, but that they will look at problems together to help him find his own solutions.

Such brief educational statements about counseling help to allay anxiety, but too much explanation should be avoided or the counselor will risk sounding defensive or affronted by the client's negativism. It is far more effective for the counselor to indicate his understanding of the client's natural anxiety. He might even generalize by remarking that clients often do feel an initial reluctance to seek help and he realizes that it is difficult at first to share feelings with and trust an unknown counselor.

With such management techniques, initial resistances can usually be resolved fairly quickly, although they may be expected to crop up again from time to time. Counselors will know their efforts have been successful if clients relax and resume talking about their problems.

Starting the Interview

The setting for interviews should be a private room, free of distraction, with a door that can be closed, where the client can be comfortable and assured that he will not be overheard. Hard office chairs are not very inviting to a client, nor should he be asked to sink into such a deep lounge chair that he feels at a disadvantage with a counselor sitting above him at a desk. Whether a counselor uses a desk depends on agency furnishings and on the counselor's personal preference and style. If the counselor sits at a desk it is best not to use it as a barrier with the client seated opposite and the desk between them. If clients sit around the corner at one end of the desk, or on a chair nearby, they are reasonably close and still not placed where the two are staring directly at one another. In the writer's experience, some clients are apt to be threatened by the closeness when both counselor and client sit in easy chairs, especially where they are almost knee-to-knee in a small office, and are more comfortable when the counselor remains at a desk.

Once a client is seated, what next? Most clients need little encouragement to start talking. It usually suffices for the counselor simply to introduce himself and pause, and clients will begin talking without further invitation. Where and how a client chooses to begin will be noted. Will he cite complaints about others, ask questions, state his problem in an orderly way, begin to cry?

If a client seems hesitant and doesn't begin to talk after a brief pause, the counselor might simply say, "You've come here because something is troubling you—do you want to tell me about it?" If the client still seems uneasy and says he doesn't know where to start, the counselor's invitation to "Begin wherever you like—we have plenty of time," will imply to his client that the interview need not be structured in a particular way and that the counselor is prepared to listen patiently without pressuring him.

Occasionally a client, reacting with anxiety to an unfamiliar situation, may inquire, "How do we go about this? Do you want to ask me questions?" He may be expecting the interview to resemble a medical consultation, with the doctor quizzing him and writing down notes in a record. The counselor can make it clear that this is a different kind of interview by saying, "Why don't you tell me about yourself in your own words—then we'll look at it together." The word "together" suggests that it is a cooperative effort.

The counselor's relaxed but interested manner, his willingness to listen and take the client's complaint seriously, will help establish a climate of acceptance in which the client can be at ease in talking about himself. To further remove the interview from the doctor-patient model, the counselor should avoid taking notes except possibly to jot down an address or phone number. Note-taking is distracting and interrupts the flow of the interview, while the client is likely to wonder uneasily what is being written about him. It is preferable to write notes from memory after the interview.

In these examples of techniques for starting an interview, observe that all are directed to encouraging the client to tell his story in his own way and to assume responsibility. This immediately confers on him an active role. It implies from the start that he will be playing a leading part in the counseling process, that the counselor respects and trusts him and is not going to direct him or take over for him. Important clues about the client are gained from observing how he presents his problem, which facts he stresses, the feelings he chooses to confide, and the degree of emotion he displays.

If instead of allowing a client to begin the interview in his own way a counselor starts out by making statements about the agency, explaining agency policy or giving personal information, he will tend to remove the focus from the client, which serves no useful purpose. If the client initially asks a question about the agency, it can be answered briefly and attention then turned to the client and his problem. Only after the client's complaint has been explored can it be determined whether the agency can offer appropriate help or whether a referral should be proposed.

Even if there are pauses when a client falls silent during an initial interview, it is best not to rush in just to fill the void. Clients often need time to think about what they want to say next or ponder about a comment from the counselor; a distracting remark is apt to close off their communication or interrupt the train of thought. If a pause continues uncomfortably the counselor might simply comment, "I wonder what you are thinking about?" or "Is it difficult to go on talking about yourself?"

(Note that while possible responses by counselors are quoted in these pages, this is not to advise that counselors use the exact words but only to suggest the kinds of remarks that might be made. Counselors should use their own words, which are comfortable and natural for them. With time and experience each will come to develop his own particular style.)

Exploring the Problem

It goes without saying that the counselor's first responsibility in talking to a client, whether on the phone or in person, is to ascertain if there is an emergency requiring immediate intervention, i.e., an emotional breakdown, suicide threat, drug overdose, etc. Ordinarily the agency will have policies for dealing with such situations and the counselor will have been apprised of these.

If the counselor is confident that no emergency exists, he will be able to focus on the client's complaint and begin to assess the nature of the problem, its significance for the client and the client's emotional state. This entails listening attentively and empathically to the statement of the complaint while exploring its duration, intensity and the current precipitant.

Clients will almost invariably begin by citing the complaints or difficulties they are experiencing that have led them to seek help. Usually they will need little encouragement to talk about their problems, while the counselor listens and asks occasional questions designed to promote fuller exploration. One will want to find out specifically:

1. How long has the problem gone on?
2. Is it chronic or of recent origin?
3. If it has occurred before how has the client handled it on previous occasions?
4. What does the client feel he can do about it?
5. What options does the client have available to him in solving or mitigating the problem?

Answers to these questions will provide clues to the client's coping resources and his relative sense of confidence and/or helplessness in the situation. Raising these questions will also begin to mobilize the client to look at the problem from a new perspective. It suggests to him that there are possible solutions and that he himself may be able to do something about his problem.

Finding the Most Pressing Concern

Occasionally a client will almost overwhelm a counselor by starting out with a recital of a multitude of problems that he seems to be dumping in the counselor's lap. While the counselor may be wondering in despair how he can possibly help with such a burden of troubles, he will often find a simple question effective. "What do you feel is the most pressing problem?" The counselor may learn to his surprise that the client is concerned with what seems the most minor of his difficulties and is not particularly troubled by the others because he has accommodated to them.

> A 22-year-old female college student began an interview, by way of introduction, telling the counselor of her father's terminal illness, a teenage brother's arrest, betrayal by her lover, recent loss of a job, and overdue car payments. When asked what problems she particularly wanted help with, she said she had to declare a major soon and wanted to talk over several choices! She appeared capable of handling the other problems but was in conflict over an important decision.

A second reason for asking a client what he feels is most troubling is that the counselor may hear what he would consider a serious or disturbing difficulty and be tempted to focus on it because of his own subjective reaction. By inquiring what is most distressing to the client, he may learn what the *client* most wants help with.

Since there is not always time in short-term counseling for a leisurely process of evaluation over several weeks, it is desirable to form as clear an assessment as possible in the first meeting. However, because inexperienced counselors feel under pressure at times, they tend to become overconcerned about the situation or symptom a client initially presents and feel a need to respond or act before they have enough information. Reserving judgment until sufficient information has been obtained requires patience and control, and allows freer rein to the evaluation process. Impressions and clues the counselor picks up along the way can be kept in the back of his mind for future reference.

> Early in an interview with a student counselor, an adolescent male voiced concern about his recent use of drugs. The counselor immediately picked up on this, began to talk about addiction and urged the client to enroll in the agency's group program on drug abuse. As it turned out, the client had only incidentally made the remark, possibly as a way to avoid or delay revealing his real problem, which involved troubling sexual conflicts.

Such premature intercession discourages clients from sharing their feelings, leading them to conclude either that the counselor does not understand them or is not concerned enough to hear what they really came to talk about.

Focusing on the Precipitant

In every initial interview it is important to learn what precipitating event or feeling finally led the client to seek help. This will often provide the key to his underlying—or core—conflict. Often an individual will have lived with a given problem for some time without undue stress, but something will happen to intensify his concern and anxiety. In other words, we want to find out what was the breaking point which occasioned the appeal for help.

To learn this a counselor might comment, for example, "You say you've had this conflict with your father for some time. I wonder why you decided only today to come and talk about it." Or, "I understand you called last Tuesday for an appointment—did something happen that day to tip the scales?"

Clients may not always be aware of the precipitant. Some may at first deny that there was any particular reason for the timing of their call to the agency, or make some vague reply, such as, "I've been thinking of getting help for a long time." In response to the latter statement a further probe might be tried: "What could have happened to make you decide that today was the day?" Obviously if the client can't answer or is resistant the counselor shouldn't persist with his questions, but may find that some information will come up later to reveal the precipitant.

When the precipitant is learned it will usually lead the client to talk further about it and to gain some understanding of its significance. This may often point to the direction or become the focus of future counseling.

> A 35-year-old male client talked initially about his dissatisfaction with his job. However, when the counselor inquired what happened the day he made the appointment, he said that his wife had enrolled in a secretarial

school on that day and he was afraid she might become independent and eventually leave him. The precipitant revealed the real problem, which was not his job but a threat to his self-esteem as the sole wage earner and to his marriage.

Asking About Client Expectations

Another question that will yield significant information about a client and should be explored at some point in every initial interview is the client's expectation of the counselor. Asking how the client feels that you can help him, or what he is expecting from counseling, will elicit clues about his attitude toward seeking help and reveal basic personality traits.

Replies might range all the way from an excessively dependent or regressed individual's statement, "I want you to tell me what to do," to a more mature, "I hoped talking it over would help me make a decision." Another reply often heard is "I don't know. I've never talked to anyone before." This client may be doubtful about his acceptance by the counselor and may be asking for reassurance that it is all right to seek help. Supportive comments from the counselor might be, "We'll explore what we can do together," or "When you have told me more about yourself, perhaps it will be clearer to you just what you want to accomplish." Both of these responses tell the client that the counselor wants to help and at the same time communicate to him that *he* will be assuming an active role in the process.

Asking a client about his feelings or expectations about counseling allows him to voice any doubts or fears he may have about this new venture and to start thinking realistically about his goals. If the question is not raised, he may be left with uncertainty or anxiety that he is unable to express, and an opportunity will be missed to stimulate in him a sense of participation.

Taking a History

The importance of getting a history of the client, as well as of the problem, cannot be overemphasized. The counselor needs to know what kind of person has come to him for help. Thus the client should be viewed in his total family, social, cultural, economic, and emotional environment, while at the same time assessing his past and present functioning in this setting. Useful as the history-taking process is to the counselor, the client is the real beneficiary as it enables him to look at himself in a new light and initiates self-examination from a broader perspective. It is the first step in problem-solving.

History can be obtained naturally as the interview proceeds. The counselor of course should avoid firing a barrage of questions at a client, but by following the direction of the client's associations he will learn most of the information he seeks as they go along. It is advisable to let the client lead while asking him to expand on and go deeper into the areas he is discussing and not to accept vague or superficial replies. The counselor might say something like, "I don't understand," or "Tell me more about this." However, it goes without saying that he should not be insistent if it becomes obvious that a client is unready or resistant about going into some personal matters. The counselor might indicate that the client may be more comfortable talking about a given subject later, thus deferring, not abandoning, the point.

The counselor's evident interest in learning all about clients is usually gratifying to them. The close inquiries about details also tell them that the counselor is not afraid to look at their problems with them, helping to ease their own fears in exploring themselves.

The order of history-taking is not important; it is important that it develop naturally and yield by the end of the first hour at least some information about most of the following:

FAMILY:	Relationship with parents. Does the client live at home? Who are current family members? Ages of siblings. What does father do for a living? Mother? Parents' educational level. Emotional climate at home. If the client is married, the nature of the marital relationship.
SCHOOL:	How well did the client function in school, or if in school, how is he doing? Family attitude toward education.
WORK:	Job history. How stable? Goals?
SOCIAL LIFE:	Does the client date? Sexual relationships. Friendships. Relative participation or reclusiveness.
HEALTH:	Major illnesses. Operations. Current complaints.
CHILDHOOD:	What does the patient remember of his childhood? How is this related to the current problem?

The counselor should not feel discouraged if he does not obtain all this information in the first interview. Nor should he feel a need to prolong the interview beyond an hour in order to get it. Sometimes in recounting a complex situation the client may take a long time to tell his story, so some history will have to be deferred for another interview. In this case the counselor can suggest that a second meeting be scheduled to learn more about the client's situation before they make any decision. If a second interview is arranged it should follow as soon as possible, at a maximum of a few days, in order to maintain momentum while the client's anxiety and motivation are at a peak level.

Observing the Client

At the same time that a counselor is listening to a new client and learning all that he can about his problem, feelings and life history, he is making continual observations of the client's manner and behavior. Even before the interview began he had gained some impressions. He knew whether the client came to the agency as a walk-in or by appointment, and if he made the appointment himself or if it was made for him by a parent, friend or other referring person. In the event that an appointment was made for him, some resistance or negative reactions may be anticipated. The client will be able to express any such feelings if the counselor asks how he feels about being sent to the agency. If the client is a walk-in, this may suggest a sense of urgency, either because the problem is so pressing or because this is an impulsive, impatient individual.

The counselor will also note a client's manner in entering the office, how he introduces himself, where he chooses to sit, and if he takes the initiative in starting the interview or waits for the counselor to speak first.

The client's manner of relating to the counselor will reveal his habitual approach to interpersonal relationships. How does he present himself? Is he dependent, looking to the counselor for cues and solutions? Is he aggressive, suspicious, defensive or resistant to opening up? An aggressive or resistant client might ask the counselor a lot of questions in an effort to turn the tables and put the counselor on the defensive. Does a client pour out too much intimate detail for a first encounter, suggesting poor judgment or lack of adequate defenses? Or is he appropriately communicative, producing relevant material about himself, while still maintaining some control? Is he insightful about the significance of his communications or feelings?

Body language is a revealing form of communication. For example, does the client's posture indicate a sense of discouragement or depression? Does he perch uneasily on the edge of his chair as if he were on the verge of fleeing, or does he nestle back comfortably? Is he able to make eye contact, or does he look down, avert his eyes or appear to look beyond or through the counselor as if the counselor didn't exist? Gestures and mannerisms should be noted as well as tone of voice, articulation in speech and use of vocabulary. Is the client verbally fluent or hesitant and ill at ease in searching for words? Does he light one cigarette after another, breathe rapidly, sigh or yawn frequently during the interview? Does he sit still in a very controlled or tense manner or continually shift about, twist his hands or behave in an agitated way?

Sometimes a client will leave on his coat, pull it

closely about him and almost seem to huddle in it as if for protection. If he removes it at some time during the interview, this will be a clear message that he is responding positively and feels less threatened. The same applies to a client who initially guards himself behind dark glasses. If he takes them off at some point, this will indicate that he is feeling less frightened or beginning to trust the counselor. After removing his glasses, a client may put them back on during an interview, alerting the counselor that he is uncomfortable about some material that has come up or some comment by the counselor.

Making a Final Assessment

In reviewing the sheer volume of information that is assembled in the initial interview, counselors may feel overwhelmed and ask if they can possibly keep in mind all they have learned about a client, integrate it and form at least a tentative evaluation by the end of the first hour.

Lest it sound dauntingly difficult, it should be explained that for learning purposes the initial interview has been broken down somewhat artificially into a number of sections. In actual practice a counselor soon learns that most of the salient information about his client comes out naturally during the interview with minimal structuring and that his impressions and observations of the client are incorporated almost automatically as the interview progresses. All of us are accustomed to note the mannerisms and characteristics of a new acquaintance almost without conscious thought, so we have already developed an observing eye and ear that will be further refined by experience in assessing clients.

Ideally by the end of the initial interview at least the salient facts about a client have been learned: the client's age, marital status, current school or job situation, his cultural and environmental setting, family makeup and general level of functioning and emotional relationships. His problem, its impact on him and possible options in handling it will have been explored. The image that emerges will then be the basis for assessing the client's ego strengths, the quality of his interpersonal relationships, his relative maturity and emotional resources.

Thus the totality—the history obtained, the client's presentation of his main complaints and the clues picked up by his behavior in the interview—will provide the three ingredients that comprise an evaluation. These are:

1. A tentative assessment of the client-problem constellation
2. A rough diagnosis
3. A treatment proposal or other plan for intervention

The evaluation process, based on the information accumulated in the first interview, is examined in detail in the following chapter. Although it is treated separately here for learning purposes, it actually goes on throughout the first interview; by the close of the interview a counselor will usually have arrived at a clinical impression of the client and drawn some conclusions about the nature and impact of his problems and probable treatment methods or other interventions.

Ending the Interview

Initial interviews are usually concluded in one of three ways:

1. The counselor and client will agree that further counseling will be helpful and the next appointment arranged. If the agency limits counseling to a given number of interviews or a given time span, this may be explained to the client. They may discuss goals then and there, or the counselor may propose that goals be talked over in the next meeting.
2. If the counselor feels he needs more information before an evaluation can be formulated, decides to test the client's motivation further, or wants to talk over the case with his supervisor before making a decision, he may make an appointment for a follow-up interview, informing the client that he would like to know more about him before they can both be clear about the kind of help he needs.
3. The counselor may conclude that his client can best be served by a referral for help that the agency can't provide. If a referral is considered, he may suggest a specific referral at once or make a second appointment to discuss available referral sources.

Summarizing the Interview

During the learning process, a counselor will ordinarily be expected to talk over interviews with his supervisor. In presenting a case to the supervisor, or for staff discussion, both counselor and listeners will find it helpful if he uses a professional form of introduction: cite first the significant data about the client—age, sex, race, marital status, school or work and living situation—followed by his principal complaint. The same form is also used to begin a written case summary.

Thus an opening statement might be: "The client is an 18-year-old single white male, a senior in high school, working 20 hours a week at a gas station, living at home with his divorced mother. He came to the agency without an appointment, appeared agitated, and complained that he had been unable to work or study since his girlfriend broke off with him ten days ago."

Note how much information has been packaged in two sentences. Use of such a précis avoids the confusion a listener experiences when a counselor begins a case discussion somewhere in the middle. It is also good discipline for the counselor to marshal his facts in this order and helps his listeners to get the case quickly in focus.

RESPONDING TO CLIENTS' QUESTIONS

In conducting an initial interview, counselors are frequently confronted with questions or comments from clients that they find difficult to respond to appropriately. The issue of confidentiality, for example, has highly important implications on which counselors must be well informed. Personal inquiries about the counselor are apt to be troubling, requiring tact as well as understanding of the client's intent in asking the questions. Techniques suggested below for responding to commonly encountered questions are applicable when they occur in subsequent counseling sessions as well as during the first interview.

"What Are Your Qualifications?"

Clients sometimes begin an interview by questioning the counselor's training or qualifications. It is reasonable for a client to want to know his counselor's background if he is to confide in him and trust him with personal revelations. However, such questions may also have undertones of which the counselor should be aware. The question may be a defensive maneuver to postpone talking about himself. Instead the client may be saying, "You do the talking." It may be a hostile or aggressive approach, revealing an individual's characteristic response to anxiety, designed to put the counselor on the defensive so he has to explain himself.

To questions about professional qualifications, a very brief, simple statement is sufficient. If the counselor is a student intern, he should say so without apology. If the counselor hesitates or goes into further explanations, the client will be aware of his insecurity and may use other manipulative means to make him uncomfortable.

Most clients do not understand the distinction between psychiatry, psychology, social work or other mental health disciplines. Unless a client specifically asks about this, there is no particular value in volunteering explanations. Should a client inquire about the distinctions or state, for instance, that he thought he ought to see a psychiatrist, it is usually sufficient to tell him that professionals in all these disciplines are trained to help clients with emotional problems. Clients are usually satisfied with this reply and respond readily to an invitation to talk about their problems. The counselor might add that, if he concludes that the client needs to consult a psychiatrist, he will help with a referral.

"Maybe My Problem Isn't Very Important?"

After sharing their complaints with a counselor, some clients seem hesitant and make such comments as, "I guess I don't have a very important problem" or "I shouldn't be taking your time—you must be very busy." These remarks call for positive reassurance. The writer has found the most effective response is to tell the client that it isn't a question of how serious his problem is as the fact that he is suffering, that if he is hurting and his problems are interfering with his life, then it is important to have help. This tells the client that he does not have to be "sick" to solicit help and that the counselor is concerned with his plight no matter how it is manifested. Such an approach is very supportive and almost invariably elicits a positive response from clients. In the event that the client is attempting to minimize his problem because he is wavering about facing it, the counselor's reassuring reply will help to bolster the healthy part of his ego and support his motivation in tackling it.

"What is the Diagnosis?"

Some clients will ask for a diagnostic label. Again the response should be that the client is troubled (or hurting, confused, anxious, unhappy, as the case may be) and that this is your primary concern as a counselor. The counselor can further make his point by adding, "How would a label help you?" Clients are relieved to learn that their counselors care about them and their feelings and are not interested in classifying them, labeling them or viewing them in terms of pathology.

One should always avoid using technical vocabulary with clients, and use simple, direct language in terms of feelings rather than intellectual constructs or mental health jargon. The client is there because of difficulties with his feelings and emotions and this is where the focus should remain.

Some clients will try to "intellectualize," using terms picked up from media periodicals or from a class in psychology as a means of rationalizing or diverting attention away from painful feelings. The counselor should be on guard not to let a client lead him into an intellectual or philosophical discussion. To clients who say, "I have an inferiority complex" or "a mother fixation" or "an oedipus complex," the writer has found it most effective to reply, "I'm not sure what you mean by this term. Maybe it will help if you tell me more about the feelings you have been experiencing." This way you don't get drawn into a discussion of terminology but turn the focus back to the emotional level.

"Are You Married?"

To such personal questions as, "Are you married?" or "Do you have children?" a counselor's best response is a simple yes or no, to which he might add "Does this make a difference to you?" or "Do you feel it will help you to know more about me?" These reponses are useful in further defining the professional relationship, turning attention back to the client and eliciting his reactions to the counselor. To temporize without replying to the client's question and instead inquiring "Why do you ask?" or "You seem interested in me," is a technique better suited to long-term therapy. In short-term counseling, it is more important that the counselor be perceived as a real person by replying briefly to personal questions than to encourage the client to develop fantasies about him by remaining anonymous.

Handling such personal questions requires tact and sensitivity and can be difficult for an inexperienced counselor. He must not reply so as to seem defensive or imply that the client's question was out of order, and, at the same time, should not be tempted to tell too much about himself. If he does, the interview will tend to shift to a friendly relationship rather than a professional dialogue. It will be helpful to the counselor to be reminded that the client is really most concerned about himself and will willingly return to a discussion of his own problems if given a slight nudge in that direction.

DEALING WITH CONFIDENTIALITY

Some clients express concern about confidentiality at the outset. Others may inquire about it at some point in counseling before disclosing what they see as a potentially damaging or embarrassing confession. It would be a simple matter for a counselor if he could promise confidentiality unhesitatingly to all clients.

Unfortunately, this is a very complex issue. Laws on confidentiality and privileged communication vary from state to state. Whether, and under what conditions, a client's record can be subpoenaed by the courts, for instance, depends on state law or judicial precedent. The rights of minors, and what protection can be promised, is another controversial area. A ticklish problem arises if a client reveals the past commission of a crime or intent to commit a crime. What is the counselor's responsibility? An extreme example is a threat of homicide or doing bodily harm to someone. Should the counselor violate confidentiality and inform the intended victim?

The California Supreme Court in 1974 set a precedent (Tarasoff v. Regents of the University of California) when they held a psychiatrist liable for failing to inform and warn a girl friend of a patient, whom the patient threatened to kill and subsequently did murder. The court concluded that "the protective privilege ends where the public peril begins."

What if a client tells of an intent to commit suicide? Is the counselor relieved of his promise of confidentiality and responsible to inform the client's family in order to insure that protective measures are instituted? How serious the threat of a self-destructive or criminal act must be for a professional to report it has not been clearly determined by the courts and is usually left to the counselor's judgment. There are many other cloudy areas and unresolved questions concerning confidentiality. The subject is exhaustively covered in *Confidentiality in Social Work*, by Suanna J. Wilson (1978).

Problems about confidentiality can be minimized if counselors are as clear as possible about this issue. They should discuss any questions with a supervisor and be fully informed about agency policy before they have any contact with clients.

Generally, counselors may assure an adult client who is self-referred and comes to the agency under his own volition that his confidences will not be shared with anyone outside the agency. Nor will the counselor disclose whether or not he has even come to the agency. This extends to parents, spouses or any person who may have advised him to seek help, no matter what the relationship. Use of the words "outside the agency" allows the counselor to be truthful if he intends to discuss the case professionally with a supervisor or staff members.

However, there will need to be some clarification if a referring person—a parent or teacher, for instance—has already spoken to the counselor before the client's appointment and has asked to be notified if the client follows through on his referral. The counselor should tell the client that the referring person will be so informed, with an assurance that he will not reveal anything the client tells him.

Moreover, if the client is a minor, the counselor may have to inform him that it is necessary to let his parents know that he has come to the agency, but again he can promise that nothing he tells the counselor will be revealed. Clarification about confidentiality is particularly important in counseling minors, since they may be hesitant to talk freely about their secrets if they suspect disclosure to parents. Whether there is any obligation to notify parents that a minor has seen a counselor will depend on agency policy and laws in each state governing the rights of minors. In some states minors have complete protection of confidentiality when they are given contraceptives or birth control or abortion information.

Supervisory conferences about clients and case discussions in staff meetings provide professional service to clients and a learning experience to counselors. This is standard accepted practice, and a client's consent is ordinarily assumed but not specifically solicited. It could be a violation of confidentiality if a client objects to disclosure to a particular supervisor or staff member(s). The client has a right to refuse to waive privilege and not allow his confidences to be disclosed to specified individuals. This is a rare occurrence but can conceivably happen if the client has some knowledge of or prior acquaintance with a supervisor or staff member(s), or for some other reason does not want his record shared with them.

Working With Outside Agencies

In addition to confidentiality issues which arise in initial interviews, often relating to parents, spouses or other close relationships, situations involving outside agencies may also confront counselors in their subsequent work with clients. For example, clinical mental health agencies are frequently requested by teachers, police or other authority figures in the community to evaluate an individual. It may be for behavior or adjustment difficulties, employment or other purposes. Clients so referred must be told by the referring person and the counselor the exact purpose of the evaluation. Although the counselor can promise the client that no personal information about him will be disclosed, he must clearly inform the client that an evaluative opinion in writing will be reported to the referring source. Of course, a release of information form signed by the client is required. Ordinarily the evaluative statement will be formulated by a consensus of staff members, including at least the director, supervisor and the counselor who interviewed the client. In the conviction that clients have a right to know the substance, if not the exact wording, of the report, the writer makes it a practice to notify clients following evaluation to share this information with them, offering them an opportunity to express and, if desired, be helped with their reactions.

Information requested by outside agencies or individuals about current or former clients may only be given with clients' written and signed permission. When possible, even though a client has signed permission for disclosure, it is advisable to consult him before responding. Client and counselor can then decide together what should be revealed and what purpose it will serve. Counselors should always use judgment as to what and how much they divulge. They should be careful not to reveal intimate details or personal confidences, but may briefly summarize the record or limit reports to relevant facts or general impressions that they believe will be helpful both to clients and the agencies desiring the information.

Many public and private agencies routinely ask individuals who apply for their services, or for employment, to sign blanket release of information forms. Applicants feel under pressure to comply without knowing what information may be sought, how it will be used, or what precautions will be taken to insure its confidentiality. For this reason the writer usually replies by telephone when asked for information about a former client, in order to learn why and what information is needed, how it will serve the client, and who will have access to it. Unless there is a good reason to believe that a fuller report will benefit the client, a brief verbal reply often suffices. It might be such a noncommittal statement, for example, as that a client was treated during a given time period for "adolescent adjustment," "family problems" or "transient anxiety," as the case may be. The client is thus protected from written reports that may go into open files or be used at some future date to discredit him. There is no absolute obligation to reveal any information about a client, even though he has signed a release form, should the counselor question its usefulness.

Particular caution should be observed in disclosing information to prospective employers. One must carefully weigh how it will be interpreted and used. If a client was seen several years ago, the counselor might explain that he has no information about the client's present functioning and advise a current evaluation. Government bureaus and officials, police and lawyers seeking information may be very intimidating to counselors. They should be advised to refer such requests to the agency director or a supervisor.

Record-Keeping

The Federal Privacy Act of 1974, which permits clients access to all personal records, has posed a serious problem regarding what information should or should not be recorded by agencies. While the act pertains only to federally funded or administered programs, it is anticipated that private agencies and programs may eventually also come under similar federal regulations. For this reason the tendency in mental health agencies has been to keep records brief, to omit confidential material as far as possible, and to use summaries that include only a statement of a client's presenting problem, a diagnosis, and a general conclusion as to the results achieved in counseling.

Student interns and beginners, who write detailed notes of interviews for the purpose of learning and supervision, should keep these separate from the official record and destroy them when a case is closed. This will protect any clients who might eventually ask to see their records from reading counselors' comments and will also afford clients protection from outside exposure, should their records ever be subpoenaed.

RECOMMENDED READING

Wilson, S. (1978), *Confidentiality in Social Work: Issues and Principles*. New York: The Free Press.

This thorough review of confidentiality issues is a useful reference guide for all mental health practitioners.

CHAPTER 3

Evaluation

THE DIAGNOSTIC PROCESS

A counselor learns a great deal about a client during their first meeting, as noted in the last chapter. This data must then be assimilated and processed, i.e., an evaluation must be made, preliminary to planning help for the client. Evaluation is a synthesis in which to view a particular client, in a particular life setting, with a particular problem, for the purpose of prescribing for him. It is both a diagnosis and a recommendation for some kind of intervention in the client's behalf.

Because subsequent work with a client rests so directly on the accuracy and soundness of the evaluation that precedes it, it forms the cornerstone of the counseling process, a firm anchor from which to proceed with confidence in offering appropriate service to a client. For a skilled clinician, evaluation begins the moment a new client walks into his office. Just as a computer sifts, correlates and integrates information that is fed into it, and comes up with an answer, so a clinician almost without conscious awareness records information and subjective impressions and assimilates these during the course of an interview. He often arrives at a tentative evaluation by the close of the interview. This is a skill acquired with long practice.

Students and beginning counselors will develop this kind of competence in evaluating clients only after considerable experience. They will be most comfortable if they focus on learning as much as possible about their clients in initial interviews without feeling any pressure to formulate evaluations at the same time.

I emphasize again that it is seldom necessary to *do* anything in the initial meeting with a client. If the counselor feels no urgency to come up with a diagnosis or make any immediate treatment proposal to the client, he can listen intently to the client's story and store up his impressions for a supervisory conference after the interview. Barring some emergency, the client can be told that the counselor would like to talk to him further and know more about him before they make plans together. They should then schedule the next appointment, in as few days as possible, especially if the client is excessively anxious or troubled.

Before seeing the client a next time the counselor will have leisure to think over the client's communications and review the material with his supervisor. With the supervisor's help he will be prepared to investigate further when the client returns. Evaluation may be continued over two or more meetings with a client; in the meantime, supervisory help should be available at each step. In practice, even experienced counselors often delay a final evaluation until they have seen a client more than once, and at times there may be a period of extended evaluation before diagnosis is clearly determined.

As counselors gain confidence with continued practice, they will find that their impressions of clients are assembled and weighed almost automatically while they listen to clients' communications. Gradually evaluation will become an integral part of interviewing.

For learning purposes, however, evaluation is reviewed here as if it were a separate process. To help counselors learn just what to look for in assessing a client and how an evaluation is derived, the diagnostic process is dissected and broken down into four components:

1. Ego assessment. This appraises an individual's personality structure, gauges his emotional strengths and resources as well as areas of vulnerability, based on his life history and functioning.
2. Problem assessment. This identifies the problem, how it is experienced by the client and why it is so troubling to him.
3. Motivation assessment. This appraises the client's motivation and capacity to use help, ability to form a client-counselor relationship, degree of insight, and problem-solving capability.
4. Disposition. This is a treatment plan or other intervention to help the client. If counseling is agreed upon, it includes the determination of goals.

Ego Assessment

Ego assessment is a method of personality inventory or diagnosis, sometimes called "psychosocial assessment." Unlike psychiatric diagnosis, which is mainly concerned with pathology, ego assessment focuses on the individual's relative strength and coping capacity. It is hopeful and positive and avoids the kind of labeling implied in standard psychiatric diagnosis. The counselor does not want to label a client—it is of no help to the client—but he does want to know what the client is like in order to individualize him.

Ego assessment takes into account the maturity a client has achieved appropriate for his age, his adjustment to his total environment, cultural, economic, racial and familial, and his ability to master stresses and disappointments and to judge reality without too much distortion. In short, it appraises the quality of his relationships and his total emotional functioning.

What is Meant by "Ego"?

In order to understand and use the ego method of diagnosis, first we need to define just what we mean by the term "ego," often so loosely used and only vaguely understood.

The ego is a theoretical concept referring to that part of the personality that perceives and adapts to reality, makes judgments, and mediates between an individual's inner wishes or drives and the demands of the society in which he lives.

An infant is born with powerful instinctual drives which demand satisfaction. His ego as such exists only in embryonic form. As the infant begins to perceive that some behavior on his part brings him gratification and other behavior is met with disapproval or disappointment, and as he becomes aware of other persons whose love and approval are important to him, an ego begins to be differentiated from his primitive instinctual drives. There is an emerging awareness of "you" and "me," of a self as distinguished from "others." While he still demands satisfaction, he learns ways to influence his environment to bring it about. In other words, he begins to relate to others.

Given a loving, reasonably consistent and encouraging climate in which to develop controls and self-esteem, the child's ego will continue to expand. He will gradually learn to adapt to his environment, appraise his world, regulate his behavior and establish a continuity of relationships. At the same time that the child's ego is adjusting to the outside world, it must also accommodate to two other forces or demands from within. The first of these are the pleasure-seeking and aggressive drives or instincts, called the "id" in dynamic theory. These desires continually clamor for expression. His ego must find some means of controlling, delaying or suppressing unacceptable drives by compromises which will allow him some satisfaction without incurring danger to the self—either loss of love or punishment. He must learn to civilize his instincts. If ego development has proceeded normally he will be able to curb or subdue his drives and still gain reasonable satisfaction. If the drives are too powerful because of constitutional factors, or the ego too weak or poorly integrated, his besieged ego will be in continual conflict with the aggressive demands flowing from the id. His adjustment will be unstable, with adequate controls lacking, or at best, uneven and unreliable.

The third agency in personality structure is the emerging conscience which sits in judgment and causes feelings of guilt. This is conceptualized as the "superego," which began its development with parents' disapproval or prohibitions. The parental voice which said "no" to unacceptable behavior, and made distinctions to the child between "good" and "bad," gradually begins to be internalized in early childhood so that the child becomes self-judging. One often hears a small child who is tempted to touch a forbidden object say, "No, no," an indication that he has already incorporated parental warnings in his emerging superego.

To the extent that the superego is harsh, uncompromising and guilt-ridden, the ego will be diminished and inhibited in its freedom to obtain gratification from the external world. A more tolerant superego will regulate behavior and observe reasonable ethical standards without bringing continual self-criticism. Inadequate superego development may result in too little self-regulation and antisocial behavior.

Freud's Terminology

The concepts of id, ego and superego are highly theoretical and may be difficult to understand, in part because of their abstract terminology.

Sigmund Freud originated the concepts but used very human and immediately understandable words to describe the three agencies of personality organization. Counselors will find Freud's ideas reassuringly clear and easy to grasp if his language is substituted for "id," "ego" and "superego." These coldly abstract terms are unfortunate English translations of Freud's German words. As Bruno Bettelheim (1982) writes in "*Freud and the Soul,*'' Freud spoke of the three aspects of personality in very personal German pronouns that reflect the spirit and intent of his thinking, and which the Latin equivalents used by the translator fail to convey.

Freud called what we know as the ego ''*das Ich,*'' by which he simply meant the ''I'' that represents what one knows as his familiar self. Freud's ''*Über-Ich,*'' the Over-I, is that part of the self that monitors and censors and acts as a restriction on the ''I.'' The word id is translated from Freud's ''*das es,*'' literally the ''it,'' a common German word for a child of either sex. Bettelheim explains that ''This fact gives the phrase ''*das es*'' a special feeling, reminding the German reader that this is how he was referred to before he learned to repress many of his sexual, aggressive and otherwise asocial impulses, before he felt guilty or ashamed because of them, before he felt an obligation to resolve contradictions and bring logical order into his thoughts; in short, it reminds him of a time when his entire existence was dominated by the It.'' Note how much more human this conception of the unconscious is than the one connoted by the abstract word ''id.''

Ego Defenses

We now have a picture of the developing ego, always struggling with the pressures exerted from within by the drives and superego and from without by the demands of the environment. In its efforts to subdue drives and protect the individual's emotional integrity, the ego employs a number of defense mechanisms.

These defenses are a normal and necessary aspect of ego functioning and are unhealthy only when they become so rigid or restricting that they are crippling to the individual's freedom of expression.

All of us use some protective mechanisms to conceal and guard our feelings. This facade or protective shell serves as a useful buffer when it fairly closely approximates, or does not totally disguise, what we are really like underneath. Thus it filters both positive and negative feelings, and allows them to be expressed to some degree or in somewhat altered form that is acceptable. Good manners, courtesy and conventional social behavior are examples of a common facade employed even when one may feel impatient or irritated. Another protective mechanism is the withholding of intimate details about oneself or one's feelings, when it might be inappropriate or damaging to share them. We tend to protect an inner core of self from revelation, and such reserve is healthy unless carried to such a degree that an individual avoids disclosing anything about his real self.

In assessing ego functions, any seriously limiting defenses will be detectable and add a further dimension to diagnosis. For example, a client who uses the defense of inhibition to excess will appear flat, emotionless, and unable to express either strong positive or negative feelings.

Denial of aggressive drives will be manifest in a variety of ways. Some clients will have a history of avoidance of situations that call for self-assertion. Others will be overly nice, undeviatingly kind and compliant under all circumstances, their assertions that they love everyone having a false or insincere quality in their desperate efforts to conceal their hostile feelings. This defense is called reaction-formation. The resulting character structure will seem bland and one-sided.

Individuals who are always belligerent and contentious, as if they had chips on their shoulders, may be masking an underlying sense of inferiority and weakness and a fear of displaying passivity. They too appear to be locked into a pattern in which only one form of expression is permitted.

Obsessive-compulsive rituals are a defense against fears of loss of control. Individuals who feel endangered by unconscious aggressive or libidinal impulses prevent these from breaking through by continual repetition of compulsive acts or torturing obsessive thoughts as a means to bind and control. This results in loss of flexibility. A simple example from childhood is the magical formula, "Step on a crack and you'll break your mother's back." The avoidance of cracks expresses both impulse and denial. Checking again and again to insure that the gas is turned off or doors locked likewise contain the wish and its prevention.

Projection is a defense against acknowledging one's liability for objectionable feelings and impulses. Instead the individual uses projection by attributing to others the feelings he wants to avoid. One often hears children use this defense by accusing others, "I didn't do it; he did." Individuals who habitually project unconsciously shift the blame for their difficulties on others, on circumstances, or on the hostile environment. The indignation they express toward others substitutes and protects them from self-criticism and guilt.

This brief review of the most common defense mechanisms indicates the protective measures individuals employ in order to maintain control and avoid danger from the demands of the id, the superego or the environment. In assessing a client's defensive structure, a counselor will recognize that one who characteristically and to an excessive and self-limiting degree uses inhibition, denial, projection, compulsive rituals or aggression, either turned against the self or others, has a poorer outlook for change and ego growth than an individual whose defenses are more benign and fluid.

It should not be anticipated that defenses will break down in counseling; nor is this desirable. Obviously an individual very much needs his particular defenses. But understanding the defenses an individual uses will help in planning a counseling approach. To a limited degree, a modification of defenses is sometimes possible in treatment. An individual who fears his aggressive impulses may be helped to accept that some expression of aggression is normal and desirable. An inhibited client may be encouraged to allow some feelings to be acknowledged. One who turns aggression on himself may be helped to examine the irrational guilt he feels and be less punitive. For the client who projects, some gentle exploration without accusation may lead him to realize that he may be contributing to the difficulties for which he blames someone or something external to himself.

Conflict and the Ego

It has been noted that the ego is always subject to some conflict. There will be a minimum of conflict if the ego has adapted to the external world with relative harmony, if it finds satisfaction without sacrificing too much pleasure and spontaneity, and if the inner drives are not too clamorous and the superego is reasonably tolerant and benign.

If the ego is too weak or immature to carry out its function as a go-between or mediator, the individual will feel uncomfortable, torn by conflicting impulses and out of harmony with himself. If the drives press too strongly, the ego may have to divert so much of its energy to inhibit them that there will be little energy left to deal with the outer world. If the superego is continually punishing so that the individual feels "bad" or worthless or guilty, he will be deficient in the self-esteem needed to perform successfully in the external world. If the ego has not been able to adapt to the demands of society, the individual will be in continual conflict and difficulty with the environment.

When clients seek help it is a signal that their egos are experiencing more conflict than is tolerable or manageable. There is a temporary breakdown of ego functions; egos are weakened and unable to maintain equilibrium. The individual will feel anxious and overwhelmed and may develop any of a variety of symptoms.

It can now be seen why a review of a client's history is important. In looking at his past performance the counselor will be able to appraise the level of ego development that was attained before the current breakdown. It will not only provide clues to the extent of the client's current regression, but be a basis for judging his strengths in handling past crises and his potential for regaining equilibrium.

If a client has been able to hold jobs successfully,

or to achieve consistently in school, this will be one indication of strength and stability. Other measures of ego assets will be the level of interpersonal relationships maintained, the extent of behavior controls, flexibility, frustration tolerance, maturity and ability to appraise reality.

Criteria of Ego Strength

Before examining specific steps in making an ego assessment, we need a model for comparison: What are the criteria for judging ego health or "ego strength," as it is commonly referred to? Mental health is sometimes simply defined as:

The ability to love.
The ability to work.
The ability to play.

The following list is a more comprehensive breakdown of the primary ego functions. Probably no individual will have attained this ideal level of functioning or be equally strong in all areas, but the following abilities or ego functions will serve as a reference scale in measuring a client's ego development:

1. To love self and others, establish stability and constancy in relationships, and give and take in these relationships.
2. To be aware of and express feelings of love as well as anger when appropriate.
3. To be reasonably assertive and feel confidence in doing so.
4. To work consistently and feel satisfaction in productivity and accomplishment.

5. To be able to concentrate, learn, and persist in order to complete tasks and achieve goals.
6. To enjoy recreation and play, relax from cares at these times and enter into social situations freely.
7. To adapt to the environment with flexibility and accept situations that cannot be changed, and conversely, to be able to take action to alter unacceptable situations when options are available.
8. To establish self-control and discipline without excessive self-limitation or rigidity.
9. To make independent decisions and assume responsibility for them.
10. To make judgments of reality with a minimum of distortion.

Appraising Ego Functions

How can a counselor now proceed to appraise a client in terms of these 10 primary ego functions? As he reviews the client's total communications, he will already have formed some general impressions, have a "feel" for what the client is like and come to some conclusions about his personality. The next step is to look at specific areas of functioning. As he asks himself how adequately the client measures up, he will note any particular points of deficit or developmental lag. From this kind of detailed analysis, a quite accurate mental health profile will emerge.

Adjustment. How relatively stable is the individual's adjustment to his environment? While his functioning may be impaired at the time he is interviewed because of the current conflict or breakdown that brings him for help, a review of his history will reveal how adequately he has adjusted in the past. To what degree has he been able to work consistently? How has he performed in school? Has he been able to complete tasks? Has he adapted with reasonable harmony to the external world? The degree to which he has adjusted will attest to his strength and resiliency. If adjustment has broken down in the past, in which areas has he faltered or failed?

Object relationships. Has there been constancy in the client's relationships with others? Has he been able to give and take, to maintain stable relationships, to express affection? Does he have a history of difficulty in establishing relationships, or maintaining them, with his own sex or the opposite sex? Is he excessively dependent on others, seeking continual support and feedback? Is he hostile or aggressive toward others; suspicious or lacking in trust?

How does the client relate to his counselor? Is he ingratiating, overanxious to please, friendly or hostile? Is he cooperative and accepting or mistrustful and resistant? In observing his behavior in the interview, the counselor should take note if he is comfortable and natural and talks easily, or seems tense and apprehensive, suggesting some inner barrier to intimacy.

Second, and of equal diagnostic significance, how do you, the counselor, react to the client? Do you find him likeable and appealing? Does he arouse your sympathy or do you feel antagonized, uncomfortable or even repelled by him? Counselors should not hesitate to admit to themselves, and to their supervisors, if they initially find some clients unsympathetic. Their reactions will reveal how the client relates to others as well, probably arousing similar negative feelings. Moreover the understanding the counselor gains by examining just what it is in the client's manner or person that alienates him will help him to overcome his own discomfort with the client.

Maturity. Has the client attained the maturity expected for his age? Maturity can be measured in ability to assume responsibility, to make judgments, to be independent and self-motivating. If he is immature, in what functions has he failed to grow? When one sees an adolescent who appears childlike, overdependent on parents or too compliant in relation to them, for example, it will indicate some arrest in the developmental process. His strivings toward independence have been at least temporarily blocked and he will need help and encouragement in taking steps toward separation and self-reliance.

Some individuals give a superficial impression of maturity and will consider themselves to be adult and responsible, but their claimed maturity has a "pseudo" quality, like an overlay. Their intellectual growth and competence to conduct their external affairs may be impressive, but have outpaced their emotional development. This is particularly noticeable in adolescents who have grown up like "little adults." They may have assumed premature responsibility for younger siblings, be considered by parents to be very reliable and acquired a facade of maturity without ever having experienced a real childhood, as if this developmental stage was bypassed. The interviewer will detect in such individuals that they seem too serious, too restricted in emotional expression, almost too good to be true. Their seeming maturity will cover an absence of a sound inner core of resilience and identity.

Aggression. Can a client recognize and express anger? How assertive is he? Does he seem inhibited and tend to deny anger when it would be appropriate to experience it? Is he overaggressive as if always on the defensive? If his aggressive drives are rigidly suppressed, he will have limited ability to deal with his world effectively. If he is unnecessarily aggressive, this may suggest that he doesn't trust others and expects hostility from them or that he may be defending against feelings of inferiority and helplessness. In either case he may need help in handling his aggressive drives more appropriately.

Frustration tolerance. How does a client respond to frustration or interference with his pleasure-seeking wishes? Does he become angry, or depressed, or tend to blame others? Is he passive and apt to give up easily in the face of disappointment? Does he act out in destructive or antisocial behavior? Does he take drugs, or get into trouble with authority?

On the other hand, can he tolerate frustration with some equanimity, accept a situation he cannot change, or take reasonable steps to alter a situation where there are options available? The latter, of course, is the healthier mode of response.

Self-esteem. Is an individual able to maintain self-esteem under adverse circumstances, loss or disappointment? Does his self-esteem depend on positive feedback from others? Does he feel worthless, a failure, and seldom think well of himself? Does he often feel guilty, unworthy or "bad"? Lack of self-esteem may be due to an overload of guilt, an early history of rejection, or failure in the nurturing that leads to self-love.

Identity. How firm is his sense of identity? Does he seem to know who he is, what he stands for, and what he wants to become or achieve? Does he have gender identity, have conviction of what it means to be a man (or a woman), or is there a diffuseness of sexual image?

Asking a client to describe himself is an excellent technique for obtaining a picture of his self-image. Will he define himself in terms of occupation, gender, familial relationships or aspirations? Will he focus positively on his personality qualities, assets and self-worth, or negatively on his flaws, complaints and dissatisfactions? Some clients will have a clear conviction of who they are and will elaborate on their qualities; others may be confused by the question, unable to come up with a ready answer, or give a superficial and sterile response, such as, "I'm a secretary," "I'm a mother," "I'm a student," or ask "What do you want to know about me?" If asked to describe their parents, the same range of replies may be expected. Some clients will talk about the qualities and interaction of their parents and siblings, while those who have never really ascribed identity to themselves or others will have conventional answers such as one female client gave, "I have a mother and father—they are just—well—parents. I love them, of course."

Strengths. In summing up an individual's qualities, examine the strengths he has displayed given his life circumstances, history and adversities. Weaknesses may be more apparent at first than the strengths an individual has been able to muster in his life situation. For this reason it is particularly important to recognize a client's coping capacities.

The counselor will often find that a client who has been subjected to severe stresses has stood up to them with remarkable fortitude. In assessing such a client an attitude of hopefulness may be felt, knowing that his strengths will be an asset and can be mobilized in the counseling process no matter how troubling his problems seem. Consider, for example, the case of a woman who was deserted by her husband after their third child was born: She functioned minimally in many areas of her life and had limited ego resources, yet for many years she had been able to care for her children with love and sensitivity to their needs. In spite of her inadequacy, the core of strength shone through.

A client's ability to seek help is, in itself, a positive indication not always recognized by counselors.

Summary. As an individual's functioning has been reviewed in detail, the complexity and uniqueness of his personality will come into focus. He will be seen not as a stereotype but as an individual, with his own particular assets and weaknesses, his strengths and areas of vulnerability. Viewing him as a whole, the counselor making the assessment will be ready to draw some tentative conclusions about the extent and kind of support this client may need to enhance his functioning. Understanding of the client's personality will be further illuminated when his presenting problem has been assessed.

Problem Assessment

Keeping in mind what has been learned about a client in the ego-assessment, the next step in evaluation is to consider the problem that is disturbing him. This provides a further dimension in personality appraisal, as the two are dynamically interrelated. A problem that is not particularly troubling to one client may be intensely painful to another, so a client's emotional functioning and the kind of difficulty that has temporarily threatened it cannot be separated.

A client's stated problem, per se, will not be very revealing until one learns how it is experienced by the client and why it is so troubling to him in the light of his particular personality and ego organization. Only when the two are viewed in conjunction can the full meaning of the problem be assessed. To illustrate, a dozen individuals might react in as many different ways to a given problem, the loss of a friend. Losing a friend might be accepted philosophically by one person. Another might feel hurt but still maintain self-esteem. A third person might be devastated by what he experienced as total rejection. The latter individual's inability to sustain a loss points to developmental failure in attaining independence and autonomy.

A college student with a history of adequate functioning may be overwhelmed by anxiety at the prospect of graduation, though graduation is a gratifying accomplishment for most students. For this student the final step toward adulthood aroused a dormant fear of separation (from alma mater-parent). Graduation coincides with a vulnerable area—failure to complete the adolescent developmental process leading to separation and identity.

A promotion to a position of authority may cause intense anxiety to a dependent individual who has previously functioned well in a structured situation. While most persons would rejoice at the promotion, this individual may be threatened by the absence of controls from superiors, fearing that he won't be able to master his aggressive impulses. He will either feel inhibited from exercising authority or be overwhelmed by an overload of aggression that he fears he won't be able to control.

In these examples—the loss of a friend, graduation, and the prospect of promotion—it was not the event itself but a particular client's reaction to the event that was significant because it touched on a vulnerable point, revealing the specific ego function which was too weak or impaired to tolerate the stress.

The clients who reacted with anxiety to the loss of a friend, graduation or promotion may not have been aware of the events which precipitated their breakdown. They may have sought counseling for other unrelated complaints or have professed total ignorance of the reason for their distress, so it is the counselor's task to ferret out the real problem. Counselors may easily recognize that something is bothering a client when he seeks help, but the problem he initially presents can't always be taken at face value. A client may not know why he is so upset. He may complain of something bland until he can test the counselor before he reveals too much about himself. High school and college students sometimes complain vaguely of study problems, a safe and acceptable subject, until they can size up the counselor and decide whether to venture on more personal concerns.

A client may initially assign his difficulty to taking drugs, when actually he is depressed, is escaping from angry feelings he can't tolerate, feels alienated or is disappointed in himself for some reason and is using drugs to evade the uncomfortable feelings. Another client may complain about his lack of friends and seek help to develop social skills. His real problem may be a conviction that he is unlovable and expects others to dislike him; he may fear rejection or be suffering from past hurts that account for his isolation.

The core problem is revealed in many cases only when one learns about the precipitant. This explains why I stressed the importance of inquiring in the initial interview what event immediately preceded a client's referral for help. When the precipitant is identified it will offer a direct clue to the underlying or core problem.

When the problem has been identified, the next question is why it is so disturbing to a particular client. What ego function is deficient? To return to the examples cited earlier, the client who was threatened by promotion had limited his self-expression by inhibiting his aggressive impulses. There was failure to develop an important ego function, the ability to express and exercise reasonable control over instinctual impulses. The client who was devastated by the loss of a friend had not acquired a firm sense of self as distinguished from others, so he relied on objects to supply identity and self-esteem. When these were withdrawn, he experienced a loss of self. The student who feared graduation had not mastered the final step in separation leading to maturity and assumption of adult responsibility. One may speculate that excessive superego guilt was a contributing factor, if success in graduating implied the realization of old hostile competitive strivings that his ego could not tolerate.

In making a client-problem assessment three factors will be weighed: (1) the precipitant or core problem; (2) the impact of the problem, that is, the degree of disequilibrium that it has caused; and (3) the specific ego functions that broke down under stress.

Ego assessment yielded a broad picture of a client's total functioning, how firmly anchored or structured his ego organization is, how far he has advanced toward maturity and his strengths and deficits. The problem, when it is identified, discloses in what areas and to what degree his ego is prone to stress. In viewing this constellation as a whole a counselor should be able to conclude what conflicts a client needs help with as well as the assets he will be able to call on in mastering his difficulties.

While it is desirable to make a client-problem assessment as quickly as possible, the counselor should be cautious about relying on an evaluation made after a single interview. It may sometimes have to be amended when the client returns for a follow-up session. An original assessment, no matter how carefully formulated, needs to be tested and is always subject to review during the counseling process as new aspects of the client's personality organization emerge.

Some clients present only a partial view of themselves initially. It may be the defensive side in some cases; in others, the turmoil underneath will be apparent with the defenses virtually inoperative. Often, to a counselor's surprise, a client who gave an impression of helplessness and inadequacy in the initial interview may return appearing more composed, integrated and with a more rational perspective on his problem. The explanation may be that controls temporarily broke down in his anxiety over facing a new experience, but that the verbalization in the first interview was effective in restoring defenses and objectivity. This indicates an ability to compensate rapidly.

Conversely, a client who seems to be well organized originally may turn out to be regressed, confused and poorly integrated when he is seen again. He was able to maintain a posture of health, with defenses under careful control at first, but could not sustain the position for long. Here one sees an ego under great stress with unreliable controls, and must alter his original assessment accordingly.

Other clients may initially present an image of helplessness in order to induce the counselor to offer help and appeal to his sympathy. Once this message has been conveyed and the counselor responds, the client will allow his healthier side to come to light in a subsequent interview.

Clients will sometimes report at the second or third interview that they have recovered and need no further help. Whether the improvement is genuine or what is known as a "flight into health" will require evaluation. It is true that clients are often able to resolve a troubling question in one or two interviews. They have no expectation and feel no need for prolonged evaluation or treatment. If there is good evidence that the client is symptom-free a counselor should be content with the gratifying results and not seek to engage the client further.

If a flight into health is suspected, it calls for careful discrimination to determine if it is justified self-protection or a form of resistance. A client may sense that his defenses are precarious and fear loss of control, so he will "get well" in order to avoid further probing. In claiming that he has recovered he can justify withdrawing from counseling to avoid endangering a brittle and shaky adjustment. In such a case the counselor should respect the client's judgment, as the client may be right in anticipating that he is too fragile to undergo possibly disrupting self-examination. He would prefer to live with his symptoms than risk falling apart. The counselor's offer to see him again when he feels that he is ready to look at his problems will leave the door open for him to return.

A client who perceives that by continuing counseling he may have to acknowledge and give up symptomatic behavior that is gratifying may also announce that he is better and seek to withdraw from counseling. In such a case the flight into health is a resistance. Carefully exploring his expectations of counseling, eliciting his fears and offering interpretation of his reluctance, and some reassurance will usually overcome the resistance.

Motivation Assessment

A client's personality structure, the nature of his problem and the particular ego weakness it exposes, were pictured in the client-problem assessment. A further factor—his motivation and capacity to use help—must then be considered before determining on a treatment plan or other disposition. In reviewing a client's communications, look for indications of flexibility, degree of insight, urgency for help and expectations of counseling.

If a client came to the agency under duress from a parent, employer, teacher or friend, or made the appointment because someone else told him he needed help, he may have little or no motivation and only be complying without real self-engagement. Clients who seem to be mainly looking for someone else to change their external circumstances are also not apt to be strongly motivated.

Those who have fairly intact egos but are currently suffering a great deal of distress are usually highly motivated and able to use counseling effectively. One clue will be their replies to questions regarding their expectations of counseling. If they see the counselor as an ally in a cooperative effort, this will be a more positive indication of motivation than if they are expecting the counselor alone to solve their problems.

Sufficient motivation may be assumed if a client seems sincerely to want to solve his problems; if he relates well to the counselor; if he is cooperative and able to accept the role of client.

If a client is hostile, suspicious and guarded or says, in effect, "No one can help me; it's a waste of time," it may be questionable whether he will be open to counseling. But even if in doubt, counselors, of course, should make the effort to engage such clients. These attitudes are sometimes defenses against fears of being rejected and a client's manner a way of testing if the counselor is really concerned before the client makes a commitment.

If a client seems hesitant and unsure what counseling may involve, it is better practice to see him several times while considering possible plans for help than to impose a program prematurely that he may not be ready to accept. Even in short-term counseling, treatment plans and goals can be evolved over several interviews while the client acclimates himself to counseling. Some clients need this time to learn to trust the counselor as well as to explore their problems and determine whether they really need further help.

Clients sometimes drop out because in a counselor's zeal to be helpful he sets up an immediate treatment plan on the mistaken assumption that the client is prepared to engage in it. Not having anticipated extended counseling, a client may feel resentful at the counselor's taking control or interpret that the counselor is telling him that he is "sick." As a result of his alarm and confusion, the client doesn't return. The same client might have been led to accept counseling after a few interviews if he himself came to the conclusion that he could profit from further help.

In assessing motivation for counseling, counselors will soon begin to recognize and discriminate between those who have promising potential for problem resolution and those who are doubtful candidates. Clients who are suffering acutely from their symptoms are most apt to respond to short-term counseling. Dependent individuals with limited ego resources welcome supportive counseling, often become attached to their counselors and return from time to time in periods of stress. Clients who have previously functioned minimally but are severely regressed at the time of referral may be able to use firm support to restore a prior level of adjustment.

Disposition

The final component of the evaluation process, the treatment plan or disposition, will be a natural outgrowth of the client-problem assessment. Counseling is only one of a number of interventions a counselor has at his disposal. Depending on his assessment of the client and the resources available in his agency or accessible in the community, he may weigh the following options:

Referral to a psychiatrist for further evaluation. This may be recommended if the counselor is in doubt about diagnosis and feels the need of a back-up opinion, or if he is convinced a client needs more intensive treatment than the agency can provide. If the agency has the services of a consultant, he may be called on to review the case or see the client for further evaluation.

Hospitalization or notification of parents or family to assume responsibility. This may be necessary if a client has expressed suicide intent, is acting out in a destructive manner or presents a threat to others. Hospitalization may also be indicated if breakdown in functioning has occurred or appears imminent.

Referral for long-term psychotherapy. This is for clients who have histories of chronic anxiety and neurotic conflict for which short-term counseling is unlikely to be effective.

Referral for medical examination. A client who complains of frequent headaches, stomach upsets, colitis, hypertension or excessive fatigue, for example, should be advised to have a thorough physical work-up to rule out organic disease, even if it is suspected that the symptoms are psychogenic. This will afford protection to counselor and client, if the counselor plans to continue seeing the client.

Environmental intervention. Some clients may need

immediate help with medical, housing, financial or other situations for which they should be referred to appropriate agencies. In cases of adolescent clients, intervention by the counselor with parents or school authorities, for instance, may be necessary as a preliminary to counseling, but should be undertaken with the adolescent's knowledge and permission.

Referral for psychological testing. In clinical interviews with children and young adolescents, their verbalizations alone cannot always be trusted, nor can parents' observations and complaints about their behavior be relied upon. Obtaining a back-up opinion and confirmation of diagnosis, based on the results of projective and intelligence testing, will be added insurance that one is on firm ground before undertaking counseling.

Short-term counseling. This will be the treatment of choice if it has been determined in the assessment that the client is sufficiently motivated and can profit from counseling. In some cases counseling may be advisable to help prepare a client for a later referral for intensive psychotherapy.

Counseling Goals

Just as physicians don't write the same prescription for all patients, so in counseling the treatment will be determined by the diagnosis. It is individualized according to the client's symptoms, level of ego development and capacities, and motivation to change. The relative activity of the counselor, focus and goals will vary from client to client. This flexibility distinguishes the psychodynamic approach from the behavioral and other therapies which have a more limited range.

Symptom relief will be a primary goal in planning a counseling approach for all clients, but additional benefits to clients in self-awareness and ego growth will also be envisaged. While treatment plans will be designed individually for each client, some general guidelines are suggested below.

In general healthy clients may be stimulated to examine their feelings more deeply and will require less activity and intervention from counselors than clients whose adjustment is precarious. Clients with well structured egos are usually able to tolerate some probing, provoking them to recall early experiences and recover old memories that may have a bearing on the conflicts that are troubling them. They will be encouraged to reflect and make connections between past and present with the goal of gaining insight.

To the degree that clients are unstable or regressed, counselors will expect to be correspondingly more active, offering firm support of weakened defenses in order to help the clients recover equilibrium as quickly as possible. Counselors may make suggestions or be directive at times. Focus will usually be on day-to-day reality; probing should be avoided since the aim is to stabilize such clients, not dissect them, which could lead to further decompensation in already shaky individuals.

Clients in crisis because of sudden and unanticipated external pressures, whose usual coping mechanisms have failed, will need immediate help to identify options and decide on a course of action to relieve environmental pressure. Referrals for other services may be indicated. Such interventions will take precedence at the outset over exploration of a client's emotional reaction to the crisis.

A client's defensive structure is a factor in designing a treatment approach. If a client's defenses against instinctual drives are inadequate, if he is impulsive, acts out or is given to outbursts of aggression, he will need to establish firmer controls and standards of conduct. Counseling will aim to help clients whose defenses are loose and unreliable to suppress their drives rather than permitting unlimited ventilation of emotions. The counselor may be firm in placing some restrictions on acting out behavior.

On the other hand, some modification and freeing of defenses will be a goal in counseling clients who are inhibited in expressing feelings, especially aggression, or who do not even recognize their angry feelings. Clients who are self-critical because of harsh superego demands will also need encouragement to modify their self-imposed and unrealistic expectations, to be more tolerant and accepting of themselves.

Characteristic behavior patterns repeatedly lead to self-defeat for some clients, though they are often totally unaware of the destructive nature of their behavior. Enabling such individuals to recognize the behavior that continually gets them into trouble, by calling attention to their actions, will be an initial goal in counseling. Clients' understanding of how they sabotage themselves may then lead them to explore the reasons and seek to establish more rewarding patterns.

Depressed clients call for warm support, the goal to enable them to restore self-esteem. They should be encouraged to verbalize their feelings, explore the precipitant and its relation to losses experienced in the past; to seek replacements for loss and be reassured that there *is* a future.

Younger adolescents regain stability and resolve transient turmoils fairly quickly by talking to an objective listener, with very little intervention required of the counselor. In helping adolescents in the later phase of development, a goal may be facilitating emotional separation from parents, and the establishment of identity and independence. Adolescents who are engaged in destructive behavior will need firm curbing of their acting out before they can be helped to identify the feelings or conflicts which they are attempting to escape by their impulsive behavior.

Talking to a calm and concerned adult is a dynamic stabilizing force in itself for many clients. Those who seek help in making a decision or who want to talk over a troubling situation may use a counselor mainly as a sounding board and find solutions in as few as two or three interviews. A counselor who listens responsively can be particularly helpful to adolescents, to elderly clients who have temporarily lost their bearings, and to clients who are confused by conflicting feelings and need an unbiased listener to help them gain objectivity.

EVALUATION OF REFERRAL REQUESTS

Mental health and crisis intervention agencies provide a major service to their communities in offering referrals to the general public who call on them for a wide variety of information. They are usually knowledgeable and up-to-date about the manifold resources in their areas. They also refer clients who come to them for help if their agencies don't offer the services needed.

The review of evaluation techniques was particularly focused on assessment of candidates for counseling, but it seems pertinent to add some remarks on the secondary but important function of counselors in responding to and evaluating individuals for referral. Answering these appeals for help demands skill and tact, although, unfortunately, the responsibility is sometimes delegated to the least experienced staff members.

In screening clients for referral, counselors serve an invaluable function in directing the right client to the right agency. However, referrals can also be a source of discouragement and frustration. Any client who has made the weary round of agencies because of a succession of casual and thoughtless referrals made without careful evaluation of the client's real needs or accurate information about the agencies to which he is referred, will testify to this.

Counselors need more than a telephone and a fat file of resource information if they are to make helpful and effective referrals. They must learn something about the client, his emotional state, the problems he wants help with, his expectations and how realistic they are. Clients who phone or come to agencies requesting a specific type of referral are often seeking help based on self-diagnosis, wishful thinking or a search for a "quick cure." They are apt to be misinformed about the efficacy of various treatments or the nature of their own problems or needs. What they do know is that something is wrong. Their inquiries convey the underlying message, "I need help."

When a client calls a "hot-line," saying that he is looking for some particular service—it may be transactional analysis, marital therapy, group counseling, the name of a behaviorist, hypnotist, or sex therapist, or even to learn where he can meet members of the opposite sex or a homosexual group—he is thus far communicating only that he is troubled. It would be a disservice if a counselor taking such a call failed to assess the caller's situation and expectations before giving him a list of resources. No matter how far out his request sounds, it should be recognized that the client is experiencing some kind of difficulty and is to be taken seriously. Even a young man's seemingly simple query about where to meet girls should raise questions in the counselor's mind. The counselor will wonder why he is having trouble meeting girls and suspect some inadequacy in his interpersonal relationships. If this is indeed the case, he will need help with his problem, whereas a referral to a church youth group might only result in further frustration for him.

Of course not all referral requests are veiled appeals for help. Some may be straightforward inquiries about community services, but this can only be ascertained by questioning. Gentle probing is not likely to alienate the caller but will be evidence of the counselor's concern and wish to be helpful.

Assessments By Phone

Since evaluation by phone is unsatisfactory at best, clients who phone for referrals should be invited to make an appointment for a personal interview whenever feasible. This will engage the client while motivation and anxiety level are high and afford opportunity for the kind of thorough assessment that should precede a referral. If a client is unwilling or unable to arrange for an interview, as complete an evaluation as possible should be conducted by phone. First, focus should be on the problem for which the client is seeking help: How and for how long has it affected him? What has he done about it? Has he had help in the past? Why has he chosen the particular kind of service he is requesting, and how does he anticipate it will help him?

Some information about the client's current situation—work, school, family involvement, level of functioning—and a picture of his cultural and social environment will be helpful. One would hope to pick up the predominant feelings he conveys. Is he anxious, depressed, angry and aggressive, discouraged and resigned, dependent, regressed, etc.? From this abbreviated evaluation one should be able to determine enough about the client's emotional state and nature of his problem to refer him for help—although it may be for another kind of service than he originally requested.

For example, returning to the young man who wants to meet girls, a focus on the history of his relations with girls would be pertinent. If investigation reveals that he has always had unsatisfactory sexual relationships, it would be appropriate to point this out and suggest that an appointment for counseling would be more helpful at this time than another disappointing experience meeting girls.

This might turn out to be exactly what he wanted to hear, but was unable to make the request directly for fear of rejection or ridicule, and was tentatively testing in hope that the counselor would understand his communication. Clients often make such an oblique approach, wishing to be offered help but not quite able to acknowledge or voice their needs. Counselors who realize that requests for referrals commonly carry such underlying communications may be able to detect the messages and respond accordingly.

Face-To-Face Assessments

A much more complete evaluation can be made when a client is seen in a personal interview, and allows the kind of psychosocial assessment outlined in this chapter to take place. As a result of the evaluation it will often transpire that the counselor can offer the client the help he needs without referral to another agency. A client asking for a "sex therapist," for instance, may turn out to have some troubling sexual questions that can be dealt with directly in a few counseling interviews. On the other hand, evaluation may reveal a need for marriage counseling, or long-term psychotherapy, for which referrals can be arranged. A client asking originally for a hypnotist may be looking for some magical cure in order to avoid coming to grips with a particular conflict. The counselor can interpret the client's unrealistic expectations, help locate and define the core problem, and then either offer to see the client in counseling or refer him to the appropriate service.

As a rule clients are not well-informed about the various treatment modes or the distinctions between professional disciplines. They may be relying on information from friends or neighbors or even from TV shows in asking for a particular kind of treatment. In a personal interview client and counselor will have an opportunity to explore together just what the client hopes to accomplish. The counselor can correct any misunderstandings and explain what kind of help might be possible or appropriate for the client's particular difficulties.

Checking Referral Sources

Successful referrals depend as much on knowledge of referral sources as on good client evaluation. Before a referral is considered, it is essential that the counselor acquire up-to-date information about referral sources, the exact nature and availability of services offered (e.g., whether they have long waiting lists), and application procedures. If this data is not complete, a counselor should make direct inquiries to an agency before making a referral. In referring to individuals, such as professionals in private practice, it is advisable to check with them to learn if a particular client's problems fall within their province and if they have time available to take on a new client.

When in doubt about a client's eligibility for a referral, it is preferable to inform him that you need time to check on the availability of the given service and request that he call you back at a specified time rather than to offer a name or names immediately. Much waste of time can be avoided by care in checking for accurate information.

The question of whether to offer a client a choice of referrals frequently arises. Some agencies protect themselves by routinely offering a choice of three names. If these choices are equally helpful, there need be no problem, but there is always the possibility that one is clearly outstanding and right for the client while two others might offer him indifferent service at best. It seems only fair to the client to point this out, since the counselor as a professional is expected to know the field, while a client has no way of judging the quality of services or the professional qualifications of personnel. For inexperienced counselors, supervisory advice as well as agency policy should be consulted about the question of making multiple referrals.

In their compassion and desire to be helpful, counselors are sometimes tempted to take the initiative in making appointments for clients they are referring to another service. On reflection it will be obvious that this is almost always contraindicated. It communicates to the client that he is too helpless to make his own arrangements, that in the counselor's view he needs to be taken care of. Such shepherding only tends to reinforce a sense of inadequacy. It is far more ego supportive to show trust in the client's strength and ability to act in his own behalf. Only if a client is so regressed or otherwise incapacitated that he is incapable of acting would it be advisable for the counselor to make the arrangements for him.

A client should, however, be informed if the counselor has contacted the agency or individual he is to be referred to and ascertained that he is eligible for their services and that a call from him will be expected. The client will then be responsible for making his own appointment.

In all cases the counselor should be prepared to give clear and accurate information about the referral source—agency name, address and phone number, name of person to be contacted, fee schedules (if applicable) and eligibility requirements.

Counselor-Initiated Referrals

The same careful procedures will be observed, of course, if it is the counselor who determines in an initial evaluation to propose a referral, even though it has not been originally requested or anticipated by the client. In that event, timing and sensitivity to the client's feelings must also be considered in informing a client that he must go elsewhere for service.

If it is obvious early in an interview that a referral will be offered, with time remaining to talk it over, there will be no reason to delay explaining the reason for proposing referral and offering help in locating the best resource for the client. He will have an opportunity to express his reaction, possibly his disappointment, talk over the kind of help he might receive at another agency, and ask any questions he may have.

Sometimes it is only at the close of a lengthy evaluation that a counselor decides that his agency cannot offer the service a client needs. By that time the client has shared extensive information about himself, so an abrupt offer of a referral would be experienced by an already anxious individual as a personal affront or rejection. He will be unprepared for the suggestion and in his disappointment might even refuse a referral. A better tactic would be the offer of another appointment to talk over the kind of help the client needs and consider the prospect. This may be more costly in terms of the counselor's time, but will pay off if as a result the client reacts positively and follows through on the referral. When clients fail to act on referrals it is often because they were made too hastily without adequate preparation or consideration of clients' feelings.

EVALUATION OF EMERGENCIES AND CRISES

Definition of Terms

Because of the nature of their clientele, community agencies and crisis intervention centers in particular are routinely faced with potential emergency and crisis situations. Counselors then are charged with the responsibility to determine fairly quickly if an emergency exists, and to discriminate between a true emergency and a crisis. This requires a cool head on the part of counselors lest they be caught up in the emotional contagion produced by excitable clients or anxiety-arousing circumstances.

"Emergency" is described by the Random House Dictionary as a "sudden, urgent, usually unforeseen circumstance or occasion requiring immediate action." The American Heritage Dictionary calls it "a situation or occurrence of a serious nature . . . and demanding immediate action," and Webster's Collegiate Dictionary defines it as "an unforeseen combination of circumstances . . . that calls for immediate action." The key words in all three definitions are the call for "immediate action."

In defining crisis, these dictionaries all use the words "turning point." To quote American Heritage, a crisis is "a crucial point or situation in the course of anything; a turning point." Webster describes it as "an emotionally significant event or radical change in status in a person's life . . . a turning point," and Random House defines it as "a condition of instability . . . leading to a decisive change." In medicine a crisis is a turning point in the disease process; in literature, it is a turning point between opposing forces. In assessing clients the same distinctions will apply. An emergency is a call for some direct and immediate action in a client's behalf. A crisis is a condition of instability, a change or turning point in a client's life for which he will need emotional support during the critical period.

Identifying a True Emergency

It would seem from the foregoing that there should be no difficulty in identifying an emergency. In fact, however, many more "emergencies" are probably perceived as such than actually occur. An emergency is often in the eye of the beholder, its designation depending on who is making the judgment, his involvement in the situation and his relative objectivity in assessing it. Is a client's problem an emergency to him, to the counselor, or so perceived by the referring source?

There are, of course, some obvious and unquestionable emergencies. If a client comes in or is brought to an agency suffering from a drug overdose or is disoriented because of reaction to a drug, emergency measures are called for. An individual who is experiencing a breakdown in functioning, who is actively hallucinating or confused and irrational presents an emergency. Threats of suicide or homicide or manic, out-of-control behavior, must always be regarded as emergencies.

Where such obvious conditions are not present, the first step in determining whether an emergency exists is to learn the facts about the client's immediate complaint. How did it come about? What precipitated it? Has a similar situation occurred in the past? If so, how did the client handle it? How is the problem affecting him?

If the client was referred to the agency, one should learn about the circumstances. What is his relationship with the referring person, their interaction; what did he tell the referring person and why was he advised to come to the agency? This will help the counselor to determine if the referring person was unduly disturbed by the client, reacting precipitously in making the referral because of his own anxiety.

The counselor will also want to find out to what extent the client's rational faculties are intact, whether his reality testing is impaired and assess his degree of control under the circumstances. What are his plans, his possible options or solutions to the problem? If he is able to look at it coherently, sees a way out or is able to make plans, it is unlikely that this is a true emergency for him. If there are no positive indications of his restoring control, however, then the counselor should consider it an emergency for the client and assume responsibility for taking action.

It is necessary to separate the facts that are obtainable from the emotional climate engendered by the client so that the counselor can gain a perspective on the client's situation. Without facts and history to guide him, the counselor is likely to be caught up in the client's emotional state and feel equally helpless.

Is it an emergency when an instructor phones in agitation to a college counseling service to report a hysterical female student in his office? Is a daughter's accusation of abuse by her mother and brother an emergency? Is a desperate mother's call to a crisis center about her daughter's threat to run away an emergency? Is it an emergency when a disoriented, excitable man tells a counselor he plans to kill his illegitimate baby? A quiet, dejected woman repeats in a flat monotone to a counselor, "There's no use going on." Is this an emergency? A young man comes to a mental health clinic without an appointment demanding to see a counselor, and because he appears to be so distressed the receptionist calls a counselor out of a meeting. He tells the counselor in dramatic terms that he is being kicked out of his home. Is this an emergency?

Case Illustrations: Emergency or Crisis?

The following are all real cases. Some were true emergencies. Others were misperceived as emergencies by one or another of the participants according to his subjective reactions. An examination of these cases will illustrate the pitfalls for an unwary counselor and the need for calm judgment in anxiety-producing situations.

Case 1. An instructor in a junior college phoned an urgent request for a member of the counseling staff to come to his office, where he was faced by a 17-year-old female student who was weeping, agitated and declaring her love for him. The instructor was a prim, scholarly and inhibited young man, threatened by the girl's emotional outburst. To him this was an emergency. He wanted to be rescued.

A counselor arrived on the scene and after a few reassuring words persuaded the student to go to the counselor's office, where the client soon calmed down and talked about her adolescent crush on the instructor. Thereafter she continued to see the counselor for several weeks during which she examined her fantasies about the instructor and began to understand the unreality of her expectations. She had had a series of such transient attachments based on romantic fantasies but had not previously embarrassed herself by declaring her feelings to the loved one. The incident represented a "crisis," or turning point, for the client.

Counseling resulted in recognition on the client's part of her inappropriate behavior and a positive step toward maturity. The only "emergency" that existed was the emergency for the besieged instructor. Immediate action was appropriately taken on his behalf.

Case 2. A volunteer counselor spent a tense and difficult two hours with a feuding mother and her 16-year-old daughter. The daughter loudly accused her mother of cruelty and also cited abuse by her elder brother. The mother was equally vociferous in her angry claims that her daughter was wayward, intractable and hostile. The only history that the counselor had been able to obtain was that the husband and father had left the family four years earlier and subsequently obtained a divorce.

The harried male counselor finally tuned in with the

daughter's charges of abuse and became so concerned about this that a red warning light, "emergency," flashed in his mind. He was contemplating the advisability of notifying a child abuse agency. Fortunately he asked the two clients to wait in a separate office while he called his supervisor for advice. She pointed out that the mother-daughter conflict had been going on for years, that the charges and countercharges were an old story, and that he had no evidence of abuse. He was advised to arrange individual appointments for mother and daughter, and when they returned to get further history to evaluate the relationship and the role of each in the conflict.

The "emergency" in this case was an emergency for the counselor who felt pressured to take action because of his own anxiety, his identification with the daughter, and his inability to maintain objectivity. As for the mother and daughter, it is probable that their appearance at a crisis center was only one of many such eruptions of emotion in a longstanding conflict. It appeared that they had existed in a state of turmoil for years and it was questionable, even though they were overwrought at the moment, whether they were motivated to examine their relationship in counseling. Nevertheless, counseling appointments were appropriately made in the hope that they would accept help.

Case 3. An agitated mother phoned a crisis agency that her 16-year-old daughter was threatening to run away with a boyfriend her own age. She asked to bring her daughter to the center at once. They were seen by a counselor on an emergency basis an hour later. At first the daughter was stubbornly mute and sullen while her mother launched into a nearly hysterical account of the girl's defiance and threats to go to an out-of-town rock

> concert in spite of her mother's prohibition. Although her reasons were not stated, the mother protested that the boyfriend had a bad influence on her daughter, and she forbade her continuing to see him. When the mother's outburst had subsided, she was asked to remain in the waiting room while the counselor talked to the girl alone. She told the counselor her mother continually criticized her boy friends and was unreasonably opposed to the boy she currently liked. She described him as a good student, stable and well liked by his peers, but attributed her mother's objections to his religious and family background. The daughter had told her mother that they were going to a rock concert the following weekend, and when she became angry and abusive the daughter said she would move into the boy's house if her mother persisted in trying to break them up. It was the counselor's impression that she had no serious intentions of running away, but in her hurt and anger had made impulsive threats to her mother. The mother was called in again, reassured about her daughter's intentions, and agreed to return the following day to try to work out a compromise about the coming weekend.

In the mother's perception, her overreaction to her daughter's boy friend, this was an emergency, but it was *her* emergency, not her daughter's. It was determined by the counselor to try to engage the mother in counseling to help her understand adolescent behavior and deal more reasonably with her daughter. Both individual and joint sessions were continued for three months, leading to a lessening of the mother's tension and improvement in communication between the two.

> *Case 4*. A man of 28 appeared at a mental health agency as a walk-in. He was distraught, excited and seemed confused. In an interview with a male counselor, he began to rage against a woman who declared he was the

father of her six-month-old baby. She was threatening a paternity suit. Then he shifted his attack, stating that it was only logical that he kill the baby, since it was the baby who was responsible for his dilemma. The counselor, perceiving this as a genuine emergency, arranged for the client's immediate admission to an in-patient psychiatric unit for evaluation. The client quieted down when this was proposed and readily agreed.

Fearful of his violent impulses and recognizing his loss of control, he had come to the agency in desperation, asking to be protected.

Ominously subdued behavior may be just as indicative of emergency as the dramatic symptoms of the client discussed above.

Case 5. A woman in her thirties, also a walk-in at a clinic, sat dejectedly and didn't raise her eyes, her only movements a tense twisting of her hands. She replied to the counselor's opening questions in an almost inaudible voice, then fell silent. All the counselor could learn about her feelings was that she was "no good" and that there was "no use." She admitted she lived alone since her male roommate left three months ago and "just couldn't go on any longer." She again fell silent. To questions as to what help she wanted and what she thought she could do, she barely shrugged and repeated, "there's no use." The counselor was finally able to elicit from her that she guessed she would take her life. She could turn on the gas and that would be the best way out.

Questions about immediate plans, friends she could turn to, family relationships, her interests, or any positive reasons for living, received only vague or negative replies. The counselor perceived the client was regressed, lacked adequate ego resources and was too severely depressed to risk letting her go home to her empty apartment. She rightfully considered this an emergency calling for immediate reaction. She arranged for hospitalization in a nearby psychiatric unit and herself drove the client to the hospital and helped her with the admission procedure.

This client had used the last strength of her nearly submerged ego to make her plea for rescue from her self-destructive impulses, and entrusted the counselor to recognize her desperation and take care of her.

Case 6. Because of his distraught manner, a 19-year-old college student's request to see a counselor at a mental health clinic was granted, even though it meant interrupting an interview with another client. The student gave a dramatic recital of an argument with his mother and brother that morning over the use of the family car. There were shouts and recriminations, ending with his mother's statement that if he could not behave more rationally he had better find another place to live. After a brief interview with the student, the counselor made another appointment with him to talk over his relationships at home. A check of the records showed several previous visits from the same student, each time with a demand for an immediate appointment. In this client's perception, every frustration was an "emergency," although on none of the previous contacts with the clinic had a real emergency existed.

Such a client's excitability and self-dramatization is often contagious enough to generate a sense of urgency and alarm in others, unless they are on guard to maintain objectivity until the client and his situation are evaluated. Either to someone in his immediate environment or to an unwary counselor the individual's behavior communicates a deceptive coloration of emergency. Likewise, an individual who characteristically acts out his conflicts in the environment may trigger anxiety, particularly if his behavior touches on a vulnerable area in others, throwing them off balance so they react as if an emergency exists. It may be a physician, a teacher, an acquaintance, a family member, or the counselor himself, whose emotional integrity is threatened by a particular form of behavior. They will feel a necessity to take action even though the individual is not in any immediate hazard.

The importance of obtaining substantiating facts about an apparent emergency is illustrated in the following case.

> *Case 7.* A 25-year-old female walk-in at a community clinic was tearful and agitated, talked hysterically about her feelings of desperation and loneliness, and said she was considering killing herself. The counselor assured her that they had time to talk it over and asked the client to tell more about herself and how she got into such a despairing state. The client's response was an immediate request that the counselor agree to see her in long-term therapy. As this seemed somewhat premature, the counselor became suspicious and inquired if the client had been, or was presently, in therapy. The story then came out that she was indeed in therapy but disliked her male therapist and didn't want to return to him. It was also learned that the therapist had cancelled their last appointment.
>
> The counselor commented that the client must be angry at him and feel abandoned, and she wondered if the client had told her therapist about her negative feelings. The client admitted she had never been able to confess to her angry feelings, which she felt would invite rejection and retaliation. The counselor then explained that she must be reacting to the cancellation and her stored-up feelings of anger, and that it was important for her to return and tell her therapist how she felt about him. She added that clients often did feel both attached

> to and also angry at their therapists and that the therapist should be able to understand and help with these mixed feelings. At this the client seemed relieved, agreed to return to her therapist, and asked the counselor if she could use her phone to call him and confirm her appointment for the following day.

In this case, as soon as the reasons for the client's acute reactions were ascertained and her feelings interpreted, her symptom subsided. The "emergency" she presented was a transient response to stress but might have been treated as a real emergency if the counselor had become alarmed and reacted before probing for the facts.

This case deserves special comment because it represents a situation frequently encountered in clinical practice. Clients in therapy who are experiencing negative reactions toward their therapists often turn up at clinics in acute distress, at times unaware of the sources of their reactions. Apart from the obvious benefit to the client for the counselor to recognize and interpret his feelings and refer him back to his therapist, these cases involve ethical considerations. To become further involved with a client who is already in treatment would be not only a discourtesy to another professional but a violation of professional ethics. The only exception would be a rare instance when there is clear evidence that a therapist has been guilty of client abuse or malpractice. Since clients under emotional stress are unreliable witnesses and apt to distort, one would usually want further and more objective confirmation to arrive at such a conclusion.

In summary, three factors must be considered in identifying a true emergency: The client's immediate situation and reaction to it; the referring person's emotional response to the client; the degree of the counselor's own equilibrium in the face of anxiety producing circumstances. Only if the counselor remains calm will he be able to judge the first two factors objectively.

Since a client gains immeasurably if he can help himself and be encouraged to mobilize his own resources in his behalf, a decision by a counselor to take emergency action should be weighed carefully. When a counselor determines that an emergency exists he is assuming control, at least for the time being. It may be tempting to the counselor to take over in order to relieve the burden of responsibility and pressure he feels, but be a disadvantage to a client who has some remaining reserves of strength which can be supported. Of course, counselors are justified in acting for clients who need immediate referrals but are too upset or insufficiently assertive and powerless to cut through bureaucratic red tape necessary for obtaining services at other agencies. Such circumstances warrant the counselor's acting for his client, since he can quickly gain access by phone to the proper authorities and expedite a referral or obtain emergency aid. Pregnant teenagers, indigent mothers and elderly clients are examples of those who may need such intercession before counseling can be undertaken.

While counselors must be alert to detect and deal with emergencies, they actually occur more rarely than one might imagine. In reviewing records of several hundred client contacts over a period of three months at a busy crisis intervention agency, the writer noted only one emergency during this period. This was a telephone plea for help by a depressed client, for whom immediate hospital admission was arranged.

CLINICAL CLASSIFICATIONS

Evaluation based on ego assessment takes into account an individual's personality traits, his adaptation to his culture, environment and family structure, his method of relating to others, his strengths and his particular manner of coping. It individualizes the client and tells a great deal about his uniqueness.

Clinical diagnostic labeling, if used without this broad understanding of a client's total functioning, is of no help to the client, focuses on his "sickness" rather than his health, and is apt to be stigmatizing and dehumanizing. Calling a client "psychotic," for instance, does not tell you to what degree he is psychotic, the intensity or pervasiveness of his condition, or anything about his traits, stengths or behavior. Once a client has been labelled, a counselor may even tend to view him in terms of the label rather than in his totality as a human being.

In *The Vital Balance*, Karl Menninger expresses his benignly human view of mental health and his objections to derogatory name-calling by conceptualizing an imaginary line extending from total mental health at one pole and total absence of mental health at the other. No individuals will be located at either extreme but will be at some point in this continuum, moving backward and forward at times during their lives. Menninger conceives of a backward movement, or regression, not as a sign of failure but as a defensive maneuver in the service of health while the individual mobilizes his resources to restore equilibrium. This can be likened to an army which retreats temporarily to consolidate its forces before another advance, or a fever in the physiological system, the body's mechanism to fight infection and regain health.

This is a positive and encouraging concept. In approaching their clients in this light, it will be reassuring to counselors to regard a temporary breakdown or regression in a client as the signal of a healthy struggle to reestablish equilibrium, rather than as an ominous sign of illness.

The objection to diagnostic labels and their implication of sickness does not deny the value or necessity of broad clinical classification. Discriminating between basic personality structures adds a further dimension to evaluation and serves as a guide in determining treatment approaches, goals and prognoses. For this reason, and also because counselors should be familiar with the main clinical entities and clinical vocabulary as part of their training and for recording requirements, six very broad categories—neuroses, behavior disorders, borderline personality disorders, psychoses, adolescent developmental reactions, and acute situational reactions—are proposed and briefly described. They are intended to be used as adjuncts to ego assessment and will be determined as a natural outgrowth of the assessment process.

The classifications are inexact, and it is emphasized that individuals do not fit neatly into slots and that all clients in a given category are by no means alike. The diagnoses should be used with discretion and with the understanding that there will be overlapping, many clients exhibiting traits that fall into several categories. An original diagnosis may shift and have to be amended as more facets of a client's personality come to light. Psychoanalysts do not believe that an accurate diagnosis can be made until the close of treatment.

The majority of clients seen in crisis intervention and community agencies tend to fall into the categories of adolescent developmental reactions, borderline personality disorders and acute situational reactions. Adolescents seek help because of the frequent turmoils and emotional upsets typical of their age group, borderline individuals because of their instability and limited capacity to maintain equilibrium under stress. Due to their disturbing behavior, those diagnosed as behavior disorders are more likely to be referred by others than to come on their own initiative. When they do seek help they are usually looking for immediate relief and are apt to drop out after a short time.

Neuroses

Most so-called normal persons have mildly neurotic traits in some areas without causing them particular difficulty, but severely neurotic conflicts can be crippling and exact a heavy toll in constricting an individual's freedom of emotional expression and activity.

A well-structured ego is the distinguishing mark of a neurotic individual. He will appear to be well-organized, responsible, and to function adequately even though he may complain of feeling that he is a failure. His conflicts are usually of long standing and are internalized, with pressures on the ego exerted by his inner drives, his superego, or both.

A neurotic may be recognized by symptoms of anxiety and depression and may suffer acutely from varying degrees of self-criticism, guilt, sexual inhibition, fears, self-doubts and compulsive behavior. He may have difficulties in expressing anger or discharge it through somatic complaints such as headaches or hypertension, among others.

In considering treatment, counseling may be helpful temporarily, for relief of a current stressful situation, but long-term psychotherapy will be required for resolution of a neurotic client's internal conflicts, since the origin of his conflicts are repressed and unconscious. Motivation will depend on the degree of suffering the individual experiences.

Behavior Disorders

Persons in this category will have a history of chronic or sporadic lapses in impulse control. Their conflicts are mainly expressed in adaptation to the environment rather than in internal struggles. They may evidence antisocial behavior, drug or alcohol addiction. They usually have well-rationalized explanations for their maladaptive functioning and seem plausible and persuasive, seldom viewing their actions as inappropriate, or experiencing guilt or remorse. Since they do not assume responsibility for their behavior, they do not usually respond well to counseling or feel the need for it except in emergencies, and motivation is seldom sustained.

One rarely sees pure types of behavior disorder. Some impulsive individuals who tend to act first and think afterward may be deficient in controls, but probably should not be classified as behavior disorders, as they do eventually recognize and feel responsible for their actions. The degree of acting out and its chronicity should be determining factors in diagnosing behavior disorder.

Individuals with behavior problems are frequently referred to counseling agencies because their behavior is troubling to others and are not as likely to seek help on their own initiative.

Borderline Personality Disorders

So-called "borderline" individuals are not easy to recognize because they often appear to be neurotic and distinction may be clear only on the occasion of a breakdown in functioning. The area of ego deficit usually stems from early deprivation or failure to have an adequately sustaining mother-child relationship. The child's ego has not had sufficient nourishing to develop a strong sense of identity and self-worth. As a result, borderline persons are apt to be dependent and especially vulnerable to separation, loss or disappointment in supportive persons in their lives.

The designation of borderline as used here does not imply that an individual is prepsychotic or on the verge of psychosis. Rather, the term is used broadly to describe a person whose ego development has been impaired at an earlier developmental level than that of a neurotic. The clinical picture of borderline clients will vary widely, ranging from those who function adequately most of their lives but experience regression under stressful situations to those who have managed to sustain only a minimal adjustment and may experience depersonalization at times.

Borderline persons can be recognized by the good

facades they often display, but one senses that something is missing underneath in terms of a firmly integrated structure. They sometimes seem flimsy, flighty and unstable, and given to superstitious beliefs, misinterpretations or distortions of reality. They may be influenced by horoscopes or take up faddish "isms" or cults from time to time. They are often friendly and responsive and in times of crisis are promising candidates for short-term counseling. They are apt to establish cooperative but dependent relationships with counselors. While there is usually an enormous amount of anger beneath their facades, this is more evident in long-term treatment and less likely to come to the surface in brief counseling.

There has been a growing tendency in recent years to treat borderline clients in extensive long-term psychotherapy and psychoanalysis. Borderline personality theory, case studies and techniques are abundantly reported in the literature. This is an important development as our culture produces more and more borderline personalities who need treatment.

Psychoses

This is indeed a broad classification, embracing individuals who may display barely perceptible psychotic traits as well as those with a pervasive psychotic structure and chronic impaired reality testing. Shallowness or instability of relationships is a distinguishing quality of persons suspected of being psychotic, as is a tendency for sudden and deep regressions with failure of reality testing and functioning. Attitudes of suspicion and mistrust of others are also symptomatic of psychosis.

Psychotic individuals may hold jobs and maintain family relationships, with occasional breakdowns requiring medication or hospitalization. In periods of remission they appear to be fairly normal and may live normal lives most of the time unless they experience undue stress in the particular areas in which they are vulnerable.

A psychotic person in a period of breakdown or regression can be readily identified. He may appear confused in his thinking or confuse the counselor with his communications, which seem distorted, irrational or bizarre. His judgments may seem askew and his perception of reality faulty. Delusions or hallucinations are common complaints. One will sense a tenuousness in his relationships, lacking constancy and genuine involvement. This is often detectable in his manner of relating to the counselor. He may avoid eye contact, seem to look through the counselor as if he were not there or avert his eyes after a fleeting glance.

These clients can often be helped in counseling to arrest a regression and recover equilibrium, or to prevent a pending breakdown. If the process is so far advanced that they are not amenable to rational exploration of their feelings, they should be referred to a psychiatrist. Medication, and possibly hospitalization, is usually necessary in the event of a psychotic break.

Adolescent Developmental Reactions

This is a diagnostic category that does not necessarily indicate pathology but rather some interruption or blocking of the normal growth process. Adolescents may present a wide range of symptoms or adjustment difficulties that are typical of their age group. Problems may be conflicts with parents or authority figures; feelings of alienation or depression; disappointing peer or sexual relationships, and symptoms of anxiety. Because of the normal turmoils of adolescence, it is often difficult to distinguish between developmental crises expected for their age and more serious pathology.

Adolescents may respond well and be helped in short-term counseling, especially in the later or integrative phases of adolescence. This form of help should be chosen unless a client appears to be seriously crippled by his symptoms, in danger of harming himself, or if there has been a long history of conflict, in which cases referral for more intensive treatment should be considered.

Acute Situational Reactions

This is not a diagnostic category but a useful classification for an individual who is temporarily overwhelmed by an acutely stressful life situation. The individual may be normal or neurotic, but so incapacitated by a traumatic situation that help with the immediate crisis will take precedence at the outset over exploration of any contributing personality difficulties.

CLASSIFICATIONS BY PRESENTING PROBLEM

A second classification, based on a client's presenting complaint, is useful to agencies for statistical purposes and for case study. While an ego assessment diagnosis is made by the counselor, classification by presenting problem reflects the *client's* original statement of his complaint. Counselors will find it instructive to record clients' statements along with their own assessments when a case is opened, and compare the two in reviewing cases following termination. Predictably, there will be wide discrepancies between clients' perceptions of their problems and counselor's evaluations. Counselors will also find it helpful to check the accuracy of their evaluations by comparing their original diagnoses with the core problem that was uncovered during counseling.

STANDARD PSYCHIATRIC DIAGNOSES

A standardized diagnostic guide, *The Diagnostic and Statistical Manual of Mental Disorders* or "DSM III," which is compiled by the American Psychiatric Association, lists and tabulates by number several hundred clinical psychiatric categories including organic and neurological conditions. Mental health clinics that charge fees and where payment is made directly to the agencies by the client's insurers, Medicare or Medicaid, usually require use of this form. Patients are initially interviewed and evaluated by a psychiatrist or other mental health professional who then enters their respective diagnostic categories (by name and number) on the patients' records. Because of the medical terminology and inclusion of organic disorders requiring medical examination, use of these forms by inexperienced counselors would not normally be expected.

Needless to say, many in the mental health profession find use of such labeling objectionable both because it dehumanizes patients, reducing them to designated numbers, and because confidentiality of these records cannot be assured. The records may pass through many hands in insurance and governmental agencies. One hopes counselors in agencies where DSM 111 is used will not be so influenced by these diagnoses that it will interfere with their views of clients' humanness, and that their treatment of clients will be based on their understanding of clients' individuality rather than on their "disorders."

RECOMMENDED READING

Bettelheim, B., Freud and the soul. *The New Yorker*, March 1, 1982. pp. 52–93.

The author presents fascinating observations on the human quality of Freud's language.

Freud, A. (1936), The ego and the mechanisms of defense. *The Writings of Anna Freud*, Vol. II. New York: International Universities Press, 1966.

This is Miss Freud's original work on classification of the defense mechanisms.

Hartman, H. (1939), *Ego Psychology and the Problem of Adaptation*. New York: International Universities Press, 1958.

This is a difficult but historically important book by the so-called "father of ego psychology."

Mahler, M., Pine, F. & Bergman, A. (1975), *The Psychological Birth of the Human Infant*. New York: Basic Books.

Observations of infants and young children form the basis for this major study of the separation process in ego development.

Menninger, K. with Mayman, M. & Pruyser, P. (1963), *The Vital Balance*. New York: Viking Press.

The author presents a history of psychiatric diagnosis as well as his own current thinking. It is a very reassuring book and recommended reading for counselors.

CHAPTER 4

Objectives: The Preparatory Phase

Short-term counseling may be as brief as two or three interviews or extend over several months. Although goals are limited, profound changes sometimes take place in a brief but intensive period of counseling at a turning point in a client's life. Counseling provides a distinct service to clients who are faced with sudden but crucial decisions or to whom an unanticipated event in their lives has created severe emotional distress. Such acute problems are often resolved very quickly. Sometimes a client may be able to weigh options and reach an important decision or resolve a conflict in as few as two sessions with a counselor. Other clients may profit from help over several months to relieve a depression or to explore old conflicts that were dormant but reawakened by some precipitating current event. For individuals whose functioning has broken down and who are temporarily regressed, brief counseling can be effective in enabling them to restore a prior level of adjustment. Emotionally unstable individuals who may need supportive help off and on for years are often repeaters at community agencies, returning for brief counseling in periods of stress.

Advantages of time-limited counseling lie in stimulating and intensifying a client's efforts to work on his problem in the knowledge that he has only so much time for the process. The dynamic interaction between client and counselor is maintained at a high level and the objective to be accomplished is kept in view. From a purely practical standpoint, the enormous cost differential between brief intervention and extended treatment is a decisive consideration, whether services are paid for by community contributions, taxpayers or client fees.

Obvious disadvantages are that as new material unfolds it cannot be as fully explored as in open-ended treatment where goals are less defined and a client's motivation and insight may stimulate him to go further into examining his problems than was originally anticipated. Evaluation is more leisurely in long-term treatment, the focus is more diffuse, and termination is determined by the client's readiness to conclude treatment rather than by setting arbitrary limits.

Three criteria will determine whether there is a promising outlook for short-term counseling in a given case: (1) the urgency the client is experiencing because of his suffering, propelling him to seek relief; (2) a readily identified problem that can be singled out for focus; and finally (3) the client's ability to form a positive relationship with the counselor fairly quickly. When these conditions obtain, counseling can be undertaken with some confidence.

Because of the necessity to engage clients and determine their core problems at an early stage, brief counseling makes exacting demands on counselors' skills and judgments. They must be prepared to assume a relatively active role, be alert to sustain movement toward the goal and to recognize and handle any client resistance without delay.

Despite these pressures inherent in short-term counseling, it should be emphasized that this is not a distinct form of therapy. The basic principles of sound counseling apply whether it is short or long-term and whatever the diagnosis. All counseling should be flexible and adaptable to each individual's personality type and needs as determined in the initial ego assessment. Even in brief counseling, aims and approach vary considerably.

CLIENT SELECTION

Three categories of clients are promising candidates for brief counseling:

1. Individuals with a history of stable adjustment who are acutely troubled by a current stressful situation.
2. At the opposite end of the mental health spectrum, individuals who have been able to function minimally but need support for a temporary incapacitating regression.
3. Individuals who have more pervasive problems than the first category but may need help to prepare them for a referral. The counseling in these cases is an extended evaluation process.

The first group of clients who can benefit from short-term counseling are relatively healthy individuals who may feel overwhelmed by a current crisis such as loss of a job, the break-up of a marriage or significant relationship, death of a parent or spouse, or the prospect of retirement. An adolescent may be undergoing a particularly difficult developmental phase, or the parent of a rebellious adolescent may be threatened by a disruption in family functioning.

In other instances the precipitant of the client's distress may not be so readily evident. A client may be intensely troubled but be totally unaware of the cause of his complaints until exploration with the counselor reveals clues to his core problem, which can then be singled out for discussion.

With the second category of clients—individuals who have never achieved more than a precarious adjustment—supportive short-term counseling in a period of regression may be enough to tip the scales and help them to recover sufficient control to maintain themselves in work or family situations, thus avoiding hospitalization or serious breakdown. In these cases, too, effort should be made to locate the immediate precipitant. However, with some confused clients this may not be clear. The focus then should be on reality testing and firm support.

For clients who do not fit these categories, for example, clients who are severely depressed, have chronic character or behavior disorders, or reveal histories of longstanding internal conflicts, more intensive psychotherapy is the treatment of choice. If this is not available because of lack of community resources or financial hardship, then short-term help may have to be undertaken as a temporary expedient. Resolution of the conflict will not be the objective, but help with the immediate situation may be offered and options explored for relief of the current distress.

IDENTIFYING THE PROBLEM

Searching out and pinpointing the cause of a client's complaints or symptoms is the essence of brief counseling. Clients' statements of their problems may be vague or diffuse. A client may assign his suffering to his marriage, his job, an adolescent child, a friend's betrayal, and so on. The question, then, is what in his situation is so upsetting? In some instances a client may have no idea why he is distraught, feels anxious or desperate. Instead of trying to deal with the symptom itself, even though symptom relief is essentially the goal of brief counseling, the counselor should seek to identify the core, or underlying, problem.

Clinical Illustrations

Case 1.

> A female high school student came to a clinic for emergency counseling, distraught because of a break-up with a boy friend. When questioned why she came for help at this particular time (the break-up had occurred two weeks before without causing a severe reaction) she could not find an answer at first. It was only when she was specifically asked what happened "today" prior to her coming to the clinic that she reluctantly stated she had had a fight with her mother at breakfast. This, then, was the core problem, and subsequently brief counseling focused on her relationship with her mother.

Case 2.

In the following case the client was assigned to a counselor for marriage counseling after an evaluation from an intake interview.

The client, a woman in her fifties, had been married for 25 years. She was tense and agitated as she complained about her failing marriage, her husband's disinterest and her feelings of being unloved, worthless and useless. She declined an offer to involve her husband in counseling, which suggested that she had some awareness that the problem was within herself.

While she appealed almost desperately to the counselor for some relief, it did not emerge until the second interview that she felt exhausted because of caring for her unmarried daughter's unruly four-year-old son. The daughter had recently moved back home and suspected that she might be pregnant again. The client had cared for her child off and on since his birth without complaint and had always given in to the daughter's impositions, however inconvenient for her. At present the daughter was going out every night and sleeping most of the day.

The core problem here was the client's anger at her daughter, her guilt about the anger, and her lifelong inability to say "no."

When the counselor pointed out that the woman had rights of her own, and the client began to relate to this, she was able to talk about her anger at being used by her daughter and to develop a healthier view of herself as a worthwhile person, with every right to enjoy her life with her husband and to assert herself. She recalled her many positive accomplishments. She also became aware that it was not helpful to her daughter to permit further dependence on her.

After several weeks she was able to tell her daughter, calmly and without anger, that she must find herself a place to live, and eventually helped the daughter to move. At the same time, she talked positively about her husband and began going out with him evenings, as they had done formerly. At termination she expressed contentment with her marriage and with herself. She was seen once a week for six weeks.

In this case the client was so immersed in her conflict that she was only dimly aware of the core problem, her resentment at being used by her daughter, her feeling of being a worthless "object" and her inability to act because of guilt. Her marriage, which she had blamed for her misery, had in fact been quite satisfactory.

Case 3.

In the following case, the client was bewildered by his breakdown and had no conscious awareness of its origin, but alerted the counselor to the core problem by several indirect allusions. It was only by picking up these obscure clues that the counselor was able to identify the conflict.

> A young man in his twenties, in graduate school and nearing his final examinations, presented a distraught appearance, had been unable to function in school or work for the past week, feared he would fail to graduate and that he was losing his mind. In his agitation he had been talking to anyone who would listen to his pleas for help—a sister, his boss, and several acquaintances. He appealed to the counselor as if this were his last resort. No immediate precipitant had been located to account for his distress until the second interview the following day, when the client appeared to be even more desperate. It was during this interview that the counselor noted he had made several references to a 13-year-old brother who was living with relatives in a small southern mining community. He was concerned that the brother was not getting an adequate education. When he again referred to his brother by remarking that his thirteenth birthday was coming up, the counselor wondered about this seemingly irrelevant statement.

The counselor asked the client how much older he was than the brother. The reply was, "thirteen years." Then the counselor asked him what happened when he, the client, was 13 and his brother was born. At this the floodgates opened and the client poured out the following:

They were very poor, his mother was ill during her pregnancy, and after his brother was born she seemed to give up and never cooked for the family anymore. Family life disintegrated from then on. He recalled at that time his father forcing him and his older brothers to go out with him in an old truck on Saturdays to pick up trash and sell it for junk. He felt angry and humiliated and blamed the birth of his brother for all his misery.

As he talked the tension visibly left his body. He had apparently been terrified that the old hostile (and repressed) wishes which had broken through at the thought of the coming birthday, his association with 13, would bring harm to his brother, and hence, his protectiveness and concern for the brother's welfare. The client was seen twice more, five interviews in all. The first three were on successive days because of his severe agitation.

Such dramatic cases are rare but serve to illustrate how the connection between symptoms and the precipitating cause may be completely unconscious to the client. This case also shows how the client's communications contained clues to the core problem, but the connection had to be made by the counselor.

Case 4.

Another vivid example demonstrates how a current precipitant may give rise to the emergence of long-buried memories. In this case the clues to the core problem were less obscure and almost immediately revealed.

A young woman college student came directly to a crisis clinic from a class where she had started crying for no known reason. She was upset but did not know why, although she had been feeling troubled and discouraged for several days. She did not date, had few friends and was supporting a five-year-old illegitimate daughter on ADC while she attended college. She lived in her own apartment but was emotionally involved with a critical mother with whom she had a poor relationship. She could not account for her distress.

The counselor was curious about the class which she had left in tears. The following exchange took place:

Counselor: "What was the subject of the class?"
Client: "Greek" (said indifferently).
Counselor: "What is the class studying?"
Client: "Greek drama."
Counselor: "What play did you discuss today?"
Client: "The Orestes Trilogy."
Counselor: "What is the play about?"
Client: "It's about a daughter, Iphigenia, who is sacrificed by her father, so he can win a stupid war and save some woman" (Helen of Troy!), this stated with emotion.
Counselor: "How did you feel about this?"

In response, the client began to pour out her anger and hurt at the memory of her father leaving the family when she was a small child, to go to live with another woman. She had identified with Iphigenia, the sacrificed daughter, and the forgotten feelings of loss and rage swept over her.

She reported in the next interview that the father of her little girl was a man in his fifties with a wife and several grown children. Their affair had long ended, and although he did not pay child support he came to visit

> his child from time to time and occasionally gave the client money. Currently he had given her the use of a car, which was important to her as it enabled her to attend classes. He had once indicated to her that he did not want her to date, and she feared that if she did so he would take away the car. After the reality of this was questioned by the counselor, the client talked to him, told him she would like to date, and he raised no objections. She also began to see her mother and establish a more friendly relationship.
>
> By the sixth interview the client said, "I feel like my old self again." She recalled that she had done well in high school, was popular and felt good about herself. Now the old feeling of well-being was restored.

In the foregoing examples, locating and focusing on the core problems led to relief for the clients. The core problems were the young girl's difficulty with her mother; the mother's guilty anger at her daughter; the young man's fear of hostility toward his baby brother; the young woman's painful memories of her father's betrayal.

CASE ANALYSIS

The very abbreviated reviews of these cases may raise questions in readers' minds as to how evaluation, goals and treatment plans were determined, what transpired that brought relief to the clients and why a decision to terminate was reached after such brief contact. It will be helpful to pause here and dissect one of these cases in depth in order to illuminate the specific steps in the counseling process.

Consider, for example, the young man whose

brother was nearing his thirteenth birthday. Close examination will show that, however condensed, evaluation and clinical judgments did indeed occur and were assimilated in the treatment. Evaluation began as soon as the client's distraught state was observed by the counselor. His helpless, pleading manner and his assertion that he had been appealing for help to anyone who would listen to him were indicative of his dependence and clinging to others for support. He had established no mature or mutually satisfying relationships, but used others to lean on, as he did the counselor. Evidence of his regressed state was his manner of approach to the counselor. Where a more mature individual might have expressed a wish to understand his problems, this client demanded that the counselor take care of him.

His choice of a career was significant. His goal was to become a pharmacist. He viewed his future as working in a drug store, which promised a structured environment and an occupation that did not present much challenge or demand creativity or imagination. Intellectually he was limited, struggling to maintain his grades. He presented a picture of an individual who was just making it, at the peak of his resources both intellectually and emotionally.

On the positive side, his achievements were notable in view of his deprived working class background. He would be the first in his family to finish college and to acquire professional standing. Evaluation gave weight to these strengths, which might be mobilized in counseling.

The obvious goals were, first, to determine what had precipitated his incapacitating anxiety, and then to effect relief as quickly as possible so he would not jeopardize his academic career. Fortunately he was able to communicate the source of his anguish, albeit in a disguised fashion, through the several allusions to his brother which appeared irrelevant and out of context, and thus took on special significance. While he claimed that he had no idea what had occasioned his mounting anxiety, he signaled where the conflict lay by the references to his brother and the number 13. This suggested that he already "knew" what was troubling him but had not been able to take the final step of conscious acknowledgment because it was so unacceptable to his monitoring superego.

It required only one question from the counselor to allow him to bridge the gap from past to present. "What was it like when you were 13?" The memories that were then recalled allowed sufficient discharge of the repressed rage and hostility to relieve the burden of fear he had been barely able to contain.

The fear derived, of course, from the magical belief commonly held by children that wishes can literally kill, as if wish and act were one. The old feelings of enmity toward the brother whose birth had had such painful consequences for him had inundated his ego in the original primitive form. This led to the fear that the old magical thoughts would somehow harm his brother. The fear was not conscious but had been converted into his symptom of anxiety.

In recalling the memories, his rational ego was able to separate past from present. As he talked of the events of his thirteenth year, he became aware that his anger at the time was justified, but was not in fact a threat to his brother now. (It can be surmised that the client's approaching graduation played a part in determining, or at least intensifying, the onset of anxiety, since it may have reactivated old hostile and competitive strivings against both brother and father. The meaning of graduation was not explored, however, as the memories surrounding his brother's birth were closer to consciousness.)

After the client reported in the fifth interview that he was functioning well, he made the decision to terminate and requested that he might return if he again felt troubled. In accepting his decision and not urging him to continue counseling, the counselor weighed the alternatives and decided that any effort to further open up old conflicts would disturb the equilibrium he had gained. He was seen as an emotionally restricted individual with ego deficits dating from early emotional deprivation, limited capacity for satisfying interpersonal relationships, poor frustration tolerance and probably a great deal of underlying anger. His defenses were brittle and precarious, but had been maintained prior to his recent breakdown and seemed currently intact. It could be predicted that treatment, if undertaken, would be a long-term prospect, might disrupt his functioning and offer questionable promise of success. Furthermore, he was not motivated and was not troubled by or aware of his limitations.

In the other cases, evaluation, ego assessment and clinical judgments were also incorporated in the treatment process. In spite of her early affair with a father representative, presumably the acting out of a fantasy, the young woman who had identified with Iphigenia evidenced ego strength in the management of her life. She had adequate self-esteem and the ability to form sustained and satisfying relationships prior to the incident that brought her to counseling. Her use of counseling to effect changes in her life, and her wish now to date men of her own age, testified to her flexibility and healthy drives. She decided to terminate counseling because a familiar sense of well-being was restored. In her words, she "felt like my old self again." Since she had successfully compensated for the trauma of her childhood, there seemed little purpose in opening up old wounds and possibly threatening the defenses she had established. Certainly there must have been early impairment in ego development and unresolved conflicts, but her relatively healthy adjustment far outweighed concern for possible pathology.

The married woman who could not say no to her daughter was also seen as an essentially healthy individual, able to make a positive decision once the cause of her anxiety was identified. While her need to serve others and to please may have originated as an early defense against (denial of) angry feelings, it had not seriously limited her functioning. Once her self-esteem was reestablished, she was not motivated to explore further, nor did it seem to the counselor that extended treatment was justified.

SETTING GOALS—THE COUNSELING CONTRACT

In the cases cited, identifying the core problem determined the goal and focus in counseling and led quickly to relief of the client's anxiety. Since these clients' presenting anxiety was so intense, problem resolution was immediately undertaken, without a preliminary agreement between client and counselor as to goals to be attained or the setting of time limits for counseling. In such brief but intensive counseling several interviews a week is often more effective than spacing interviews a week apart. With other clients who have an immediate need to make an important decision, two or three interviews closely spaced may be sufficient to effect resolutions.

For clients whose needs are not so urgent, a more structured counseling program may be proposed. Objectives are defined and often a time limit agreed upon after initial evaluation has indicated that the client can profit from counseling. Asking the client what he would like to accomplish in counseling is the first step in setting a goal and eliciting his participation in the counseling process.

If the client has unreasonable expectations, for instance that a parent or spouse will change or an external condition will alter, this should be pointed out to him. Explaining to him, however, that he has options in dealing with parents or spouse, or in changing or adapting to the conditions in his environment, will shift the focus to the client and what he can realistically expect to do for himself. Then a goal can be mutually agreed upon.

A goal should not be insisted on or contrived by the counselor so that it seems artificial. If the client has no specific goal, such as breaking off a relationship or leaving home, but is seeking symptom relief or just "to feel better about myself," it is preferable to allow the client to experience a period of counseling and then propose setting goals for termination.

If the agency limits counseling to a specific number of interviews or a specific time span, this should be explained to the client so he knows that there is a given length of time to work together.

To maintain the momentum in time-limited counseling, an extension of the period of time contracted for should not be offered unless there is some pressing circumstance. Once established, the structure should be maintained as evidence both of the counselor's predictability and consistency and as indication of his trust in the client's ability to work out his problem in a given time.

Appointment times and the length of the sessions should be agreed upon at the outset. Interviews should not extend over 50 or, at most, 60 minutes, and should be ended promptly by the counselor. This too provides a predictable working structure. Interviews longer than one hour are not productive, as neither client nor counselor can maintain the desired tension. The time limit impels the client to communicate what he has to say promptly, knowing that he cannot wait until the end of the hour and then manipulate the counselor to extend the time for him. When an important communication is made at the end of the hour, the counselor might comment, "I wonder why you brought that up so late? Let's discuss it at our next meeting when we will have more time to look at it."

PREPARING FOR REFERRAL

Short-term counseling as a preparation for more intensive psychotherapy is a valuable preliminary step for some clients. It may be evident in an initial evaluation that a client could profit from long-term treatment but an immediate proposal for referral would be rejected. For individuals who are unaware of the extent of their conflicts, who have suppressed or denied their feelings and are unsophisticated about psychological processes, a suggestion that they need extended treatment could be alarming, implying they are abnormal or sick. As a result they might withdraw or go to another agency. An offer of short-term counseling in such cases provides clients with an introductory experience in which to develop readiness for referral. These clients have sought counseling knowing that something is wrong, it is true, but they need time to recognize and acknowledge their problems, as is illustrated in the following case.

A 28-year-old married woman began counseling rather hesitatingly, complaining about her lack of direction in her career as an artist and vague dissatisfaction with her life. In appearance, manner and behavior she resembled a lively and intelligent adolescent. Her marriage of six years had not brought her much gratification; her husband was emotionally distant and inhibited and their communication superficial. However, she had not considered separation.

She was third of six children of conventional Catholic parents, with three very successful brothers. She had always felt a need to please and give in to others' demands, especially to "protect" her mother from her father's frequent angry outbursts. She was brought up to regard marriage and children as primary goals in a woman's life.

Prior to counseling she had little knowledge of psychology and, though imaginative and given to fantasies, had hardly dared to probe her deeper motives and feel-

> ings. She was therefore surprised and shaken as she gradually became aware in counseling of the complexity of her emotions—the anger she felt toward her mother, her attachment to her father, her sexual fears which had prompted her to marry a "safe" man who made few demands, and her self-imposed subjection to others' needs.

While her conflicts were apparent to the counselor who made the initial evaluation, it is doubtful if this immature woman would have accepted a referral for psychotherapy at that time. It was only after several months of counseling, which she had begun tentatively, that she became aware of, or could admit to, the turmoil of emotions which she had kept under check, or believe that she was justified in seeking self-realization and independence by making a commitment to psychotherapy.

> A woman in her middle thirties was profoundly disturbed when she sought counseling. She complained of sleep difficulties and described symptoms of depersonalization, repeating during the initial interview that she felt as if she was "falling apart." She was married, the mother of two children, and was a competent poet with recognition for her published work. Her symptoms erupted three weeks previously after her mother was admitted to a psychiatric hospital because of irrational thinking and behavior and some paranoid ideation. The mother had been discharged when the client started counseling. It appeared that when her mother was strong, the client was strong, but when her mother's functioning broke down all the client's props were removed. If she had been immediately referred for the long-term treatment she needed it would have confirmed her fear that she was "going crazy." Instead she was offered counseling. After three months, during which she stabilized

and began to recognize both her anger at her mother and her dependence, she agreed to a referral. Four years of therapy then ensued until she could separate from the symbiotic relationship with her mother.

In proposing a referral for such clients after several weeks of counseling, counselors must handle both their own and their clients' feelings. A relationship has been established, the client has developed an attachment to the counselor, and the counselor has an emotional investment in the client. Unless the counselor has examined and is aware of his own feelings, he may sound apologetic and defensive in advising a referral to someone else. The prospect of referral will be more readily acceptable and viewed as a constructive move if the counselor presents it positively and out of his concern for the client. The client's reaction should of course be explored, allowing him time to ventilate his disappointment. Rather than an abrupt (and rejecting) termination, several further interviews may be needed to prepare the client for the transfer and ease the separation.

RECOMMENDED READING

Freud, S. (1914), Further recommendations in the technique of psycho-analysis: On beginning the treatment. *Standard Edition*, 12:121–145. London: Hogarth Press, 1953.

This is an interesting early paper on Freud's method of beginning treatment and setting the treatment contract.

Sterba, R. (1951), A case of brief psychotherapy by Sigmund Freud. *The Psychoanalytic Review*, 38:76–80.

The author presents the first recorded case of short-term dynamic treatment, conducted by Freud in 1906.

Tarachow, S. (1963), *Introduction to Psychotherapy*. New York: International Universities Press.

This is a clearly written book addressed to beginning medical students, but is also applicable for counselors using a psychodynamic approach.

CHAPTER 5

Techniques: The Problem Solving Phase

In the initial or preparatory phase of counseling, the foundation is laid for the treatment process to follow. Evaluation has determined that the client can profit from short-term counseling. Ideally, the precipitant has been identified and the core problem has been selected as a focus. Client and counselor have formed an alliance to work together, often in a given time span, which is explained to the client. Regular appointment times have been arranged.

The ensuing phase of counseling—problem solving—is a continuum of the initial phase, but the counselor implies "let's get down to work" by asking more searching questions, analyzing with the client in detail the situations that are troubling him, encouraging him to speculate on the reasons for his reactions and behavior and to search for solutions. In short, the counselor promotes movement toward the goal.

It may sound paradoxical to say that while a counselor is quite active in short-term counseling, he is primarily a listener. He should be alert, raise questions and maintain a tension and focus on the problem; at the same time, his interventions are primarily directed to engage the client in self-examination, to keep him talking.

An apt term might be "active listening," as a counselor looks for meanings in a client's disclosures, manner and behavior, notes any evasions or avoidances of certain subjects, and remains on guard lest counseling stagnate in monotonous repetitions without movement. If a counselor feels bored at times, it may be a sign that progress has been stalled for some reason and intervention is called for.

In some of the cases cited in the previous chapter, the counselor's main activity was directed to locating the core problems. From then on this was minimal as the clients explored their feelings and sought solutions. The counselor did not tell the clients what to do, or advise them, but encouraged them to examine their situations and options, to understand the feelings that were troubling them and the sources of those feelings.

Some clients come to an agency for help in the expectation that it will be like visiting their doctors. They will be given a "prescription" and told what to do. A counselor's best response to a request for advice is to ask the client what he thinks will be best for him. Turning a client's questions back to him will imply that he is capable of answers and choices. This may be the first time he has thought of himself as competent to solve his own problems and it will tend to reinforce his self-esteem and confidence.

Taking over and directing a client, on the other hand, only intensifies his feelings of helplessness and dependence. Giving him "homework" in general is not advocated for the same reason, as it suggests a teacher-child situation. The only clients for whom a counselor should serve as a temporary parent-substitute are acutely disturbed or regressed individuals who are for the time being incapable of action.

INTERVENTIONS

Counselors have a number of interventions or technical tools at their disposal to stimulate movement in counseling. Any response, statement or activity by the counselor is an intervention, since it singles out and directs the client's attention to some particular statement or aspect of his behavior. Interventions range from simple questions to the occasional use of interpretation. All have their place in counseling but should be used selectively according to counseling goals and the client's ego organization and capacity for insight. One would be more likely to limit interventions to questions, suggestion, and pointing out reality to disturbed or regressed individuals, while interpretation is reserved for clients who have a capacity for insight and can tolerate more probing self-examination.

Questions

Questions are a counselor's single most used and useful device. Counselors constantly ask clients to explain, to enlarge on a subject under discussion, to examine their reactions, and to explore feelings.

A simple question may be, "Can you tell me more about your relationship with your mother?" More probing questions are asking a client why he felt so upset about a particular situation, or why he behaved in a certain way. Such questions start clients thinking about their reactions, what prompted them and whether they seemed appropriate. Counselors continually ask:

"What are you afraid of?"

"Why were you so angry at your father?"

"How do you feel about it?"

"What might you have done instead?"

"Do you remember feeling like this in the past?"

An opening statement by a client that he didn't sleep well the previous night, for example, might develop and broaden into a discussion continuing for an entire counseling hour. The counselor may initially question what kept the client awake or what his thoughts were while lying awake. The client's responses might lead into a number of possible directions—events of the day before, fantasies that preoccupied him, feelings about the counseling hour the following day, or even, disturbing reactions from the previous counseling session. The client's associations with the sleepless night may raise further questions, expanding and developing the discussion into material not heretofore explored. If the questions are not asked and the subject dropped prematurely, a valuable opportunity may be lost for the client to connect up and understand some feelings that have a bearing on his problems. However, if a counselor does fail to pick up some significant communication and only realizes it after the interview, he should not be dismayed. The client will bring it up again if it is important, and there will be another opportunity to examine the matter.

A client might begin a counseling hour by reporting a marital quarrel. Asking how it started may initiate close examination of the incident and be followed by further inquiries about the client's feelings, how he behaved, if there were other ways he might have responded, and if similar quarrels had occurred in the past. Such expanded discussions will throw light on the marital interaction and the client's characteristic way of reacting to anger in himself and others. It may revive memories or associations from childhood that are relevant to the client's reactions.

Clients will sometimes start with a seemingly casual remark and then change the subject. Why was the subject brought up and then abandoned? It might, for instance, have to do with a sexual experience which the client was hesitant to talk about, even though his opening statement had alerted the counselor to his concern. If the counselor fails to take note of it and ask why he changed the subject, this may convey to the client that the counselor is not comfortable talking about sex and the client may be embarrassed to return to the subject in the future. Conversely, a client will occasionally make a statement that is designed to turn the counselor's attention from a subject he wants to avoid. It is introduced as a distraction and caution should be observed in pursuing it. The following is an illustration.

> A young woman had admitted to some uncomfortable homosexual fantasies at the close of the previous session, and it was agreed that she and the counselor might talk more about it at their next meeting. Instead, however, she began by discussing a course she considered taking. Had the counselor picked up on this and asked more about the subject, it would have abetted the client in her evasion. The counselor listened a few minutes to the client's rather desultory remarks, which ended in a long pause. The counselor then asked the client if she might

be avoiding something. After a few thoughtful moments the client agreed, saying she was embarrassed but knew she should talk about the feelings she had admitted in the last hour.

Of course, counselors should not bombard clients with questions or challenge every statement they make so that counseling turns into a quiz session or a harassment. However, once a subject is opened up it is almost always good tactics to go into it more deeply, to expand it and help a client look at it from all angles.

The searching questions counselors ask are gratifying to clients because they are evidence of the counselor's interest and desire to understand. Clients will usually respond positively and soon learn to explore and examine themselves with less and less help from the counselor. One frequently hears a client comment with surprise at how much he learned about himself in going thoroughly into an incident that did not seem very important in itself.

Suggestions

Suggestion is not the same as offering advice or directing a client to undertake some course of action. It is often implied rather than presented directly. It is useful in raising a question in a client's mind as to a possible option or alternative and is often prefaced by "What if—?" For example, "What if you stood up to your father when he criticized you?" "Have you thought of returning to school?" "What about looking for a new job if you are so dissatisfied?" Sometimes when a client feels helpless to change, the counselor might suggest a number of possible options for him to consider. Clients may not act on such suggestions, but they do initiate a train of thought and convey that there are alternatives and other possibilities that may be open to them. This proved sufficient to lead to some movement in the following case.

> A 50-year-old married woman complained of feeling desolate and lost since her children left home. Her life was empty, she had little communication with her husband who was only interested in sports, and she insisted there was nothing she could do. She felt hopeless.
>
> The counselor then pointed out a number of courses open to her: Although she had not worked since her marriage, she might find satisfaction in volunteer work, and local agencies in need of volunteers were mentioned; as she had once been interested in art, she could enroll in extension courses in drawing or painting, alternatively, she might try to reestablish communication with her husband by going to sports events with him and sharing his interest in local teams.
>
> The client at first denied interest in any of these activities and rejected them outright. After thinking them over, however, she eventually made some inquiries about classes and signed up for one at the local community center. As her mood improved following this move, she made some tentative approaches to her husband about sports, went to some ballgames with him and started to read the sports pages. She then invited some of his sports friends and their wives to dinner. Her husband responded, and she found that he was willing to take her to movies and concerts she liked and to share her interests once a basis of communication was established. Her marriage improved, as did her mood and outlook, after a three-month period of counseling.

POINTING OUT REALITY

The crux of mental health counseling, both short- and long-term, is helping clients distinguish reality—the possible—from their wishful thinking, distortions and fantasies. Counselors need to be on the alert to question clients who express hopes for impossible changes in their environment or in the persons close to them, have dreams of unattainable goals, and especially, have misconceptions of themselves. An endless list of misrepresentations of reality—belief in superstitions and old wives' tales, unfounded fears, misjudgments of others' motives, imagined wrongs, guilt without cause—plague emotionally troubled individuals. Helping clients to assess their world in the light of reality, to dispel myths and fears, frees them for real problem solving.

It is not suggested that one should ever attack clients' beliefs, but questions may be raised that help them make distinctions between reality and fancy. A client who feels guilty about admitting anger toward parents in a counseling session, or views his criticisms of them as a betrayal, may be asked if it will really hurt his parents to talk about his feelings. The client will usually agree that since the feelings exist anyway, discussing them will do no harm to his parents and may eventually lead to improvement in their relationship.

To a client who says, "If only my husband would change, things wouldn't be so bad," the counselor might ask if she really thinks her husband will change. Admitting this is unlikely, the client is then encouraged to consider what she can do to help herself. Another client may view the world as hostile and feel unable to trust anyone. When he is asked just what he is afraid of, what is really so dangerous out there, and is reminded that other people don't feel this way, he is helped to realize it may be his misperception of the world and other people that is causing him to be so mistrustful.

> A young man of 20, of middle-European parentage and living in a working-class suburb, presented some irrational attitudes. He had never ventured into the central city and even feared to drive through the city streets. He imagined all kinds of dangers, being assaulted on the streets or robbed, as if "downtown" was a jungle. These fears did not derive from his own experiences but from his parents' attitudes with which he had been inculcated. His parents were bigoted, suspicious of neighbors, and had often warned their children that "everyone is out for himself" and will take advantage of them. This young man had never examined reality until his fears were addressed by the counselor. Only after his misperceptions were questioned was he able to correct his attitudes and begin to feel freer to venture into unknown territory and to meet more comfortably with people outside of his own culture, which he found was not so threatening after all.

Another typical distortion is the complaint, "I'm just unlucky." Again the reality of this needs to be questioned. Is it "bad luck" or something the client does that is responsible for his woes? In pointing out reality to a young teenager who dreams of being a car mechanic but is failing school, an obvious question is, how can he hope to enter a trade school and reach this goal unless he first masters his ninth grade subjects?

"People don't like me." "My parents are too strict." "If only I'd studied harder"—and many other "if onlys"—all need to be examined in the light of reality. It might be suggested, for example, that the client who didn't study hard enough had learned a valuable lesson; it doesn't mean that he can't go back and repair his educational deficiencies.

In the following case, more deeply ingrained misperceptions had to be challenged by pointing out reality to a woman who persisted in an image of herself as "abused" and a victim because of her unfortunate childhood experiences.

> A female client in her thirties made no friends, rejected others' overtures and complained of her boring job, but refused to look for more rewarding work although she was well qualified by her college education. In counseling she dwelled for weeks on her childhood memories, reviled her father, stepmother and aunts for their neglect, and cited her many deprivations while tears of self-pity often streamed down her face.
>
> The counselor was sympathetic, acknowledging that her childhood had indeed been bleak, but intervened when the client repeatedly insisted she had been "abused." It was pointed out that her father had never deliberately hurt her, that he had done his best to provide for her physical well-being and offered her educational opportunities even though he was incapable of sensitivity to her emotional needs. A stepmother had also done her best and within her limitations had been affectionate, patient and reasonably indulgent.
>
> The client was angry at these reminders of reality and even more so when the counselor commented on her strength in leaving home, supporting herself for a number of years, and managing to work her way through college. She didn't want to give up her perception that she was a victim and that the world owed her compensation for her suffering. Only with repeated assurances from the counselor that she couldn't relive her child-

hood, but that she did have control of her life now and of her future, was she gradually willing to relinquish her martyrdom and fantasies of "getting even" and begin to make some positive changes in her life.

CONFRONTATION

It is sometimes necessary to confront a client with repetitive behavior that gets him into trouble. It is a technique used when a counselor feels that a client must face facts directly in order to understand the consequences of his acts. "Is it surprising that you lose jobs when you are constantly late to work?" Or, "You refuse to help with any tasks at home, yet you complain that it is unfair when your father won't let you use the car." A client who wants to achieve a certain goal might be confronted with his refusal to take the first steps leading to it.

Confrontation should not be communicated as a criticism of a client, but as a means to help him understand how he may be continually sabotaging or defeating himself. It should be used only when the behavior pattern has been clearly demonstrated and the client is aware both of the behavior and the self-defeat, but has not viewed them as cause and effect.

A young man who dropped out of a junior college after his freshman year and had been working for two years seemed strongly motivated to return to school. He had a meager but adequate income to support his education if he budgeted carefully, but for three consecutive semesters when the time came for registration and payment of tuition he had unaccountably spent all his savings and had accumulated debts. When he was confronted with these facts, he had to acknowledge that he was setting himself up for failure. With this realization he was able to explore the fears that caused him to avoid completing school.

A repetitive behavior pattern established in childhood, and the use of confrontation to bring it to a client's attention, is illustrated in the case of a woman whose marriage was failing.

A female client, in her early thirties, had been disappointed in her marriage for several years. The marriage had been tolerable while the client was working but had become increasingly frustrating in recent months during which the client had to stay home to recover from a back injury. Her principal complaint was her husband's failure to spend any time with her. He was always away from home on one pretext or another on the Sundays and two weekend evenings that he didn't work. Longing for his companionship, his wife blamed herself, her complaints and demands, for driving him away. She determined she had to change, to be more tolerant and understanding of his needs and to talk to him reasonably and calmly about their relationship; to discuss what he wanted in the marriage, and to explain how much his companionship meant to her. For five successive weeks in counseling the client reported her attempts to involve her husband in examining their relationship, his evasions, vague promises to make weekend plans with her, and failure to do so. When the weekends came he invariably made some excuse to leave the house to see someone on business or to "shoot a little pool" for an hour or so, and invariably failed to return home until long after his wife had given up and gone to bed.

The client's principal memories of her childhood were the painful recollections of holidays and birthdays when she ever hopefully waited for her alcoholic father to appear. Her dreams of a happy family life and her excited anticipation of special occasions always ended in bitter disappointment. She couldn't recall one occasion when her father actually turned up for a special event.

The counselor's comments to the client that she still seemed to be waiting for something to happen, just as she had in her childhood, didn't elicit a response until several more weeks when the same scenario was repeated. But it became clear that the counselor's confrontation had been heard when the client appeared for her eighth counseling session. There was a dramatic change in the client's appearance and manner as she said that it had dawned on her in the preceding week that her husband wasn't going to change and there was no hope to patch up the marriage. She had talked to her former employer about going back to work, made some concrete financial plans and told her husband of her decision to separate.

In the following weeks while she carried out her plans, many more connections between her early experiences and her marital situation came to light. Her husband was not alcoholic, but a passive man with whom the client had reenacted the old disappointing patterns of her childhood.

Confrontation may be used in the form of a gentle reminder of contradictory statements or feelings a client has expressed. A client may be very critical of his parents one day and extol their virtues and defend them on another occasion. By pointing out the discrepancies in the client's communication, the counselor draws his attention to his conflicting feelings. A counselor might remark to a client that his depression always seems to occur on particular days or after particular incidents, impelling him to recognize and examine a relationship between the precipitant and the depression.

A woman of 26 initiated counseling because of her dissatisfaction with a live-in relationship with a man. She complained that they no longer shared any interests, he showed no tenderness toward her and seldom talked to her. Furthermore, she was offended by his personal habits, but whenever she considered leaving him she recalled all the positive aspects of the relationship, his generosity in the past and her fondness for him. In confronting her with her dual feelings, the counselor was able to help her realize how she justified staying with him and hung onto the unrewarding relationship because of her dependence and fear of separation.

Interpretation

Interpretation is used in making a connection, of which the client is unaware, between two sets of feelings, impulses, experiences or memories. It may call the client's attention to a forgotten event from the past in order to explain or throw some light on current feelings or behavior. Usually the client is conscious of one element but not the other, or he may be aware of both but not the link between the two. Interpretation is used sparingly in counseling, but is effective when a client is invaded by apparently irrational feelings that he cannot understand until the connection with old feelings from which they derive are explained.

An interpretation should only be made when a counselor has sufficient evidence for it from the client's associations and when the connection is already close to consciousness. It should be suggested tentatively, often in the form of a question or speculation, so that the client can reject it if it is disturbing or unacceptable. Sometimes a client will spontaneously make his own interpretation when some insight has broken through, like a light dawning, without intervention by the counselor, as in the following example of a simple use of interpretation.

> A female client was concerned about her unaccountable anger at her husband. Since she had talked earlier in counseling about her mother's neglect when she was a child, the counselor inquired whether the irrational anger at her husband could be a displacement of the anger she had once felt toward her mother. This interpretation was confirmed by the client in her associations, helping her to refocus the anger on her mother where it originated.

Interpretation in the following case led to insight for a divorced woman who was considering remarrying but had many misgivings because of her disastrous first marriage.

> An attractive and intelligent woman of 36 volunteered little information about her childhood and parents, discussing almost exclusively the confusion and doubts she was feeling about her relationship with a slightly younger man who wanted to marry her. Only with prompting from the counselor did she reveal some history of earlier years, particularly recalling her father's distance and detachment from his six children. He never talked at the dinner table or played with his children and was emotionally cold. The counselor interpreted that her description of her father sounded like the way she had depicted her former husband. The client was surprised, had never made this connection herself, but once aware of it began to reexamine her second choice of a partner. What was unconscious was her attraction to a man resembling the father who had disappointed her.

An interpretation involving a client's relationship

with his female counselor was made at a time when counseling had come to an impasse, and there was a likelihood that the male client would break off treatment unless his resistance could be overcome.

> A 20-year-old client had been insightful in relating memories and fantasies to the depression he suffered after the break-up of his first intense love affair. One day during the sixth month of counseling he came late, and instead of sitting in his usual chair near the counselor's desk he took a chair close to the door, explaining that he could see the counselor better from there.
>
> He missed his next appointment entirely, again came late for the following interview and again sat by the door. He appeared uneasy and was uncommunicative. The counselor commented on his lateness, his missed appointment and his decision to change his seat. Since the counselor had acquired a great deal of information about him, she felt on firm ground in making an interpretation. She asked him if he might be afraid to be close to her. When he agreed, she reminded him of some pictures he had drawn as a child showing his mother with fangs, and his fantasies of his mother as a frightening witch. Could it be that he was viewing the counselor the same way and confusing her with the threatening mother of his childhood? He immediately confirmed that this was true and relaxed as he talked about his irrational fears of the counselor. At their next meeting he resumed his usual chair, laughingly remarking that he no longer felt a need to escape. In this case, what had been unconscious was his confusion of the counselor with a childhood image of his mother.

Counselors should not be concerned if a client fails to react or seems not to hear an interpretation. Clients sometimes seem to have selective hearing and will ignore an interpretation that is incorrect or that they are not ready to accept. The counselor may be surprised to hear the same interpretation offered by the client several weeks later, as if he had thought of it himself, suggesting that he had heard the counselor's words subliminally but they had taken some time to percolate into conscious recognition.

Environmental Intervention

Clients who seek help at community agencies often present multiple complaints. They may need medical care, financial aid, help with housing, employment or school authorities. Disrupting family situations, illness of a parent, an unmanageable child or serious conflict between family members may be causing acute distress.

Assessment of these external pressures will take priority at the outset. Indeed, it is not always possible to discriminate in the original evaluation the degree to which these very real difficulties may account for a client's complaints of depression, anxiety or other emotional problems. Relief of these immediate and pressing environmental problems is a necessary preliminary step in counseling. Referral to other agencies and intercession with school authorities, parents or spouses, are among the active interventions to be considered.

A counselor should be on guard, however, about inviting the participation of the family until he is sufficiently clear about their role in the client's problems. Some clients will initially assign their difficulties to the behavior of someone in their immediate circle—blaming husband or wife, parents, adolescent children—when the problems lie instead in their own conflicts or provocations. A few exploratory interviews may help a client to recognize and clear up some of his distortions, if such is the case, thus avoiding premature family involvement which would have supported his projections.

Extensive environmental intervention was undertaken in the following case of a woman who needed immediate help in applying for financial aid, obtaining medical treatment for her daughter and arranging care for her near senile mother.

> A divorced mother of three children sought help because she was depressed and anxious and felt so beset by the daily demands of child care, an inadequate income and worry about her mother that she had been functioning poorly at work and feared losing her job. It was determined that she was eligible for ADC. She had been reluctant to consider applying but agreed to accept aid temporarily until she completed training to qualify her for better paying employment. She was referred to a clinic where her ten-year-old daughter could get shots and medication she needed for a severe allergy. Her mother, who had been living alone in an apartment, was functioning minimally. With the counselor's help, a daycare center was found where her mother could get hot meals, needed companionship and supervision.
> Relieved of these pressing concerns, the client was able to recover equilibrium and restore her self-esteem during the three months of counseling which followed.

If an adolescent client has been in trouble for misdemeanors at school, or is failing, it may be advisable for his counselor to obtain his permission to talk to school authorities, to get a clear picture of what is going on and, if appropriate, to act as intermediary for the client. An adolescent may welcome his counselor's offer to talk to his parents if he complains of their overstrictness or there is evidence of continuous strife between parent and child.

In some cases of marital conflict, or serious disagreement between parents over child management, for example, involving the spouse may be indicated. It is often possible to clear up misunderstandings or help those involved to modify their attitudes in one or two consultations with a counselor who acts as an unbiased go-between.

> A married woman of 30 began counseling because she was torn by indecision over accepting a promising offer of a full-time job. She felt her husband had strenuous objections to her working. They had two sons, aged 11 and 13. Because it wasn't clear either to the client or counselor just why her husband took this position, the counselor suggested he come in with his wife to talk over his feelings. It turned out in the discussion that he did not object and was quite comfortable about his wife taking the job, but it was the client who was ambivalent. After this had been clarified she was able to focus in counseling on her guilt about leaving her children and the doubts she felt about her own adequacy.

If a client has physical symptoms for which he is not receiving medical care, it is always good practice for the counselor to propose a physical check-up and, if necessary, make a referral for that purpose. This will insure that the client is getting needed care and also help client and counselor to determine to what extent, if any, the symptoms may be psychological in origin.

Counselors should be aware of the difference between psychosomatic and psychogenic conditions. Psychogenic symptoms are solely the expression of emotional stress, which finds its outlet in various bodily complaints such as headaches, backaches, or in rare cases, of hysterical paralysis, for which there is no medical evidence of disease. In psychosomatic illnesses, on the other hand, a detectable disease process does exist, even though it is thought to be induced by psychological pressure. It may take the form of skin rashes, ulcers, hypertension, allergies or colitis, among others.

It is important that the distinction be made since a counselor may need to consult and cooperate with a client's physician if the client is suffering from a psychosomatic disorder. If the illness is serious the counselor should consider referring the client for treatment by a psychiatrist who can monitor the patient's medical condition. Psychogenic complaints can, of course, be investigated in counseling in order to help a client understand the relationship of his symptoms with the emotional precipitant.

LETTING THE CLIENT BEGIN

It is good practice to allow clients to open counseling interviews. A client may be on the verge of communicating some feeling or introducing a new subject he has been pondering about, which the counselor would not learn if he started to talk first, asked the client how he was feeling, or directed the conversation into some other channel of his own choosing. Furthermore, a client's initial remarks will tell something about his attitude toward counseling. Will he begin on a positive note or with complaints and negative attitudes? If a client seems uncomfortable or waits for the counselor to speak first, a simple question, "What would you like to talk about?" will invite the client to begin. After a few interviews clients will usually start talking without prompting.

If a client continues where he left off the last time, brings up memories or feelings stimulated by the previous session, recounts incidents relevant to his problems or new insights he has gained, the counselor can be assured the interview is off to a positive start and can be content to listen attentively. If, on the other hand, the client begins with a defensive posture and makes negative observations, cites a litany of complaints (counseling is not helping me?), says he was reluctant to come that day, fills the first few minutes with small talk (evading feelings?), or claims he has nothing to say or doesn't know where to begin, this is a cue for the counselor to come to his aid.

A comment on the client's apparent discomfort and a question about the attitudes he has expressed will allow him to acknowledge and examine any negative feelings and thus lead to some relief of his anxiety. A client's defenses must be dealt with first in order to clear the way for positive work to resume. If a client seems to be on dead center and unable to proceed, a tactic that usually works well is to suggest that he go back and review his problems. Thus, "What do you see as the main problems you want help with?" or "What do you hope to accomplish here?" will give him something concrete to work on.

LINKING PAST AND PRESENT

Unless the sole aim in counseling is to help a regressed individual regain equilibrium, in which case treatment will usually be focused on current reality, even very brief counseling will uncover some relationship between a client's complaints and his early life experiences. If a client has a relatively intact ego he should be helped to incorporate old memories that will bridge the emotional gap between past and present.

It will be recalled that a client's total life history was taken into account in the initial evaluation. His complaints and behavior were assessed in the light of his emotional development, his early experiences and his cultural and family milieu. What is learned about the client's past should be kept in sight as counseling unfolds. Since every individual's emotional reactions and characteristic behavior patterns are outgrowths of what went before, his current symptoms must be assumed to have some connection with the past.

Ideally, in counseling, a client's attention will range from present to past, back and forth, at times dwelling on current incidents, then reminiscing and associating old feelings with present behavior. As past and present are linked up and the connections understood, his often irrational feelings or puzzling symptoms can be explained. Questions like "Do you remember feeling like this before?" "How did you express your anger in the past?" "I wonder if you felt so misunderstood as a child?" may stimulate a series of memories; first may be recollections of the more recent experiences of adolescence, then ones further back to childhood incidents and, eventually, even very early memories. A forgotten hospitalization, the birth of a sibling, or some seemingly insignificant event recalled may arouse emotions which can be directly related to a client's symptoms.

A client may complain of feeling depressed or

lonely because of the loss of an important person in his life. Asking him if he remembers being left before may recall memories of feeling abandoned when his mother was away. Perhaps there were multiple losses over the years, and echoes of these feelings of rejection or desertion may be contributing to his present sadness.

> A female client in her thirties seemed irrationally depressed after the death of a 12-year-old dog which had been a cherished companion since she acquired him as a puppy. She made an elaborate ceremonial of his burial, buying a new blanket to wrap his body in and planting flowers over his grave. When asked if she had felt so emotional in the past over the loss of an animal, she recalled her desolation at the death of a pet cat when she was 13. Soon after this she began to visit a local cemetery every few days, dressed in black when she came to her counseling sessions, and told the counselor, "I think I am in mourning." Further questions led to her realization that she must be experiencing for the first time the depression and grief she felt at her mother's death when she was five, and whom she had never been able to mourn. A period of painful depression ensued for several weeks as she relived the early and heretofore suppressed feelings of loss. Eventually she experienced a marked improvement in her social life and sense of well-being.

Another client may react to failure at some enterprise by heaping unjustified criticism on himself. The question "Did you always feel so worthless when you failed?" may remind him of some impossible parental expectations, criticisms of his school reports or humiliating remarks about his clumsiness or ineptitude that made him feel inadequate and unloved. Clients are often heard to remark sadly that their parents only valued them for their achievements but never loved them "just for being me." The resulting anger may be expressed in self-sabotage, as in the following case:

> A youth of 19 was unable to complete the written work required to graduate from a trade school, although he very much wanted to qualify as a patternmaker. Asked if he recalled similar situations in the past, he remembered failing to make the high school football team. He knew he had the ability but always seemed to sabotage his performance. His father had boasted of his athletic prowess and had set his heart on his son's being a star. The client then reported an earlier memory of taking home an all-A report card in the second grade and his father regaling friends and relatives about his son's achievement. When he learned to walk at an earlier age than usual, his father was elated and had often spoken of this accomplishment.
>
> As he recounted these incidents the client began to feel angry at his father because his father had always taken all the credit, and he never felt he achieved anything for himself. By failing he had both frustrated his father and punished himself for his anger. It was only by putting together all this information that he could see a pattern in his present behavior and realize that he could finally succeed for himself.

Sometimes a current stressful situation may seem sufficient reason to account for a client's presenting complaints and a decision will be made to focus counseling exclusively on resolution of the present crisis. This might have offered temporary relief in the following case, but would have failed to uncover the origin of the problem from which valuable insight was gained for the client:

> A 23-year-old woman was urged by her family to get

help because of several months of severe depression following an affair with an older man who broke off their relationship. The counselor might have offered support during the mourning period to help the client find substitute gratifications and restore her wounded self-esteem. However, questions about past relationships and disappointments going back to her childhood revealed that the particular man had been chosen by the client not for his attributes but to fulfill a childhood fantasy and he was destined to disappoint and fail her. The man represented an idealized father figure, a replacement for the disappointing father of her childhood. The understanding this insightful young woman gained, as she recognized the reasons for her unhappy attachment, enabled her to recover from her depression fairly quickly and a few months later to choose a more suitable partner her own age.

As shown in the case studies presented above, clients' insights into the links between past and present enabled them to gain perspective on and master their problems. Desirable as such understanding is, counselors should be cautioned against encouraging too much ventilation of feelings and fantasies in clients whose defenses are loose or inoperative. Such clients may pour out instinctual material that can beguile the counselor into thinking they are highly insightful, while in reality their egos are too weak to integrate these revelations. They may sound like textbook examples, but insight that comes very quickly should be suspect. Often it is not real insight but an uncontrolled expression of id derivatives. The following case illustrates the danger of regression that can occur.

A young man of 25 talked first about his anger and resentment at bosses, then recalled his hatred of his father when he was a child. He described fantasies of destroying his father, then almost gleefully told of driving a nail through a picture of his father's face. His father was proud of this group picture in which he appeared as a member of an athletic team.

Three days later the client phoned the counselor to report that he had beaten up a man in a bar the night before. This frightened him as he had not been in a fight for years. His calling to report the incident rightfully implied reproach to the counselor for allowing him to spill out so much uncontrolled aggression. Subsequent counseling, needless to say, focused on curbing his behavior and establishing controls in handling day-to-day reality situations.

MEANING AND USE OF EGO SUPPORT

All counseling is supportive in that it fosters self-esteem, self-trust and self-reliance, thus nurturing ego growth. The term "support" as frequently used in these pages, however, describes a precise clinical tool, requiring that the term be more accurately defined lest it be loosely interpreted as simple "encouragement." Because it is sometimes misunderstood, one may hear "support" as a treatment method spoken of depreciatively as "merely" supportive, suggesting that it is a superficial approach placing little demand on a counselor's skill.

On the contrary it is a disciplined form of treatment requiring skilled techniques. It presupposes a knowledge of a client's ego structure and awareness of the particular ego functions of a given client that are to be singled out for support. Using the writer's preferred term "ego support" will help to clarify just what it does, and does not, mean.

Use of support as a disciplined and purposeful approach does not mean flattery. It does not mean glossing over a client's problems or telling him how well he is doing or how many assets he has. It doesn't mean avoiding painful subjects that are distressing to him.

It does mean implying a trust in the client's ability to face his problems and find solutions. For example, when a client asks what he should do, a supportive technique is to reply, "What do *you* think about it?" This informs the client that he is capable of finding some answers. If the counselor directly advised him what he should do, there would be no movement in counseling and the client would be no better off.

It does mean that a client's disturbing feelings can be discussed freely and that it is acceptable to have such feelings, however shameful or embarrassing they may seem to him. Were the counselor not willing to listen and respond to all intimate disclosures, the client's possible embarrassment or shame would be reinforced by the counselor's avoidance, which might be inferred as his disapproval.

It is supportive to ask clients who are hesitant to try new ventures or who complain that they can't change, "What are you afraid of?" This question is asked again and again in counseling. The client is then impelled to examine what there really is to fear. The question suggests that he needn't be so afraid.

Another response to a client who feels unable to make a positive move is to ask him, "What is the worst than can happen?" In thinking this over the client may conclude that nothing disastrous will happen to him even if he makes a poor decision or fails at an enterprise the first time he tries. This question, asked of a young man who couldn't bring himself to stand up to his father, brought the reply, "Well he wouldn't beat me . . . and he wouldn't throw me out . . . he might be angry . . . or he might be surprised. I guess it wouldn't be so terrible after all."

A counselor's understanding of how a client feels is supportive insofar as it is very gratifying to find that someone understands. Clients often comment with pleasure and relief when a counselor's response indicates that he understands: "No one has ever understood how lonely I felt"; "My family keep telling me to cheer up, but you understand."

> A young female client, after expressing a great deal of anguish because of her mother's seeming indifference and failure to understand her when she was small, came to the reluctant conclusion that her mother didn't love her. This was a most painful admission. It would not have been supportive for the counselor to deny this and try to convince her that her mother must have loved her; it *was* supportive to remind the client of her mother's emotional deficiencies and to point out that she must have done her best within her limited capacity.

An observation made to a man early in counseling became the central theme in the following weeks of treatment:

> The client was desolate because his wife left him and wouldn't consider reconciliation. He felt lonely and rejected and missed his children. He was an only child of older parents who were austere and undemonstrative. When the counselor remarked to him, "You must have felt unloveable as a child," it was as if an emotional door had been opened for him. The counselor "understood" feelings that he had never consciously acknowl-

edged or put into words. As he recalled and reflected on this statement over the next weeks, memories were revived and the self-examination that ensued helped him develop a more secure sense of self-worth.

It is supportive to remind a discouraged client of his past accomplishments, suggesting that he may do equally well again. Ability he has shown to hold jobs, to make friends, to succeed in school, to cope with losses or disappointments, for instance, might be commented on. There should be good evidence for such statements, however, so the remarks don't sound false or as if the counselor is just trying to cheer up the client. Such observations as, "Badly as you say you failed, you did find the strength to finish school" (or hold a job or manage to care for your children, etc., as the case may be) will enable a client to look at his situation from a wider perspective so he can see that things were not always as bad. This kind of reminder speaks to the healthy part of the client, which is your ally in counseling. Like the other supportive techniques that have been reviewed, it implies to the client the existence of a positive part of himself that wants to get well and that "other" or interfering part that he must overcome. This split may be reinforced by a statement from the counselor that they will work together to try to understand what gets in the client's way. This is an effective technique as it enables a client to gain some distance or step back, as it were, and become an observer of part of himself. As his conscious "I" examines and recognizes the other or alien part, the counselor can then support his efforts to master and gain control over the immature or self-defeating aspects of himself.

Educating the Client

Educating clients about emotional functioning is a supportive technique not always given sufficient emphasis. We refer, of course, to information imparted by the counselor about normal sexual and emotional development in childhood and the adolescent development process. It is not appropriate to suggest that a client read psychological material outside the counseling hour, which would be analogous to handing a child a book to read when he asked a question about sex. The information should be shared and communicated so that clients' responses can be discussed.

Many clients do not understand their own feelings; some would be unwilling to admit to what they consider unacceptable feelings of anger or ambivalence or disturbing sexual fantasies. For the counselor to suggest to these clients that they have such feelings might be resented as an accusation, but some impersonal information about young children's sexual concerns and the ambivalence they normally experience informs clients how others have felt as they grew up. As clients learn about emotional processes they eventually will be able to relate this information to themselves and to acknowledge that they, too, may have had similar feelings. A client who might be quick to deny rivalrous impulses toward siblings, for example, can be helped indirectly to recognize hostile memories he has suppressed, if it is explained to him how children in general react to being displaced by the birth of a sibling.

Children's intense curiosity about sex, their often distorted perceptions of sexuality, common fears, ambivalence because of attachment to powerful parents and anger at their own sense of helplessness as well as adolescents' rebelliousness and urge for independence, are all subjects that may profitably be introduced in counseling. It is particularly helpful to parents of young children and adolescents to learn about normal psychosexual development; it will enable them to be more understanding and tolerant of their children's behavior and may help them to understand themselves better as well. Educational information about parents, their normal conflicts and preoccupations, also helps adolescents to be more accepting of their parents' imperfections.

OVERCOMING RESISTANCE

Client Resistance

The positive alliance between client and counselor in short-term counseling usually assures that they will work together harmoniously. Resistances will occur less frequently than in long-term psychotherapy, but when they do happen counseling may come to a temporary standstill unless the resistances can be understood and cleared up quickly. The limited time span in counseling does not permit counselors to sit back and await developments as they might in long-term treatment.

Resistances at times are inevitable because clients are in conflict, which is the reason they seek help. While there is a conscious wish to change, unconscious forces cling to old, familiar, and safe behavior patterns. To give them up is threatening to the very defenses that were instituted early in life to protect the individual from unmanageable impulses, hurt and danger. A forward step in counseling may awaken old anxieties, which then announce themselves as resistances. Even though a positive move is gratifying to a client, it may be followed by a period of doubt and resistance before he can consolidate his gains and gather strength to move forward again. Thus, there is often a fluctuation between two forces; the urge to change predominates at one time, the defenses take over at another.

In the dynamic relationship between client and counselor, the counselor becomes allied with that part of the client which wants to overcome his problems; he also comes to represent the danger, opposing the part of the client which fears change. This is one reason resistances are often manifested as a reaction to the counselor. The second reason is that clients displace onto counselors old feelings toward parents. A client may want the counselor all to himself, as he once did his mother, or want the counselor to gratify all his fantasies for love and indulgence, and feel frustrated when this doesn't happen. At the same time, he may resent his own helplessness in relation to the counselor's power and feel angry and rebellious. The attachment to the counselor thus arouses all the ambivalence once felt toward parents.

How are resistances recognized? A client may talk of superficial matters or skip from one topic to another at random. He may tell the counselor he can't think of anything to say. He may be silent. He may cancel, come late, or ask for frequent changes of appointment time. He may wonder if counseling is really helping him, minimize his problems or claim that they are not bothering him much. A client may also stare at the counselor, as if provoking him to do or say something, causing him to feel vaguely uncomfortable. As a result, the counselor will sense that he and the usually cooperative client are somehow at odds.

Whenever a resistance is suspected it should be inquired into. A comment about a client's late arrival or questions about his reasons for cancelling or missing an appointment may be sufficient stimulus for him to voice his doubts or negative feelings. If not, the counselor might ask him directly if he may have felt some reluctance to come to his appointment and encourage him to discuss his feelings about counseling.

If resistance is evident in a client's behavior during the counseling hour, the counselor can bring it to his attention by asking if anything is getting in his way or remarking that something seems to be troubling him today. Telling a client directly that he seems resistant is helpful at times, but may be denied because clients are often not even consciously aware of the resistance, much less the reason for it. Nonetheless, the counselor's reminder of the client's apparent unease will initiate some reflection and help him to recognize it so he can go on to explore its cause.

Given the central and intensive relationship with the counselor, a good starting point, when no specific reason for resistance is uncovered, is to ask the client if he is having some uncomfortable feelings about you. The counselor should also try to recall what he may have said, or left unsaid, during the last interview, which might account for the client's reaction. Did he keep the client waiting before the interview, change an appointment time or announce his vacation plans? Inexperienced counselors will be surprised at the intense reactions clients often have to a few minutes' delay, to a brief interruption or phone call during their hour, or the counselor's unavoidable cancellation of an appointment. If any such situations have occurred, a client's resistance may be cleared up by asking how he felt about it or suggesting that he may have been disappointed or angry about the particular occurrence. Given this kind of opening clients will usually feel free to confess to something that may have annoyed them about the counselor's behavior.

> A female client in her early twenties was dissatisfied with her marriage but fearful of separation and independence. She was the middle of seven children. She remarked at the end of an interview that she felt "just like a book on a shelf." She referred to this the next hour, saying she was uncomfortable about "what I said last time." She seemed to be guilty as if she had made a hostile statement. The counselor asked, "I wonder if you have ever thought of my other clients?" This brought the resentful response that the client imagined the counselor just classified them and compared her with them, adding that the counselor didn't know what she was like in real life, and finally that she felt angry at the counselor's power. Noting her resentful feeling of being one in many, the counselor then asked her if this is the way she felt with all her brothers and sisters. What was a potential resistance in this case was forestalled by immediately helping her to express her angry feelings and then relating them to the childhood situation where they originated.

While some clients are able to express anger at their counselors, others can't even admit to negative feelings. There are indirect ways, however, that counselors can assure a client that anger is acceptable. "I can understand that it is annoying to be kept waiting.'' ''Clients often do feel angry at their counselors,'' or ''It wouldn't be surprising if you felt frustrated.'' Such statements indicate the counselor's understanding without pressing the client for an admission.

Simple recognition of a client's feelings often removes the obstacle even if no further response or explanation is forthcoming from the client. If the client resumes talking, the counselor can be assured that the resistance has been overcome.

Reactions to Counselor Vacations

Counselors' vacations will almost always arouse reactions in clients. One shouldn't be misled by a client's assurance that he will welcome the break from treatment or hopes the counselor will have a good trip, but should understand that these responses may be denials, or ''sour grapes,'' and be prepared for negative reactions to appear. Announcing vacation plans at least three weeks in advance will allow clients to ventilate feelings during the intervening two weeks. There may be no overt expression of disappointment but more subtle indications of feelings. These come in many forms. Clients may talk about how well they are doing, which can be interpreted as ''I don't need you.'' With others new problems may crop up, as if reproaching the counselor, ''You are leaving me when I am having so much trouble.'' Clients may complain about counseling or wonder if they should try something else. They may cancel or come late for their next appointment.

Whether or not resistances are evident, clients

should be reminded at succeeding interviews about the counselor's plans, allowing them an opportunity to talk about the coming separation. Clients who are fearful of dependency and attachment to the counselor may not admit their disappointment about his going away, but the counselor's concern and understanding will still be heard and recorded.

The same kinds of reactions may be anticipated when the counselor returns from a vacation. The first appointment may be cancelled or a client arrive late. There may be complaints about depression in his absence, or conversely, denials of missing the counselor by assuring him how well things went without him. Whatever the reactions, clients' feelings should be solicited. Resistances occurring either before or after a counselor's vacations may need interpretation. "You are silent today. Is it because you missed me and are angry that I left you?" "I can understand that you may have felt abandoned."

Clients are not always aware of the connection between their resistances and the counselor's absence until it is pointed out to them. Most will then be able to recognize and admit how lonely, resentful or disappointed they felt. If a client should persist in denying he was affected by the counselor's absence, however, the counselor should not press the point. The client will feel accused of feelings he is not conscious of and reply angrily, resenting the implication that the counselor is important to him. Whatever the client's reactions, they yield valuable information and lead to exploration of feelings that may only be uncovered under such circumstances.

A male client, who was emotionally inhibited and unable to form close attachments, expressed total indifference on several occasions when the counselor cancelled their appointments. After the fourth cancellation, he admitted wondering if the counselor saw other clients on those days. This was as much of an admission of feeling as he could allow himself, but it led to recognition of his jealousy of his younger siblings, which he had never acknowledged before.

While the exact time a counselor will be gone should be specified, a question arises as to whether he should tell clients how or where he is going to spend his vacation. A regressed or borderline client, who might feel that the counselor has just disappeared, will be reassured if he knows where the counselor will be so he can picture him in a particular place. There is a clinical reason, however, to withhold this information from healthier clients; in this way, their fantasies about the counselor's vacation can be elicited. For example, a young woman who had an inadequate and rejecting mother imagined the counselor and the counselor's daughter taking a trip together (although she had no knowledge of the latter's existence), revealing the longing for such a union with her own mother. Another client thought the counselor had been attending a professional meeting, which was more acceptable than the thought of her leaving him for an enjoyable vacation.

Not only do clients react to counselors' extended vacations, but a single cancellation or even a change of the usual appointment hour can arouse resistances.

A female client was asked to change her usual hour on Monday to Friday for one week. On her arrival on Friday, she asked the counselor if all clients felt so much fear about coming to their sessions. She admitted she was always anxious, but felt more so than usual this day. Asked how she felt about the change of time, she shrugged off any feelings but then remarked that her previous counselor was always changing their appointments "as if she fitted me in when she didn't have anything else to do." At their next meeting she brought up the subject again, saying she thought the counselor was right about her being affected by the time change. She recalled crying at night the week before "as if I was crying for myself." This then took her back to early feelings of loss and abandonment when her mother had been too busy to give her attention.

Resistance as Avoidance

Resistances are sometimes due to a client's avoidance of a painful or embarrassing subject. Clients may squirm and talk of trivial matters until it is obvious they are blocking. They may be unaware of the reason until the counselor asks them about it. The question "Is it possible you are avoiding something you are uncomfortable about?" may evoke an acknowledgment that the client has been hesitant to bring up a subject he finds difficult to talk about. Introducing an important topic at the end of an interview is another form of avoidance. Here, the client does mention it, but too late for discussion.

A male client talked for nearly 45 minutes, mainly about his weekend activities, then recalled a dream of the night before which appeared to be related to his father's serious illness. He had heretofore denied concern about his father's condition, although he expressed guilt at the lack of feelings. Deferring mention of the dream until the end of the interview revealed resistance to opening up a painful subject. The counselor questioned him about this at their next meeting. Bringing it to the client's attention both enabled him to explore his reasons for delay and prepared him to recognize future temptations to avoidance.

Clients who note that a counselor is interested in their past experiences may dwell on early memories exclusively, ostensibly to please the counselor, but really to avoid telling him what is going on in their current lives. This is a subtle form of resistance which is not easily detectable. The client may be acting out, engaging in some new venture or withholding information about some significant event of which the counselor is entirely unaware, lulled into thinking the client is deeply involved in self-examination. His suspicions should be aroused if a client becomes absorbed in reminiscences, whereupon the counselor should make inquiries about the missing daily life events. If indeed the client has been withholding, this will need to be interpreted as a resistance.

Since clients' negative reactions toward counselors are usually reflections of feelings experienced in relation to important persons early in their lives, their expressions of anger, dependence or attachment are useful keys to the past. Such remarks as "This must be the way you felt when your mother left you" or "Perhaps this is how you used to react to your father" will inform clients that the feelings really belong elsewhere and that old patterns of behavior persist even when not warranted by current situations.

MANAGEMENT TECHNIQUES FOR TYPICAL CLINICAL SITUATIONS

Situations frequently rise in counseling which pose technical difficulties, and counselors may be at a loss when they observe certain client behaviors. For example, expected emotional responses may be absent, or clients will talk about their dreams, to which the counselor is not prepared to respond, or a client may bring his counselor a gift. Clinical procedures are proposed to help counselors meet some of these commonly encountered situations.

Significant Omissions

Sometimes an emotion seems to be missing from a client's responses. For example, a client may talk about a situation which would ordinarily be expected to arouse anger but does not express this. To ask, "Weren't you angry?" may sound like an accusation, but a milder comment such as, "Many people would have been angry if they were treated like this," tends to generalize and be more acceptable. Clients who have difficulty in dealing with anger and are fearful of acknowledging it will often accept terms such as "resentful" or "frustrated," where the words "hostile" or "angry" will be vehemently denied. To them these feelings seem to convey destructive impulses. "Aggression" is another word some clients may interpret as destructive and unacceptable. It is helpful to point out that aggression can be viewed in a positive sense as a needed and healthy drive to accomplish a goal, and is only hostile if directed against a person.

Clients who can express anger freely may be fearful of the opposite, acknowledging their positive or love feelings. One sometimes notes that a client's face will momentarily light up with pleasure after the counselor has made a particularly helpful comment. Then he will quickly resume his normal expression, fall silent, tell the counselor he has nothing more to say or look at the clock and wish the hour were over. A suggestion from the counselor that the client is perhaps experiencing some positive feelings might bring a quick denial, but may help him to talk about his difficulty with such feelings.

> After such an exchange took place with a female client, she began to weep. She admitted that whenever she felt close to someone or was tempted to allow her love feelings to show, she immediately withdrew or became defiant. She recalled as a very young child longing to show her love for her mother. At the point of approaching her mother, however, she was stubborn, willful and rejecting. She was so fearful of capitulating, of being vulnerable to possible rejection from her mother and to being dependent, that she had continued to repeat this behavior pattern in all her future relationships.

In other instances an important person may be omitted in a client's associations. It may be a parent or sibling who is never mentioned, and the question will eventually arise as to why.

> A married client in her thirties, embroiled in an intense love-hate conflict with her mother from whom she had never been able to separate emotionally, talked about her mother, father, husband and two children. However, a younger brother was never mentioned, as if he did not exist. When this was commented on, the client first said

she had almost no memories of her brother and appeared to have literally cut him out of her life. The talk then began to turn to her feelings at the time of his birth, which became the focus of counseling and was directly related to her problems with her mother.

Dreams

Dreams may be reported early in counseling by clients intuitively aware of their significance. Others relate disturbing dreams to which they attach significance during counseling. Although dream interpretation is not ordinarily undertaken in short-term counseling, counselors who are recipients of unsolicited dreams must be prepared to listen, allow clients to speculate on them and, as with any other communications from clients, hope to glean some useful information from them. Dreams may yield clues to clients' current preoccupations or their reactions to counseling, especially if they occur the night just preceding or following a counseling session. Dreams in which the counselor appears usually contain some commentary on the dreamer's reactions to him. Apprehension about a coming event, such as an examination or job interview, also may be revealed. If the setting of a dream is a familiar house or location where the dreamer lived as a child, it may refer to a childhood memory or an old feeling evoked by a current event. Even though the counselor does not intend to interpret the dream, he may learn something about the trend of the client's concern.

Since dreams are highly disguised statements, one should never be misled into taking them as literal expressions of the dreamer's thoughts. Like riddles, their meanings are, to varying degrees, hidden and obscure. The dreamer converts some impulses, wishes or conflictual feelings (called the latent dream) into an altered form, the actual or manifest dream which he remembers. The manifest dream still contains some kernels of the underlying message but these are often hidden so as to be unintelligible. The dream process, conversion of the latent dream into the manifest dream, is called the "dream work."

The keys which unlock the riddle the dream presents are the dreamer's own associations to it. If a dream is only lightly disguised, a client's associations may enable him to unravel the dream work and interpret his dream spontaneously. All dreams cannot be understood, however, even with the help of a therapist skilled in dream interpretation; the dreamer may have few or no associations to a dream because of resistance or anxiety, or the dream will be too obscure. This is particularly true of long, rambling dreams.

Occasionally a dream will be so transparent that its meaning will be quickly evident both to the dreamer and the counselor. An example is the following dream reported at the start of an interview by a female client.

> The client dreamed the preceding night that a stern voice (possibly a woman's voice) insistently pressed her to tell what psychological theory she subscribed to. The dreamer replied, "Jung, because of his symbolism and magic." The voice continued to quiz her in an intimidating manner.
>
> In thinking about the dream, the client first volunteered that it might be the counselor who was speaking. Or could it be the other way around, the client quizzing the counselor? The client confirmed the correctness of this explanation by recalling that she had wondered the

> day before if the counselor was the right person to help her. Maybe she should be seeing someone who would tell her what to do, perhaps a behavioral therapist. This was a typical resistance dream, which opened the way for the client to talk about her misgivings and disappointment that counseling was not progressing faster.

Dreams and nightmares sometimes arouse so much anxiety in a client that an explanation about dreams or even a partial interpretation will be reassuring. A dream that he is being threatened, abandoned or betrayed by an important person in his life may be so real to the dreamer that he actually believes this person wants to harm him. Reminding the client that it is *his* dream and that he himself contrived the situation will be a relief. If a client is acutely disturbed by his own behavior or thoughts in a dream, his fears can be allayed by informing him that dreams cannot be taken literally but mean something quite different from their content, in some cases, even the opposite.

If a dream clearly represents both unacceptable id impulses, such as undisguised aggression, and defensive or ego elements, support and focus on the latter is sometimes advisable to reduce the client's anxiety. This is what is meant by partial interpretation. In the following example, the dreamer's superego defense, his rescue of his victims, was stressed:

> A young woman with two small sons frequently dreamed that her children were in some mortal peril and that she had to make desperate efforts to save them, which she always managed to do. As the oldest of six children, the client's role in her family had been as the "little mother" who was very good at caring for the babies as they came along. She received praise from her mother, and the

respect and affection of her siblings, enjoying the sense of importance her position gave her. Though she had often spoken of how much she had loved her sisters and brother, she had recently expressed envy of married sisters who had bigger houses than hers and was resentful of her parents' indulgence of two teenaged sisters still living at home, contrasting it with their strictness toward her when she was their age.

The next time she reported a frightening dream of rescuing her sons she was asked if the dream might be an expression of her jealousy of her siblings, by first placing them in jeopardy and then saving them. This was more acceptable to her than her fear that she might have hostile impulses toward her own children, which seemed to be implied in her dreams. The client already had enough conscious awareness of her resentment of her siblings, so her ego could accept this explanation of her dream and make use of it to explore old suppressed feelings of jealousy. The interpretation of the dream was correct as far as it went. Shifting the emphasis from her children to her siblings and the counselor's reminding the client that she always came to the rescue were supportive, while to have probed into the destructive elements in her dream would have been an attack on her defenses and aroused resistance and anxiety.

A series of dreams reported during counseling are often useful pointers, signalling progressive steps a client is making. For example, a client in mourning after the death of a loved one may first dream of the lost object as still alive and well, perhaps as he or she appeared in youth. A later dream may depict the same individual as living but ill or on his death bed. If the client finally dreams that he has died, this will confirm that the client is beginning to relinquish him and accept his death.

Many dreams will not require any comment from

the counselor except to observe that they must have been disturbing. Simply by allowing a client to relate nightmares or frightening dreams will offer enough discharge to relieve his anxiety.

HUMOR

Clients who are witty, make humorous remarks about their experiences or at their own expense, may tempt the counselor to laugh with them. While a smile at a client's witticism is sometimes appropriate, one should be cautious in reacting to a client's smiles and jokes. Their laughter may have many connotations. It may be a way of covering up embarrassment or pain, or be used to seduce the counselor into a kind of camaraderie in the relationship.

> A recently divorced young woman client talked in a very animated way, smiling and often chuckling gaily during several interviews. This was especially noted as she recounted some disturbing incidents in her late adolescence just prior to her marriage, culminating with her mother's remark when the client told her she was going to be married, "Good, I won't have you to worry about any more." The counselor replied, "But this must have hurt," and asked her why she laughed when she talked about it. Several weeks later the client observed that she had begun to recognize this mannerism and to realize that it was a way of denying or covering up painful feelings.

A counselor may be misled by the appealing manner of a constantly smiling client until it becomes obvious that it is inappropriate and that a comment is called for.

A rather childish-looking, 30-year-old woman complained about her inability to be in touch with her feelings. She often said she didn't know how to respond to others because she didn't know what she was feeling or how others felt toward her. As counseling progressed and she began to recognize and admit to long suppressed anger, it occurred to her that the smiling, which the counselor had commented on several times, was a means to disguise and deny anger that she had never been aware of.

SILENCE

Inexperienced counselors may be uncomfortable with silences and feel a need to make some remark to fill a void. Some silences by a client should be tolerated to enable him to reflect on what has been said or to mobilize himself to bring up a painful or embarrassing subject he has been avoiding. He may need time to think how to phrase a remark. If the counselor interrupts at this point, he may cut off this communication or permit the client to evade something he is hesitant to bring up. Long, empty silences are best avoided, however, as a silent, waiting counselor may be experienced as hostile. If a silence is prolonged, the counselor might simply say, "You are quiet. I wonder what you are thinking of?" If there are repeated silences during an interview and the client seems to be blocked, this may be a sign of resistance and call for further intervention.

GIFT-BRINGING

Clients bringing gifts pose a delicate problem to counselors. Tact and clinical judgment must be exercised in deciding how to respond, what the gift might signify, and whether to accept or refuse the gift.

Gifts have a multitude of meanings. They may be an appeasement for hidden and unexpressed hostile feelings, bribes, manipulative means of putting the counselor under obligation, or genuine expressions of appreciation. In general, difficult as it may be for counselors to do so, they must almost always inquire into the reason for even a very small gift. Whatever the value of a gift, it has clinical significance and requires investigation just as any other material a client brings to counseling. The only exceptions are gestures of appreciation or symbolic gifts from emotionally disturbed clients, signalling real progress, and which must be accepted with grace and without question.

Refusal of an expensive or valuable gift is always warranted, but must be managed so as not to humiliate or offend the client. This may be accomplished by an explanation that counselors cannot accept gifts from clients but that they can talk over what it means to the client and why he wanted the counselor to have it.

How a counselor responds to an offer of a gift requires careful discrimination, determined by his knowledge of the particular client and what has been transpiring in counseling. It is seldom sufficient to accept a client's explanation that he just wanted to bring the counselor something in return for his help. The matter requires further examination in the context of the current counseling situation. Has the client expressed disappointment in his lack of progress, been obstructive or unresponsive; has he, or the counselor, cancelled an appointment recently; or has there been a positive move by the client? In the latter case, the gift offering might ostensibly be a gesture of appreciation, but it could also imply, "I've pleased you by making progress . . . now let's be friends and don't ask any more of me."

If the client is angry or disappointed in the counselor, he may be using the gift to pacify the counselor in advance, thus avoiding acknowledgment of his negative feelings. A client may be bribing the counselor to ease his pressure on him, or be manipulating the counselor, subtly trying to undermine the professional relationship. If the counselor is indebted to him, the client will gain control.

Inquiries as to the client's thoughts and motives in buying a gift, his feelings in bringing it, and what it would mean to him if the counselor accepted it, will usually lead to the underlying meaning, which the counselor can then clarify to the client.

> A female client in her thirties who repudiated everyone making friendly advances to her, was angry at the world, and begrudged others more fortunate than she, had a habit of bringing a single rose or other flower in a florist box to her counseling sessions. The counselor could do no less than thank her and put it in a vase on her desk, then ask the client her reasons for buying the flower today. After some typical provocative evasions from the client, examination usually revealed that the flower meant, on one level, a peace offering and on a deeper level, "Thanks for nothing . . . you aren't helping me any more than the others did."
>
> On one occasion when the client presented the counselor with a rose, she made the revealing remark that roses were her dead mother's favorite flower and that there had been many roses at her funeral. This seemed to say that she both wanted the counselor to be her lost mother and, at the same time, to destroy the counselor

because she failed to fulfill this wish. Reviewing these incidents made a valuable contribution to counseling as it brought out the client's ambivalent feelings, first to the counselor and then to the mother who abandoned her in death.

Inexperienced counselors may be understandably embarrassed by their seeming ingratitude in questioning clients who bring gifts, but failure to do so can seriously interfere or even sabotage counseling. The following is an extreme example.

An error of this kind was committed by a counselor who was recently divorced and lonely and allowed her personal problems to interfere with her clinical judgment. She accepted lavish gifts of flowers and candy from an older bachelor client, without question, so that counseling took on the nature of a courtship. Since the professional relationship could not be salvaged after this, counseling was terminated in a stalemate. The rejected "suitor" client was referred to another agency, resulting in damage to the client and a painful learning experience for the counselor.

Many clients do feel an obligation to make some return for services at clinics which do not charge fees. They are uncomfortable or feel their dignity affronted at receiving something for nothing.

Out of respect for a client's feelings, a tactful solution was found by a counselor when, near the end of counseling, a middle-aged male client brought her a fairly expensive desk set. It was obvious that it was important to his self-esteem to show his gratitude. Since the counselor felt that accepting the gift would impair their professional relationship, she thanked him warmly but suggested that instead of giving her something, he might wish to make a contribution to the agency's emergency fund for teenage runaways. This satisfied his need and protected the integrity of the relationship.

As mentioned earlier there are exceptional situations in which gifts should be accepted without question, as illustrated in the following two cases.

A male client in his early twenties was referred for counseling because of his serious difficulties in completing an industrial arts program. He had had a severely traumatic childhood and adolescence. His father was a violent man who had been committed to a psychiatric institution, where he committed suicide by slashing his throat. The mother barely functioned and committed suicide when the client was 16. The son, the oldest of six children, was so emotionally impaired he had never formed an enduring relationship, had no friends or social skills and lived alone in a trailer. During his three months in counseling he formed a dependent relationship with the counselor, whose firm support and interest helped him to finish school. He arrived for the last session with a little potted plant for the counselor that he had grown from seed in a botany class. This was a moving experience for the counselor as well as for the client, as this must have been the first time in his life he had spontaneously proffered a gift, which expressed the "thank you" for which he had no adequate words.

A gift had an important symbolic meaning to an unstable female client as a representative of her emotional link with the counselor.

The client, an attractive and gifted graduate student then in her thirties, had been hospitalized many times since the age of 17 for psychotic breaks, depression and several suicide attempts. She was in fair remission but had

> occasional erratic episodes which she was able to overcome with firm support. Halfway through a six-month period of counseling she went to Florida for a vacation, and on her return brought the counselor a pretty shell she had picked up on the beach. The counselor admired the shell and from then on kept it on her desk, which the client often noted. The client sometimes brought in pictures she had painted depicting her feelings, just as some clients bring in dreams. One day she arrived with a painting of a small white boat almost engulfed on a stormy-looking, dark blue sea. In a lower corner was the shell. The client explained that the boat was herself, trying to stay afloat and "the shell is my anchor." The shell referred, of course, to the counselor. It had become a symbol of the counselor's ego, which gave the client strength.

One additional type of "gift" deserves mention. Clients sometimes offer a counselor poems or stories they have written and ask the counselor to read them. Instead of accepting such material to be read later, it should be shared in the counseling hour. The counselor might suggest that they look it over together or ask the client to read it aloud so they can talk about it. There are sound clinical reasons for this. It would not benefit the client for the counselor to read the material alone after the interview, when the client's reactions could not be elicited. Furthermore, if the counselor devoted an extra hour or two to the client between regular meetings, this might give rise to fantasies of gaining special favors denied to the counselor's other clients.

THE TELEPHONE IN COUNSELING

It is common practice for counselors not to take phone calls during interviews with clients. They argue that it is disrupting to the interview and annoying to the client. Instead, a receptionist takes the caller's phone number with the assurance that the counselor will return the call later. While realizing that this may be controversial, the writer disagrees, having learned from long experience that accepting all phone calls from clients has benefits that outweigh the objections.

There are two compelling reasons for this practice. One, a depressed client may try to reach the counselor as a last resort before making a suicide attempt. When the counselor is unavailable, the client in his irrational state of mind may interpret that the counselor doesn't care, is too busy for him, or is more concerned with some other client. He will often hang up in dejection, without leaving a number where he can be reached. If the counselor had been willing to speak to him and offered to see him on an emergency basis, a very brief conversation might have made all the difference at a time of crisis. The client had called because he wanted to be saved from an irrational and frightening impulse to harm himself, and he had trusted the counselor to respond.

The second reason for accepting calls is to deal directly with a client who phones to cancel an appointment. If a receptionist accepts the cancellation without question, instead of putting the call through to the counselor, the opportunity will be lost to find out the client's feelings about cancellation. He may be angry at the counselor, upset about material that came up in the previous interview, resistant to talking about something that is troubling him or feel immobilized by depression.

When his call is taken by the counselor, the client can be questioned about his reasons for cancelling.

Clients often use such excuses as lack of transportation, being too busy, not feeling well, or being "too depressed." Of course there may be a genuine reason why it is impossible for the client to keep his appointment, but in many more instances it has something to do with his reaction to counseling or the counselor, and the counselor should probe enough to ascertain if this is so. Such questions as, "Are you really too sick to come?" or "Could it be you have some negative feelings you don't want to talk about?" or "Perhaps you are feeling resistant because of the material we talked about last week," will often bring a reluctant admission that such is the case. The counselor can then urge the client to come in and discuss these feelings. More often than not, the client will agree to keep his appointment. Furthermore, when clients do come in under these circumstances they almost always admit they feel better after talking it over, say they are glad the counselor insisted and tell the counselor they really did want to come.

Had the client been allowed to cancel without question, a valuable opportunity to cement the counseling relationship would have been lost, the client's resistance might have been intensified, and he might never have returned. The counselor's speaking to him at the crucial moment communicates to him that the counselor is concerned and cares about him.

What about the client who overhears such conversations in the counselor's office? He may well be annoyed at the interruption, and the counselor should of course invite him to express these feelings. But something else has occurred. He has noted the counselor's concerned response to a depressed client or his careful questioning of one who wants to cancel and his urgency that the client come in and talk about his feelings. He is impressed by the counselor's interest and assured that the counselor will be equally concerned with him if he ever finds himself in a similar situation.

Many times clients who had overheard such exchanges have told the writer at some later date they too thought of cancelling, but knowing the kind of questions they would be asked decided they might as well come in.

Such phone calls do not occur often enough to present serious disruptions of counseling sessions. The conversations are usually brief. Sometimes a regressed or depressed client just needs the reassurance of hearing the counselor's voice. If a client calls who is not in crisis but wants to discuss some issue, the counselor can take his number and call back when he is free. Of course, calls from individuals who are not clients can be handled by the receptionist.

USE—AND MISUSE—OF MEDICATION

Clients frequently ask for medication—a tranquilizer, for example, to relieve tension. If the counselor asks, "How will this help you?" or "Do you think this will solve your problems?" clients will usually agree that it is better to deal with their problems than to rely on drugs as a temporary expedient. A tranquilized client whose anxiety is reduced by drugs, or who may be in a state of torpor, is not in very promising condition for a real investment in problem solving. He may feel sufficiently better because of the medication to dismiss his problems or feel that they are not very pressing.

The writer has almost never found it necessary to advocate the use of drugs in treating many quite disturbed clinic patients. In times of stress they might be seen more frequently and were aware that they could phone the counselor in a crisis. But unless they were on the verge of a psychotic breakdown, or were chronic psychotics on medication following hospitalization, they were able to function and profit from counseling without medication.

When drugs are used, it should be in cooperation with a physician who is aware that the client is in counseling and can consult with the counselor. A counselor might ask a physician to give a client a prescription if the client is faced with a particularly anxiety arousing situation—excessive worry over an exam or a job interview or a lonely weekend approaching. On a few such occasions the writer has advised that clients be given a very limited number of pills to tide them over a trying period until the next counseling appointment. In almost every case the clients returned to say that they had not taken the drugs but felt reassurance in having them. The pills in these cases represented a kind of psychological support, as if the client carried with him a bit of the counselor's ego, which was sufficient to give him strength. This is an effective use of drugs in very selected situations. In general, however, medication is too often overused or misused, since it is a temporary palliative, reinforces the client's feelings of helplessness and his unrealistic wish for a magic cure, and tends to interfere with his active efforts at problem solving.

COUNSELORS' EMOTIONAL REACTIONS

In spite of counselors' efforts to cultivate professional objectivity, they are bound to find some clients less appealing than others. Certain clients may arouse personal antagonism or be incompatible with a counselor's values, temperament or cultural orientation. While counselors will tune in and feel immediate rapport with most of their clients, it is human and natural to experience occasional negative reactions, discomfort or disapproval. Clients' resistances, criticisms and obstructiveness are sometimes hard to accept with equanimity, arousing irritation and a temptation to be defensive and retaliatory.

Since counselors prepare to work with a broad spectrum of the population, it is particularly important that they develop self-awareness by observing their own reactions and examining what it is in themselves, and in their clients, that sometimes causes them discomfort. They need not be embarrassed or disturbed by their negative responses to some clients, but rather, should attempt to understand them.

Whenever a counselor feels ill at ease with a client, for any reason, he should not hesitate to talk over these feelings with his supervisor so that together they can try to identify the cause. A counselor's reactions are diagnostically significant, indicating how the client relates, possibly antagonizing and alienating others as he does the counselor. If a client arouses anxiety in the counselor that can be attributed to some prejudice or sensitive area in the counselor's personality, exploration will be of value in fostering self-awareness.

A frank and open review of his negative feelings

will usually be sufficient to overcome a counselor's initial misgivings and enable him to continue working with the client more comfortably. Only under rare circumstances of a severe personality clash should a transfer to another counselor be considered. It may come as a pleasant surprise to inexperienced counselors to learn how often they begin to like and feel empathy for a client who was originally unappealing, after the client has confided in him for a few interviews and the counselor begins to understand, identify with and genuinely want to help him.

Negative counselor reactions that may develop during the course of counseling will be easily recognized if he is tense on the day he expects to see a particular client, is reluctant to face the interview, or feels relieved if the client cancels.

The demands of very dependent clients often cause discomfort. These clients may gaze almost hungrily at the counselor as if pleading with him to do or say something. Their intense oral longings to be "fed" can be threatening because of the hostile undertones. Other clients defend against their fear of passivity by arguing and belligerently challenging counselors' statements, sometimes questioning their methods and even their competence. Counselors may feel ill at ease or frustrated with these clients, and with others who behave seductively or provocatively toward them, unless they develop self-awareness and also understand the dynamics of the clients who elicit these reactions.

It is understandably difficult for counselors to remain imperturbable when faced with clients' provocations and sometimes irritating and obstructive behaviors. But it is in the nature of clients, because of their conflicts and insecurity, to test their counselors, to provoke and at times react negatively. Understanding and allowing for this will gradually enable counselors to control their own impulses to defend themselves. Counselors who are sensitive to a client's criticisms or complaints about counseling will be particularly vulnerable and need to struggle with their own feelings. If they learn to recognize that a client's attacks are due to his own anxiety, and are manifestations of his resistance rather than of the counselor's failure, they can turn such situations to advantage by commenting on a client's dissatisfaction and inquiring why he feels so discouraged or disappointed. An attitude of defensiveness or show of irritation by the counselor would only expose the counselor's vulnerability and shake the client's faith in his strength and objectivity.

Clients who are older than their counselor, especially if they have professional or social status, may be intimidating to a young counselor who is not confident of his own position. It will reassure him to examine his reactions and to tell himself that these clients are present because, despite their seeming assets, they are troubled and need his help and that he has something to offer them.

Since few counselors will be entirely free of emotional conflicts and sensitivities, however well they may be compensated, there are bound to be some clients whose conflicts mesh with those of the counselor. When this happens the counselor may experience anxiety and have difficulty in maintaining objectivity. He may be tempted to gloss over or avoid exploration of certain areas that are threatening to him.

If the counselor is uncomfortable about acknowledging and expressing his own anger, for example, he may fail to recognize anger in his clients or to encourage clients to ventilate their anger. The message to the client may be that anger is not acceptable and therefore to be suppressed. An important aspect of the client's conflict, his handling of aggression, will thus be ignored in counseling.

An adolescent's rebellion against parents is another area which may be troubling for a counselor, if he has not resolved his ambivalent feelings toward his own parents or accomplished a healthy separation from them in his adolescence. His tendency will then be to back away from helping an adolescent client to resolve his separation anxiety.

A client's sexual behavior or conflicts about his sexuality can also trigger anxiety in a counselor who has not come to terms with his own sexuality, making him uncomfortable or reluctant to explore fully the client's sexual feelings or activities. The client may then interpret the counselor's attitude as an echo of the communications he received in childhood, that sex is not "nice" or cannot be talked about openly.

Whenever a counselor feels a temptation to foreclose certain topics, he should examine his reasons for this and ask himself why he is uncomfortable. If he becomes aware of a connection between his own problems and those a client is struggling with, this insight will help him to overcome his hesitation in tackling the subject and to regain his objectivity.

Finally, counselors should be reminded that the course of counseling does not always run smoothly. Clients who seem to have been making gratifying progress may unexpectedly become resistant and even drop out. They do not always react as anticipated; nor do counselors' interventions always hit the mark. Occasional mishaps and disappointments on the part of both clients and counselors are inevitable. They happen to all counselors and should not be regarded as personal failures.

Many of the cases chosen for clinical illustration in these pages were selected because of their successful outcomes. It is hoped that counselors will not be influenced by these examples to form unrealistic expectations that all cases turn out so well; nor should they feel inadequate if they are not always able to duplicate such satisfying results.

RECOMMENDED READING

Altman, L. (1969), *The Dream in Psychoanalysis*. New York: International Universities Press.

This volume presents dream theory and the application of dream interpretation in therapy, useful for counselors who wish to enhance their knowledge and understanding of dreams.

Greenson, R. (1967), *The Technique and Practice of Psychoanalysis*, Vol. 1. New York: International Universities Press.

This book is excellent throughout and contains an especially helpful section on resistance.

CHAPTER 6

Termination: The Final Phase

Short-term counseling falls into three phases: evaluation, problem-solving, and termination. Termination is a process in itself to dissolve the relationship that was so carefully nurtured at the beginning. Even though it covers a brief time span, counseling is to many clients a moving and significant experience at a time of crisis in their lives, and its ending will be correspondingly emotional. If a client was deeply involved in counseling and developed an emotional attachment to the counselor, termination may arouse intense feelings, often entwined as it is with old memories of separation and loss.

Unless a termination date was specifically agreed upon at the start of counseling, it may be the client who expresses a wish to terminate when he feels he can carry on alone, or the counselor may propose at some point during counseling that they consider setting a termination date. If a time limit had been determined at the beginning, clients should be reminded intermittently of the number of weeks left so that the date is kept in sight to allow clients to talk over their feelings about it. At least in the final three or four weeks the coming separation may be the principal focus.

EVALUATING READINESS TO TERMINATE

When the client is the one who proposes termination, the counselor should offer to talk it over with him. However, he should not agree too quickly lest his concurrence be viewed as the counselor's wish for the client to leave. The client's readiness to terminate can then be examined. Inviting the client to set his own date for termination some weeks ahead, allowing him time to explore his feelings about ending treatment, will insure his active participation in the termination process.

A client's abrupt decision to terminate should always be questioned and the client asked to think it over until it is clear why he wants to leave now and if he is ready to manage alone. If it is suspected that a sudden proposal to terminate is due to resistance, an impulse to run away from feelings that have provoked anxiety, this should be explored and the resistance interpreted.

If a client has become excessively dependent on a counselor, or appears to be deferring positive moves and clinging to symptoms in order to perpetuate the counseling relationship, it is particularly important that his attention be called to the inevitable ending. The counselor may initiate the subject of termination by suggesting that the client consider what he has accomplished and think over when he would like to terminate. The termination phase that follows may then be very productive, impelling the client to recognize his dependence and to examine the feelings that the coming separation is likely to evoke.

A female client of 32 complained continually of her lack

of friends, her social isolation, her boring job, her unhappy childhood and her anger at all the persons in her past who had failed her. She made no moves to change, refused to consider her options when pressed to do so, but seemed to bask in counseling and settle in as though it would last forever. After three and a half months the counselor suggested that she think about setting a termination date. The client seemed shocked, demanded angrily that the counselor predict when she would be cured, but failed to pursue the subject. After it was raised several more times, the client finally, and reluctantly, suggested a date three months hence.

During the next sessions she was angry and accused the counselor of telling her to "shape up or get out." When the counselor explained that good parents let their children go and don't cling to them, the client recalled leaving home impulsively in defiance of her father when she was in her early twenties. Since then almost the only communications from her father have been letters a few times a year urging her to come home, which she was still receiving.

The counselor's gesture of freeing her had a positive effect. The client began to see that she could have a life of her own and in the following weeks approached some acquaintances, involved herself in new activities, and thought about training for a better job. Though she was sometimes sad, and was apprehensive about leaving, her relationship with the counselor was positive during the final weeks, as if the counselor's push to gain independence was a needed incentive that no one else had offered her.

Criteria for Termination

What are the criteria for termination? If symptoms have abated, the immediate problem is resolved and a client has gained some understanding of his own behavior or conflicts for which he sought help, the goals of short-term counseling have probably been met. The degree of independence, identity and self-esteem the client has acquired will be a factor in evaluating progress. If a regressed individual has restored equilibrium and is functioning adequately, he should be encouraged to carry on without further tampering.

It may be evident to his counselor that a client has problems which were not resolved in counseling, but these need not be touched on if they are not particularly troubling or consciously recognized by the client. The problems may become more apparent to the client at a later date as a result of the original gains made in counseling, at which time he will be more ready to seek help with them. Borderline clients in particular need some time to elapse after counseling while they test themselves and consolidate gains; they may then decide to return for another period of counseling. Short-term counseling that succeeds in overcoming immediate problems is often a steppingstone to more intensive treatment at a later date. This is frequently true of clients who have had effective short-term treatment during adolescence. As they mature and become aware of conflicts they did not recognize or were not ready to deal with earlier, they become motivated to explore more deeply in long-term psychotherapy.

For clients who have suffered significant early losses, or who have not accomplished adequate separation during adolescence, an extended period of termination—two or three months—is desirable to allow them to review and work through old unresolved attachments. In the following case, almost the entire duration of counseling was focused on termination, while a client resolved separation anxiety that had not been mastered in an earlier period of counseling.

> A very immature, dependent and docile young woman was able to leave home, support herself and function adequately following three years of counseling during her undergraduate years in college. She returned to counseling in a panic five years later, at age 27, however, when an opportunity arose to attend graduate school in another state. She was intensely anxious and complained of some debilitating somatic symptoms. Because of her fear, she had passed up such an opportunity to continue her education a year ago; this time she was again in desperate conflict over making the decision. While she had appeared to be independent in the past five years, she had lived in various apartments all within a ten-mile radius of her parents' home. She was resentful of her parents and seldom saw them, but was terrified of leaving the familiar area.
>
> The client was encouraged in the first two months of counseling to complete her application for graduate school for the following fall and, though apprehensive, she did make the formal arrangements for enrollment, loans and housing. The five intervening months before she was to leave for the fall term provided a natural termination period during which to work through her separation from the counselor and her underlying ambivalent attachment to her mother. Old memories were revived. Bouts of rage, and finally some tender feelings, which she had been too inhibited to express in her earlier period of counseling, poured out during these months.
>
> At times she was deeply depressed and at other times shouted her fury at the counselor for letting her go (unlike the mother who had clung to her). It was an intense and anguishing experience, but she had matured enough to face the emotional storm. Her somatic symptoms cleared up, and when the time came for departure she was reasonably composed and left by herself, having

stoutly refused her parents' offer to drive her to the new campus. She made many comparisons between this emotional termination and the ending of her previous treatment when she had been apprehensive but unable even to recognize her feelings.

Question of Tapering Off

Once a termination date has been agreed on, an extension of the time should not be considered except under some pressing circumstance such as a death or other crisis in a client's life. Clients sometimes ask if counseling can be tapered off with a period of less frequent sessions. Except for borderline clients whose adjustment is shaky at best, and who may need to maintain contact at intervals for an extended period, tapering off is contraindicated. It would permit deferral or avoidance of working through the separation anxiety which is an important final phase of the counseling process. While a counselor's vacation might seem a natural termination date, a better plan is to terminate several weeks after the counselor returns. The temporary separation will serve as a testing period during which the client can experience the separation and then have time to react to it.

ELICITING CLIENTS' REACTIONS

Clients may express a variety of feelings about a coming termination—disappointment, resentment at being left, loss and abandonment as well as positive feelings. Their reactions sometimes imply a reproach to their counselor, "You let me get attached to you; now you are leaving me." Clients may act out during the final weeks, miss or come late to appointments, or regress or complain of new problems to appeal to the counselor by communicating how needy they still are. These reactions must be discussed and interpreted as a reaction and resistance to terminating.

If there have been past experiences in a client's life of being left, or other losses with their painful memories, the termination period will stimulate him to work through the old memories. The absence of mother when she went to a hospital to have a new baby, deaths in the family, loss of or separation from close friends, or a series of losses a client experienced through his life may be recalled and the feelings revived during the process of separation from the counselor. If separation from parents was not fully accomplished during adolescence, leaving the counselor, and the counselor's permission to leave, will help a client resolve the separation conflict.

Even if a client denies any reactions to termination, it should not be assumed that it doesn't have meaning for him. He may be unwilling to admit that the counselor has been important to him and instead assume an off-hand attitude as if to say, "Why should I care for you. You are leaving me." While the counselor shouldn't probe in such a case or insist that the client express feelings, the very fact that the counselor asked about his reactions and recognized that he may feel some loss, informs him that the counselor understands. Some clients have particular difficulty in expressing tender feelings, for fear of rejection or of becoming too close to another person who might be in a position to reject them. If the counselor suspects such is the case, he might touch on the subject by remarking that clients are often sad at leaving, even though they are pleased that counseling has been helpful. Whether or not the client responds, he has heard and understood.

SAYING GOOD-BYE

A client may seem tense during the final interview, knowing that he will soon have to say good-bye. He may feel awkward, be making an effort to hold back tears or be mistrustful of his ability to walk out without showing emotion. The counselor can be helpful by not provoking emotion at the very last. By standing up and shaking hands when the client is ready to leave, he is putting a seal on this episode in the client's life and the handshake is, in itself, an expression of good will, more effective than any parting remarks of good luck or hopes for the client's future. It may take restraint just to say, "good-bye," but seems a better ending than any hearty parting wishes.

Counselors' Reactions: Letting Go

It is also important at termination *not* to ask the client to let you know how he is getting along. At this point, when the client is willing to part, the counselor would in effect be saying that he's the one who can't quite let go! This raises the issue of the counselor's own problems in terminating with a client. If the counselor has for some reason become attached to a client, he may find it difficult to let go, or feel guilty as if he is letting the client down. If he is not aware of these feelings he may delay dealing with termination until the last minute or fail to allow the client to ventilate his feelings, with the result that the termination phase of counseling will become difficult for both client and counselor. The same awkwardness may arise if the counselor has had some negative feelings about the client, so that he may feel guilty about the relief he experiences that the end is near. In either case his tension will be alleviated and the termination process facilitated if he examines and understands his own feelings and doesn't allow them to get in his way.

AFTER TERMINATION

Should the counselor leave the door open for further help when a client terminates? Generally if the counseling has been helpful and the client has regained control and feels confident, it is just as well not to raise the question. If the counselor offers future help at the time of termination, it may suggest to the client that the counselor is not sure that all is well, and is predicting further difficulties. It is usually more supportive to assume that the client is able to carry on; he knows where he can come for help if he needs it.

In cases of individuals who have precarious adjustments and may feel a need for continued identification with a helpful person, it is appropriate to let them know that you will be there in case of future need. This does not mean that dependence on the counselor should be encouraged or that the counselor is offering to take care of the client, but just a reminder that the counselor will be there is supportive.

A client's wish to maintain friendship with the counselor after termination should be viewed clinically as a manifestation of separation anxiety and a desire to prolong dependency. Asking the client about his fantasies will help him place the wish in the context of his treatment so his feelings about leaving can be examined. If a friendship were encouraged it would blur the necessary separation process and also prohibit the client from returning for further counseling. A request that the counselor see a spouse, other relative, or close friend after termination must also be handled as a clinical problem. The client may want to perpetuate the relationship vicariously through a substitute. A referral to another counselor should be advised, just as would be the case if a client had asked the counselor to see someone close to him while he was in counseling.

RECOMMENDED READING

Freud, S. (1937), Analysis terminable and interminable. *Standard Edition*, 23:209–253. London: Hogarth Press, 1953.

This is an important work for its discussion of the problem of terminating treatment and wide-ranging observations on psychoanalysis written near the close of Freud's career.

CHAPTER 7

Counseling Special Populations

Clients who are highly gratifying to counselors—often referred to as "good clients"—are those who are strongly motivated because of their suffering, are able to grasp their problems fairly quickly, and use counseling effectively to find solutions and relief. Because of ego limitations and character structure, many of the clients of mental health agencies are not equipped to respond so positively to counseling. Therefore, counseling techniques, with illustrative case studies, are discussed to help counselors work with some of the clinical categories of clients who have limited potential or are particularly difficult to engage in a working alliance. Other specific populations include elderly and minority clients, and those with chronic marginal adjustments, who so frequently appeal for help at community agencies. Unlike "difficult" clients, these groups are usually responsive and promising candidates for counseling but require specialized approaches and understanding.

CLIENTS WITH LIMITED PROGNOSIS

Individuals who have developed deeply ingrained character traits seem restricted to one mode of response in all situations. Because they view their reactions as normal and are not aware of the narrow range or inflexibility of their behavior patterns, they have limited capacity for insight and change. Compulsive, aggressive, oral, inhibited and emotionally restricted character types fall into this group.

A second clinical group who do not readily respond to counseling and are not strongly motivated to engage in self-examination are individuals who are impulsive and tend to act out their conflicts in the environment.

Counselors working with clients who are resistant or weakly motivated must be prepared for occasional disappointments, but unless they undertake each case hopefully they will not be able to help clients with a marginal prognosis. In approaching their more discouraging clients, counselors will be able to maintain positive attitudes if they recognize that these are needy and troubled individuals whose complaints are real and painful, despite their sometimes combative, demanding or negative responses.

Compulsive Characters

Compulsive characters are difficult to treat in short-term counseling because of their resistance or inability to communicate on an emotional level. They are neat and orderly, often restricted in their life patterns, have rigidly organized personality structures and rationalized explanations for their acts. Some obsessive-compulsive individuals expend a great deal of energy in repeated rituals or complain of obsessive thoughts. In counseling they may produce material freely that one would expect to be emotionally charged, but the emotions are missing as if isolated from the events or situations the clients experience or recall.

A tendency to intellectualize is characteristic of compulsive individuals. They will digress into philosophical discussions or introduce psychological constructs picked up in the classroom or the media and devote counseling time to abstract subjects as a diversion from talking about their feelings. Counselors must use care not to get drawn into such discussions and remind the clients that they have come to counseling to examine their problems. If a client uses psychological jargon, the counselor should ask the client to describe what he feels when he says he has some complex or other, to avoid getting involved in a discussion of terminology.

In short-term counseling, clients whose time and energy are absorbed in compulsive rituals or who have restricted themselves to an excessive degree can sometimes be helped to modify their behavior if the destructive nature of their activities is pointed out to them. If a client is asked directly what would happen if he didn't check and recheck his locks or follow some circumscribed pattern, he may venture to relax his compulsive habits and to recognize their irrationality, even without gaining insight into the underlying conflicts.

In general, individuals with rigid, compulsive character structures are most promising as clients if they seek help in an acute crisis which can be resolved in very brief counseling. Deeper insight and personality change are usually only possible in long-term psychotherapy, for which referral should be considered if clients are sufficiently motivated.

Clients Who Externalize Problems

Applicants to mental health agencies frequently attribute their difficulties to something or someone external to themselves. They may blame their problems on their bosses, working conditions, spouses or economic situations. To say they are not motivated is not quite accurate, as they have come for help in their distress, but they do not visualize this as entailing any changes in themselves. Somehow something outside will be changed to accommodate them. Since their projections on outside causes serve them as defenses, they will be resistant if the reality of their projections is questioned early in counseling.

If a counselor listens to their complaints with empathy, however, and encourages the development of a positive relationship, he should eventually have enough evidence to make such a comment as, "This same difficulty seems to have happened so many times in your life. I wonder why?" Or the counselor might ask, "Do you feel there is anything you may have done to contribute to the trouble?" Questions like these, without accusing the client, tend to turn his attention to his own behavior. If he is resistant, the matter is best dropped for the time being but may be brought up again when additional material comes to light.

> A man in his thirties complained bitterly about an autocratic boss who criticized him, made unreasonable demands, and with whom he seemed to be in constant conflict. He feared he might lose his job. As his problem was explored and his history of prior employment began to emerge, it was learned that he had changed jobs frequently and attributed this to a series of bosses, like the present one, who seemed to be continually on his back.

Eventually the counselor commented on how unusual it seemed that all his bosses had been so difficult to get along with. What was it about them that upset him so? He rationalized for a time, but finally began talking about how they all seemed to resemble his demanding, critical and authoritarian father. As he talked about his father he began to realize that he was reacting to all his employers as he had reacted to his father when he was a child. Once the connection was made he recognized that he may have provoked some of his difficulties because he had misperceived his bosses as father figures. This led to some behavior changes and his job situation improved. (It can be speculated that this young man was initially attracted to bosses like his father in an unconscious attempt to work out old conflicts with a different ending, but this was not touched on in counseling.)

In another example a young man blamed his economic situation for his continued dependence on his mother.

The client was a 19-year-old high school graduate who lived with a nagging mother given to violent temper outbursts, usually directed at him. His divorced alcoholic father took little interest in him. He submitted to his mother's tantrums, seldom argued with her, and said he had no choice as he was economically dependent on her. In fact, he had a fairly good job but had recently bought a new car, and his payments and insurance took most of his earnings. He vaguely expected to leave home in a couple of years. What he mainly wanted from the counselor was to persuade his mother to change.

At first he was not open to examining his relationship with his mother, saying that he could do nothing about it until his car was paid for and he could move out. A sympathetic male counselor with whom he developed a warm relationship was eventually able to question why he had bought such an expensive car, knowing that it

> would make him economically dependent. The client resisted the idea that he may have created his own dilemma, but was gradually led to examine his fear of leaving home and of separating from his mother. The purchase of the car had been an indirect way to prolong his dependence. As this was explored, he began to stand up to his mother more assertively, reexamined his economic situation, and decided he could afford to move to a small apartment with a roommate to share expenses.

There are some unhappy individuals to whom woes always seem to befall, as if their world conspired to disappoint them. Such clients who have a lifelong history of displacing their misery on outside circumstances are often so entrenched in their perceptions of a hostile or unfair world that their defenses will not yield, no matter what the counselor does. They will go from one agency to another for relief, with the same complaints. They seem, perversely, to gain some satisfaction from their plights, which they are unwilling to give up. Pointing this out to them should be attempted, and may occasionally yield enough insight for some clients to be motivated to change. Others may simply regard the counselor's failure to alter the external situation as another proof that everyone lets them down, and they will terminate yet another disappointing service.

Aggressive Characters

Individuals who defend against their fear of passivity by belligerence may be particularly difficult for some counselors who are sensitive to the clients' criticisms and challenging behavior. Counselors can avert head-on collisions with an argumentative and aggressive client by allowing him to talk freely and refraining from comments that the client might challenge. The counselor's calm manner and absence of defensiveness will disarm such a person for the time being. As the relationship develops and the client begins to feel less threatened and more trustful that the counselor is not going to dominate him, the counselor may remark mildly on his belligerence and need to control and inquire if this is the way he always reacts. If he is able to recognize and acknowledge his characteristic behavior, it will be a helpful prelude to his examining the fears that underlie his aggressive attitudes.

On the other side of the coin, excessively passive individuals seem continually to be awaiting some word of advice or response from the counselor, as if pleading with him for nourishment. Their oral longing has a hostile, devouring quality, provoking in counselors a temptation to give, to try to satisfy their needs. It requires patience and control to withhold from such clients and still offer them some gratification by a warm encouragement to express their feelings. When they ask the counselor what he thinks, or what they should do, he must gently tell them that he would like to know what they think about the question, or what they feel they might do. These clients also need to be made aware of the demands they make. A comment from the counselor that they seem to want something from him, and asking them to verbalize what it is they may be seeking, will initiate some self-examination. With patience and firmness, passive individuals may be enabled to recognize their longing, express their disappointment in the counselor, and begin to volunteer their own thinking.

The Emotionally Restricted

Physicians often refer clients who repeatedly complain to them of somatic symptoms or "nerves," for which no organic cause can be found. Their doctors prescribe drugs which usually prove ineffective, and finally, out of their frustration with the complaining patients, send them to mental health clinics. These clients repeat the same complaints to counselors, still expecting a prescription. They seem unable to relate their distress to emotions, and are resistant to any suggestion that their difficulties might be due to something as frightening as what they call "mental" problems.

Counselors should try to communicate with such a client in feeling terms by asking him, as he reviews his current life circumstances, if he might feel sad, or unhappy, or lonely. Some educational explanation by the counselor that disappointments and frustrations in their daily lives can cause people to feel nervous may be helpful, since the remarks can be generalized and do not directly accuse the client of emotional problems.

If a client remains unresponsive to this approach, the alternative is to listen patiently to his complaints and examine his family and living situation in detail, in the hope that some concrete reason for dissatisfaction or tension can be found. If so, the client can be helped to look for changes in his external circumstances that will bring some relief.

> A female client in her late fifties, who insisted her problem was her "nerves," lived an empty, shut-in life with her retired husband. Without attempting to confront her self-diagnosis, the counselor suggested that this woman go out for a walk every day, since she did not drive and

had no friends in her neighborhood. The woman was skeptical about this prescription, but did follow it and eventually was also persuaded to offer service at a nearby convalescent home. Though feelings were never directly addressed, the activity helped her to gain self-esteem, and her complaints subsided.

Some clients like this, who view their troubles as somatic and strongly deny emotional causes, can be reached indirectly in counseling; others are unable to respond to a counseling relationship. They are not looking for self-help or changes in themselves and instead will seek still another physician for relief through medication.

Clients Who Act Out

So-called "acting out" individuals react to stress by externalizing their anxiety in the form of constant and often inappropriate behavior that may be destructive. Their drive to act out conflicts serves as a defense against experiencing inner pain, which they can thus escape and remain virtually unaware of.

In psychoanalytic theory, acting out is used in a narrower sense to refer to individuals who act out a specific unconscious fantasy in their therapy. Here we give it a wider meaning to describe a variety of individuals who are impulsive and impatient, and who express their drives in behavior of all kinds. Persons who act out may lose or change jobs often, drop out of school, run away, be sexually promiscuous or change partners frequently. They are restless and seem to be continually on the move.

Clients who act out are frequently seen at crisis centers because they come for help on impulse just as they do everything else. They are difficult and sometimes impossible to engage in counseling. They often get embroiled in new situations and drop out, rationalizing that the problem they sought help with no longer exists.

The adult client to whom acting out has become a characteristic way of life in response to stress is rarely conscious of the acting out nature of his behavior and will tend to deny it when it is brought to his attention. Typical individuals who repeatedly choose inappropriate sex partners, flit from job to job and get into desperate financial binds, for example, have well rationalized explanations for their distressing situations. These persons are seldom sufficiently motivated for counseling unless their plights become extremely painful.

Adolescents are particularly prone to acting out, and unless it is continuous or destructive it can be considered a normal and transient aspect of behavior. Activity is an expression of drives or conflicts that are temporarily unmanageable and may be alternated periodically with periods of withdrawal, both of which are typical of this phase of development. Only when the acting out has become excessive, seriously harmful, or unremitting should it be considered an alarming symptom. In the latter case it is unlikely to yield to short-term counseling. Milder or occasional acting out may cease with help from a counselor in locating the underlying problem, gaining some understanding of it and then reinstating controls. Since acting out may be a screen for depression, this possibility should be explored in assessing and counseling adolescents.

Success in treating acting out adolescents and young adults is most promising if they are able to forge a strong relationship with a counselor. Once a trusting relationship had been established the counselor must take firm steps to curb the acting out and at times even forbid it. These clients need to be seen oftener than once a week at first because they cannot contain their impulses for more than a few days.

It is typical of a young acting out client to talk to a number of other persons about his problems between appointments with his counselor, which of course dilutes the effectiveness of counseling. Clients should be told that this is not helpful and that they must try to control their need to talk until they can see the counselor again.

So much happens to an acting out client in even a few days that the entire hour may be taken up in his recital of events as he brings the counselor up to date, and there is little time left to discuss the meaning of his behavior. In other cases, a client may focus on past events or fantasies, as if to please the counselor with how earnestly he is working on his problem. If the counselor becomes suspicious and asks what is going on now, he may find that the client has withheld important information about current activities that he wants to avoid talking about.

In the following case the counselor was lulled into a belief that an acting out client was making gains in counseling.

> A 17-year-old girl asked for help because she had not been going to school for several weeks and was having an affair with an older and quite unsuitable man. She said she wanted to get her life in order. After four in-

terviews she had returned to school, seemed more stable, and told the counselor she was breaking off with the man.

However, one evening a few days later when her divorced mother went out and left her home alone, she suddenly decided to go to the man's home to tell him she wanted to break off the relationship. She ended up having a few drinks and spending the night with him. She phoned the counselor the next morning to say she could not go home and face her mother. Here she could not tolerate the frustration of being alone, so chose the most inappropriate way to end an affair by going to the man's house at night to tell him she did not want to see him!

The counselor saw her later in the day, helped her make peace with her mother by calling her mother while the client was in her office, and pointed out the unreality of her behavior. She was asked in future to communicate with the counselor before making such an impulsive move and told she must curb her behavior if she wanted to get control of her life. Her relationship with her mother was the focus in counseling in succeeding interviews, as her acting out seemed to be related to her mother's leaving her. She eventually settled down in counseling and felt more in control of herself by termination three months later.

Another client could not deal with the intolerable conflict which precipitated her acting out and dropped out of treatment.

A 17-year-old high school girl was having affairs with two men, one in his middle twenties, the other 35. She asked for help in choosing between them.

Her father left the family when she was 11 and soon after this her mother became involved with a man of 19. The daughter began her affair with the younger of the two men when she was 15. Both men were dependent, inadequate and passive. Here the mother's acting out was echoed in the daughter's behavior. The client had no stable model in her life and could not internalize the painful feelings occasioned by her father's leaving and her mother's apparent competitiveness with her.

In counseling she broke off after four interviews, which followed a session in which she talked about her feelings when her father left, saying she had decided on one of the two men and no longer had a problem.

A young man seen for several months in counseling because of anxiety and depression continually acted out in counseling whenever the material under discussion became too painful.

A 21-year-old client dropped out of college after his first intense love affair had failed and was working at an unsatisfactory part-time job until he had enough money to attend art school. He wanted help because he was depressed and anxious, did not have a girl friend, still longed for the old idealized girl, and felt he was a failure in comparison to his two brothers. In counseling he was insightful and brought in significant material about the past, which was pertinent to his current difficulties. However, he lost or changed jobs several times, which necessitated his either changing appointment times or cancelling. He also impulsively spent the money that was set aside for his counseling fees, and had to cancel at times because of lack of funds. It seemed that whenever his associations became painful or close to the source of his anxiety he would act out in such a way as to sabotage his treatment. He had not been aware of this connection until his counselor interpreted his behavior as a resistance, which he could then recognize and bring under some control.

CLIENTS WITH MARGINAL ADJUSTMENTS

Clients whose adjustments are precarious are frequent repeaters at community agencies. They recognize when coping powers falter, appeal for help and are usually able to use counseling effectively to restore equilibrium. Such clients are gratifying to counselors because they are cooperative, relate well and are often able to resolve immediate problems fairly quickly.

Those who are prone to breakdown under stress range from individuals who maintain only a shaky adjustment at best and seem chronically on the verge of emotional collapse, to others who function adequately under optimum conditions so that their ego deficits are only evident when their coping resources fail. Whether the diagnosis is normal or borderline, or barely detectable indications of psychosis are suspected, these clients need firm support in counseling. Counselors must be prepared at times to be directive or, if the situation warrants, to take over temporarily and make decisions for them. The specific event which precipitated the crisis should be located whenever possible, although in some cases the precipitant cannot be identified.

The following example illustrates how brief counseling helped to restore the client's equilibrium even though the precipitant of her crisis was never discovered.

> A young woman of 21 sought help because she felt confused and complained that people were following her. She was living at home, taking some college courses; a fiancé was in the army stationed in a foreign country for a year. The client often quarreled with her

mother, who was quite volatile. She reported she dreamed in technicolor and had recently had a series of violent, bloody dreams. She could not identify the persons who followed her or assign any reason for it, but felt threatened.

In this case no precipitant could be discovered. The client had a history of poor reality testing and minimal adjustment, but there was no evidence of a prior psychotic episode. She had managed to keep up with her college work fairly well.

The counselor let her talk about her relations with her mother, her feelings of missing her fiancé and the circumstances in which she felt she had been followed. The counselor also listened as she related her dreams, but did not comment on them except to sympathize that they had been frightening. No attempt was made to dissuade her from the belief she had been followed, or express open skepticism, but the counselor did once ask why she felt so sure she was being followed and why anyone would want to follow her.

The client had no ready answers, and in fact no longer complained of being followed after the second or third interview. The subject was never raised again. The client went on talking about the present, especially her complaints about her mother, for several more interviews and then proposed terminating. She appeared to feel comfortable again and the counseling ended without any insight into her delusion of being followed. The act of talking to a sympathetic, stable and reality-focused counselor had been sufficient for her to recover equilibrium.

In the following example, a young woman had such a fragile hold on reality that even a minor incident in a vulnerable area could lead to collapse of functioning.

A 23-year-old woman had been living in a precarious Bohemian style for a number of years, sometimes at-

> tending college, sometimes working at menial jobs, moving often from one shabby apartment to another. She lived with a series of inadequate men, but the relationships were short-lived and unsatisfactory.
>
> Over the years the client had sought counseling on several occasions for brief periods. At these times the support she received was sufficient for her to gain control until a new and unmanageable stress occurred. She seemed like a waif and was once described by one of her counselors as "the poor little match girl."
>
> Her father had left the family when she was 12, and her mother supported the five children. The client never felt she "belonged," in the family or elsewhere, and was confused about her parents' marriage and her own identity. Most of the problems she sought help with were complaints of being victimized as a woman. She refused to accept herself as a female and insisted on her right to be a "person" of neither gender.
>
> A new crisis was precipitated after she had been getting along fairly well for over a year in a job she liked, working for the post office as a mail carrier. One day while delivering mail she was taunted by some children as the "mail-girl," which she heard naturally as "male-girl." This was enough to send her into near collapse, having felt ridiculed, exposed and humiliated, and she could not go back to work the next day. A period of counseling helped her to get some hold again on reality, to realize that her inner feelings had not been exposed, and that delivering mail was an appropriate job for her at the time.

A client like this often needs help over the years at times of crisis, and the assistance afforded may mean the difference between even a marginal adjustment and a complete breakdown. It is instructive to note the evidence of strength in such clients as the one above, in that they do recognize their need for help and seek it. This particular client stabilized enough a year or so after the episode described to undergo a long period of treatment, which resulted in her finishing college, holding a more responsible job, and coming to better terms with her sexual identity. However, she is still vulnerable and conceivably may need help at a later date, given sufficient stress. The fact that she maintains occasional very brief contact with her last therapist (often only a phone call) indicates continued need to make use of the therapist's sustaining ego to bolster her own. This is an appropriate and valuable service to such clients.

The following case, in which a counselor had to take a client firmly in hand and make an immediate decision for her, illustrates the need to be directive with a regressed client.

> The client was a single woman in her early thirties who had been hospitalized for brief periods on two occasions in the past. She came to the agency without an appointment, seemed agitated, declared that she was frightened of losing control and questioned whether she could go to work. If she did not go she might jeopardize her job. After a short evaluation in which her intense anxiety and degree of regression were noted, the counselor decided to make the decision for her, in effect, to act as her good parent. The counselor phoned her female apartment mate who agreed to come and take the client home. The counselor also phoned her employer to explain the client was ill and might need a few days to recuperate. Arrangements were made with the client for an appointment the following day to talk over the upsetting conditions at work. The client was visibly relieved to have the matter taken out of her hands and to be told that temporarily the counselor was in a better position than she to judge what was best for her.
>
> When the client returned the next day she was able

to talk more coherently about what upset her at work. She thought a woman coworker had been talking about her and hinting to other staff members that she was having a sexual alliance with the boss' son. There was no truth in this and it became questionable as the situation was explored further whether the woman had in fact been talking about the client or had malicious intent toward her. The client revealed that the son had a seductive manner toward women and resembled a former boyfriend with whom the client had had a brief sexual relationship. She felt guilty about this, had the illusion that her guilty secrets were evident to others, and displaced the conflict onto her work situation. After this was clarified for her, she was able to go to work the next day. She continued for three more sessions of supportive counseling aimed at reinforcing her reality testing and relieving her guilt.

The case that follows illustrates how an apparently stable and successful adjustment can break down under stress in a vulnerable area.

The client was a woman in her fifties who had raised seven children, had a reasonably supportive husband, and was currently working for an advanced college degree. She complained of being a victim of sexist prejudice, of feeling used all her life, and of resentment at her mother's teaching that childbearing and duty to husband and family were a woman's destiny. She was angry at everyone. She said she had always hated being a mother and seriously considered leaving her husband and family.

This seemed out of character for a woman who had been active in community affairs and successful as a wife and mother, much as she deplored it. It turned out that she had had a hysterectomy several months earlier. She insisted this was a boon to her, and she was glad to be freed of having to bear any more children. At first she denied vehemently that she experienced it as a loss of her femininity and was angry when it was suggested that she might be depressed about it. On reflection, however, she began to talk of her sense of inadequacy in her girlhood and her anger that her mother had reinforced this by comparing her disparagingly to her brother. She had had to continually prove herself by having children, and when she could no longer do so she felt worthless. As a defense she became angry at men, espoused feminist causes and repudiated her husband.

Three months of supportive counseling, in which her achievements were noted and she could discharge pent-up anger and frustration, led to better acceptance of herself and resumption of family life.

MINORITY CLIENTS

Much has been written about counseling so-called "minority" clients, but one wonders if the difficulties are not magnified. All human beings, whatever their ethnic, racial or religious origins, have the same feelings, impulses and emotional needs. All experience guilt and anger, sorrow and loneliness, are torn by emotional conflict and family tensions, and strive for love, independence and self-esteem. If counselors understand this, regard their minority clients as troubled human beings, are comfortable with them and respect them, counseling should not present serious problems.

Of course, it is important that the clients' differences from the counselor be recognized, that both client and counselor feel free to talk about it and clients be encouraged to express any feelings they have. For example, even if black clients appear to be comfortable and accepting of a white counselor, or vice versa, sometime during the treatment the subject will come up. It may be in the form of a remark by the client, or some resistance he shows which might be attributed to his reactions to the counselor's race. The counselor should be alert to elicit his feelings, recognize that their racial differences may trouble him, and allow him to talk about his experiences and possible mistrust or alienation in relation to race. Naturally the counselor should not protest his lack of prejudice, which by its very admission might sound false, but convey his acceptance and understanding of the client's feelings. Such discussions are usually sufficient to clear up tensions so that counseling can proceed. In the case of any ethnic or cultural difference, the same techniques will apply.

The writer has found it helpful to clients, and also instructive to the counselor, to ask clients questions about their cultural, ethnic or religious observances. The clients are pleased by the counselor's interest, and their roles as instructors give them a gratifying sense of esteem and participation in the relationship with the counselor. If a non-Jewish counselor does not ask about Jewish rituals and their historical significance, for example, he may fail to understand some of his Jewish clients' realities. The same is true, of course, in counseling Oriental or middle Eastern clients whose religious and family patterns may have a direct bearing on the emotional difficulties they experience in our culture.

Minority clients who are suffering from environmental deprivation, with its accompanying assault on their self-esteem, will often need referrals for help with their external circumstances, as an adjunct to counseling.

THE ELDERLY

While men and women over 60 are subject to the whole gamut of emotional problems experienced by other age groups, they are particularly prone to depression because of the many losses they suffer—illness or death of relatives and friends, loss of prestige and function at time of retirement, physical disability, loneliness and feelings of rejection.

While they may or may not verbalize that they feel depressed, older clients frequently present complaints of apathy, disinterest, memory failure, physical impairment and hopelessness. Some in their dejection have retreated from activity as if they have erected a protective cocoon around themselves to ward off painful feelings. Their posture, attitudes and behavior may even resemble symptoms of senility. However, counselors should not be misled into assuming irreversible impairment and dismissing these clients as untreatable and unable to change. What may resemble deterioration is often a manifestation of depression.

Elderly individuals can and do change in the benign environment and stimulation of a counseling relationship. The techniques used in short-term counseling in general are applicable in fostering self-examination, exploration of options, reminders of past strengths and coping powers, reality testing, and encouragement to seek solutions. Older individuals are capable of understanding and insight into conflicts. Sexual feelings, anger, guilt, as well as sadness and loss may all be explored and expressed, just as in treatment of younger clients.

Counselors should not make the error of behaving

in an overcheerful, jollying and falsely optimistic manner with elderly clients, which would be a denial and belittling of the client's real distress. Their complaints should be taken seriously, with an understanding that the clients are really suffering. At the same time, counselors should hold out hope via their questions, interest and encouragement, that clients' temporary distress is reversible and solutions available.

IMPORTANCE OF LISTENING

Elderly clients need a particularly warm, concerned, and firmly confident attitude on the part of counselors, who should be patient in exploring with them and listening to them. Listening is especially important as these clients often live alone and have few others to talk to or who are willing to listen. In obtaining a history, the counselor should encourage reminiscence, a review of the past, of achievements and successes, of memories, both pleasant and painful. It will be ego enhancing for clients to recall their strengths and successes and the positive relationships they established. This review, in turn, can help restore confidence in seeking new relationships and satisfactions in their present environment. It can be emphasized that although their current situation is changed, the new phase in their lives can offer gratification and be met with challenge.

Those who have suffered losses need time for mourning, for reviewing memories of the lost objects, for the gradual relinquishing of the old attachments, and eventual substitution of new satisfactions. This is equally helpful whether a client has suffered loss from a recent death or multiple losses over a period of time. As an example of sensitive and helpful service, a volunteer phone-in crisis agency offered a client, who had recently lost her husband, daily contact via phone for a limited period.

> A woman in her late sixties had apparently functioned adequately until she was devastated by her husband's death. As she did not drive and had no available transportation to the agency, which was 20 miles from her home, it was arranged that she call at a given hour each day. She used the time to talk over repetitively and work through, to the unseen listener, her grief, her guilt, and eventually her feelings of anger at her husband. This opportunity of an outlet for her feelings provided a most important bridge during a critical time, until she could begin to put her life together again. After six weeks of daily calls, the contacts were reduced to once or twice a week, and finally she accepted a referral to a community center near her home which she could reach by bus.

Environmental Intervention

As a supplement to individual counseling for emotional problems, elderly clients will often need help with environmental concerns—managing finances, locating community resources for health care, finding recreational activities, volunteer work or other sources of stimulation and challenge in their daily lives.

In helping in these areas, the counselor's aim should be to engage the client's participation and initiative in seeking out such services. Steps the client takes for himself are ego building, whereas too much solicitousness and taking over by the counselor would tend to reinforce a client's sense of dependence and helplessness. As a rule, elderly clients can and do find resources within themselves to initiate changes if they are given a nudge.

Often it will be sufficient to point out the availability of services or activities, the possibility of using public transportation, or means to initiate better neighborhood or family communication. The counselor's implied faith in the client's resourcefulness will enhance his feeling of satisfaction and sense of adventure in taking these steps for himself.

RECOMMENDED READING

Blanck, G. & Blanck, R. (1974), *Ego Psychology: Theory and Practice*. New York: Columbia University Press.

This volume is rich in clinical material, and is particularly recommended for its emphasis on ego building techniques in treating borderline and unmotivated clients.

Kernberg, O. (1975), *Borderline Conditions and Pathological Narcissism*. New York: Jason Aronson.

This major work introduces new theoretical concepts in identifying and treating borderline personalities.

CHAPTER 8

Counseling Depressed Clients

Depression is one of the most common problems in our society. Most of us experience transient depression at times and recover in a few days, but when depression is more severe or lasting it can be extremely painful and brings thousands of sufferers to mental health agencies for relief.

Interviewing a depressed client imposes a serious demand on a crisis intervention or mental health counselor. It is incumbent on him to evaluate, often fairly quickly, the severity of the depression and potential suicide danger. In his assessment he must discriminate between transitory depression in a relatively stable personality and more ominous chronic depression in a susceptible individual. It goes without saying that depression should always be taken seriously.

Depression is a state of feeling, an affect, characterized by such symptoms as apathy, loss of interest, loss of appetite, withdrawal from normal activity or relationships, excessive sleeping, inability to concentrate, dissatisfaction with the self and low self-esteem. A depressed person may exhibit an attitude of pessimism about the future and express various degrees of self-criticism, a sense of worthlessness and being "bad."

Depression is a normal affect in response to a real, or external, loss. The loss of a friend, parent or lover due to separation or death will lead naturally to sadness, grief and disappointment. So will failure in some enterprise, loss of prestige or money, or remorse, at least temporarily lower a person's self-esteem. All of us need some emotional supplies from the environment to maintain healthy self-feeling. This may be in the form of appreciation, recognition, affection, love. When these supplies have been denied through adverse circumstances, the individual will respond with feelings of loss and complaints of being "blue" or "moody" or "low."

While an objective, identifiable loss or disappointment accounts for normal depression, another and chronic form of depression arises from internal conflict. Since the conflict is unconscious, the individual will be unable to explain why he feels depressed. The symptoms may range from mild but pervasive depressive reactions to severe impairment with suicidal tendencies; or there may be wild swings of mood, from bouts of dark depression to elation.

Clients are not always aware when they are suffering from depression but may enumerate a variety of complaints such as lack of energy, sleeping and eating difficulties, dissatisfaction with work or their life in general, and uncomfortable physical symptoms, from which an underlying depression can be inferred. Others, in their effort to compensate for or deny the painful affects, may engage in continual restless activity, as though by excessive distraction they can escape recognition of their despair.

In children and young adults particularly, depression may be masked by other symptoms. Acting out, aggressive behavior, hyperactivity or withdrawal into intellectual preoccupations in young clients should be carefully evaluated and raise the suspicion that the symptoms may be disguises for depression.

THEORY OF DEPRESSION

A brief review of psychodynamic theory of personality development in depression-prone individuals will provide a foundation for understanding and evaluating depressive reactions and recognizing danger signs. We begin with the premise that the affect of depression is always a reaction to loss, but an important differentiation is made between two sources of loss: (1) a real, external and current loss which can be recognized and eventually overcome, and (2) an internal loss originating from deprivation or severe disappointment in early stages of ego development. The second loss, which is unconscious, may have been the absence or death of a mother or failure of the nurturing person to meet the infant's needs. Whatever the cause, the developing ego of the child will be to some degree impaired or impoverished.

Normal reaction to external loss is the mourning process, in which the loved one is gradually given up and replacements or substitutes found over a period of time. However, if there is predisposition to depression due to early life trauma involving failure of good mothering or other severe disappointments during early stages of ego development, then a current loss can trigger a revival of, or regression to, an early state of emptiness and despair. Thus, the loss experienced will be the old internal loss in addition to the current precipitating event.

Loss in Early Infancy

While the concept of early infantile ego development is complex, we endeavor here to describe in simple terms the dynamic view of the infant's psychic state. Try to imagine the newborn in which there is no "I" or "you." The infant experiences his mother as an extension of himself so that the two are felt as a global unity. As he takes in nourishment, he also takes in good feelings of warmth and satiety and thus feels "good." If there is a failure of mothering and need fulfillment, he feels cold and empty, abandoned and "bad." In effect, the infant incorporates within himself the mother's image, taking her in through his mouth in the total nourishing process. His then unformed ego is a merged mother-infant self and his rudimentary identity. A depressed mother will be incorporated in the merged mother-child ego and lead to predisposition to depression in the infant.

If through repeated disappointment in the nourishing mother there is more "bad" feeling than the infant can tolerate, the development of his ego will be impaired. As a result he will tend to lose trust in others, and fail to develop adequate self-esteem, a sense of being loved and good.

Aggression plays a part, too, because the infant's frustration will bring about aggression toward the loving-disappointing object. Since the object, the nourishing mother, is part of him in the merged mother-child union, he will take in and incorporate the ambivalently experienced mother, so that the aggression will then be internalized and turned on himself. The hated mother image within him thus becomes self-hatred.

Given a child's experience of unbearable loss or disappointment in early life, when he was only able to internalize conflicting feelings, he will be in an unfavorable position to deal adequately with loss later in life. He will be predisposed to react to it in the original manner. The early feelings will be revived and there may be regression to the early emotional state, with its feelings of emptiness and aggressiveness toward the self, or rather, toward the "bad" mother incorporated within the self.

While all depressed individuals will express some self-dissatisfaction, those who suffered an overload of deprivation in infancy are more likely to show repeated self-condemnation and self-contempt and to feel themselves as unloveable or worthless.

Inability to accept disappointment and resulting depressive reactions are also sometimes seen in individuals who have been overprotected, indulged and gratified in early years. While their oral needs were met, they were infantilized by parental failure to help them deal with normal frustration. With all their wishes granted, no demands were made on them to develop controls, to accept some disappointments and to move on from the infantile phase to more structured levels of development. They remain like demanding infants, lacking inner resources to compensate for frustration, and in their failure to achieve self-esteem and independence, may turn their anger inward in later life in the form of depression.

Loss at Later Developmental Levels

Deprivation in early infancy is the most ominous loss and a prototype of severe depressive reactions later in life because it occurs when the undifferentiated ego is most vulnerable. However, this is only one of a series of disappointments that may be precursors of depression. Each succeeding developmental level brings its own potential for traumatic reactions to loss.

This can best be illustrated by examining the vicissitudes of normal childhood development. Every child, however benign his environment, suffers a series of disappointments beginning with the original loss of the blissful union with mother as he begins to distinguish and separate "self" from "others." Submission to parental demands during toilet training imposes a sacrifice of his autonomy over his bodily functions. He is the loser in the clash of wills and must give up a pleasurable freedom. His dawning realization that he cannot fulfill his fantasies of possessing the parent of the opposite sex as a cherished sexual object is a humiliating blow to his self-esteem. With the birth of siblings the child loses his unique position as the exclusive object of his parents' regard.

If excessive and traumatic reactions are experienced at any of these crucial levels of development, a child's ego will be correspondingly impoverished and he will be less well prepared to deal with the inevitable losses later in life. The old feelings will be reactivated and accentuate his suffering. The normal depression adolescents experience with the loss of the idealized parents and recognition of parents' fallibility will be heightened if they are already depression-prone as a result of losses to self-esteem in early years.

Gratifying as progress may be as a child acquires new skills, gains mastery over his behavior, and adapts to the external world, each new step in ego development has a price. Something is always given up along the way. Earlier modes of behavior and fantasies of omnipotence and magical powers must yield to the demands of reality that the child subdue his impulses and recognize that he is small, helpless and dependent.

In each later stage of life, too, losses are sustained, accompanied by varying degrees of depression according to how successfully an individual's ego accommodated to the early losses in childhood. In middle life men and women must come to an acceptance that once dreamed of aspirations may not be realized. The end of child-bearing years for a woman represents a loss of function. Retirement will bring to some individuals a loss of prestige, especially if they associated their identity with their occupation. With advancing years diminution of physical strength, loss of energy, friends and family members and limitations of activities are seed beds for depressive reactions.

Superego Guilt and Depression

It will be recalled that while a child's ego is expanding it begins to incorporate another agency, the superego, which censors his behavior and arouses guilt. If the superego is harsh and makes demands he cannot fulfill, an individual may acquire an overload of guilt and continually punish himself by feeling unworthy and "bad." He becomes aggressive toward himself, but cannot account for the depression he complains of because the conflict between the ego which seeks gratification and the superego which denies it is internal and unconscious. The depression may have little or no relation to external causes, although the prospect of success or fulfillment may sometimes account for depression because the individual will be guilty for gratification he feels he doesn't deserve. Following is a typical example of depression caused by superego guilt.

> A married woman of 60 was depressed since a near car accident, in which she was forced to brake and skid dangerously to avoid another car while driving to work in a snowstorm. She feared driving again and dated her breakdown from this incident. Questioned about her fear of accidents, she recalled her sister's death three years previously and her guilt because she had not done enough to care for her sister. In an irrational way she felt responsible for her sister's death. Further exploration elicited a memory of a near accident her younger brother had when he first learned to drive. Going further back, she spoke of unhappy early years when her widowed mother had had to work. They had little money except for basic needs, and she felt angry and deprived. If it had not been for her two younger siblings she and her mother would have been able to live in comfortable circumstances. For many years she had dreamed of accidents and violence happening to her.
>
> Her recent near accident had revived and intensified old superego guilt because of her wish to be the only child and eliminate her siblings. This accounted for her depression, which she could not explain until the old memories were uncovered in counseling.

Personality Traits

Because the chronic depressive individual never developed a firm sense of self-esteem, he seems to perpetually seek from others the nourishing supplies he lacked in infancy. He demands continual reassurance that he is loved, that he is successful, that he is appreciated, and no matter how well he may actually be performing, he is never convinced of it without external confirmation. He is apt to be more concerned about being loved than in loving, and indeed may seem unable to love. However, he may behave in an ingratiating manner in order to gain the supplies he needs to maintain equilibrium.

An individual who is ever demanding and manipulating others for reward also surreptitiously expresses his hostility and gets his revenge by annoying others and making them feel guilty and responsible for him if they do not respond. At the least he may make others feel uncomfortable, yet guilty if they withhold support. The counselor, too, who empathizes with a depressed client's misery and feels genuinely sorry for him may feel pressure to do something to relieve his suffering and, at the same time, feel helpless and frustrated.

Since a tendency to depressive reactions later in life so often originates from disappointments in early childhood during the oral phase of development, a depressed individual will usually exhibit "oral" personality traits, thus, his demands for "feeding" from others in the form of expressions of love, approval, sympathy and attention. Often resorting to drugs or alcohol may be used as a means to soothe the pain and fill up the emptiness he experiences. Both excessive eating and greed, and its opposite, anorexia, are common in depressive persons. Stuffing himself gives a temporary sense of relief, while at the same time serving a destructive purpose in causing him to further despise himself for his overweight. Anorexia is, of course, more directly destructive. Use of either drugs or alcohol are in the end self-destructive and may indirectly serve suicidal impulses.

Another indirect acting out of suicidal impulses takes the form of frequent accidents that some people chronically suffer. Accident-prone individuals may never kill themselves but they are continually placing themselves in jeopardy and gambling with serious injury or death.

Delayed Mourning

A common cause of depression is delayed mourning, particularly when loss of a parent has occurred during childhood or adolescence. The mourning may then show up in depressed adult clients who have dealt with the pain of loss by repressing their feelings or as a psychological denial of the death of a loved one. The depression may occur months or even years after the actual loss.

> Delayed mourning occurred in the case of a young woman in her early twenties whose mother committed suicide when the daughter was 16. She reported very bland reactions to her mother's death at the time, managed to complete high school and college and to marry. However, when she considered having a child she became extremely anxious, feared she might harm her baby, and this fear spread to obsessive thoughts of hurting others. She felt depressed, worthless, and had many suicidal fantasies associated with particular dates, especially the Christmas season.
>
> It was only after months of treatment that she was

able to recognize and deal with the long-suppressed feeling of loss, and with her anger at her mother, both in relation to the suicide and to an early ambivalent attachment to her mother. In this case she had identified as a child with a depressed mother which made the mother's suicide the more disastrous for her. Her healthy protective mechanisms, however, came to her rescue in enabling her to suppress the affects aroused by her mother's death until she was strong and mature enough to deal with them in therapy.

In the following example of delayed mourning, the client had actually denied that a death had occurred.

The client was a 19-year-old female student, immature and childish in appearance, who was referred by her advisor because she was on probation and in danger of flunking out of college. She talked about her parents, her school difficulties and her dissatisfaction with a boyfriend who was critical and unloving but with whom she could not bring herself to break off. She had been refusing dates with a boy she liked and who seemed interested in her. Her principal focus was on her worry over school and grades.

The counselor was completely taken by surprise after the third counseling session when her advisor phoned to ask if the client had followed through on his referral and mentioned that the client's mother had died several months ago. The client had maintained the pretense that her mother was still living and only acknowledged her death when the counselor brought it up in their next meeting. She could not explain why she had denied it, but with encouragement began to talk about the circumstances and her feelings.

After several weeks she began going to the cemetery where her mother was buried, sitting for long hours by the grave. Up to then she had been immobilized by unbearable feelings of loss, but once the mourning pro-

> cess was undertaken and she could allow herself to experience her grief, she was able to make some positive decisions for herself. She transferred to a small college where the standards were less demanding, broke off with the punitive boyfriend and began seeing the young man she had previously turned down. Though she terminated counseling at that time, the counselor learned later that she eventually finished college and married the second young man.

In other less dramatic and traumatic cases, delayed mourning reactions may occur and be treated on a relatively short-term basis. In exploring the reasons for a seemingly unaccountable bout of depression, it will sometimes come as a surprise to a client to realize that it is related to a death he had not considered particularly painful at the time. Once the connection is made he may experience a short period of deep grief and emotional suffering and then be able to recover control and undergo a normal mourning process.

RESCUE FANTASY

However obliquely or belatedly he gets his message across, a suicidal individual wants to be saved. This is demonstrated by the frequent appeals for rescue received by suicide prevention and crisis agencies. Paradoxically, would-be suicides are communicating both an impending suicide attempt and a plea for rescue. These may be last-ditch efforts for intervention after other chosen rescuers may have failed to respond or to act.

Studies reported in the literature on depression and suicide have shown that in almost all cases of suicide or suicide attempts, warning messages were given to chosen rescuers in some form, through direct hints, gestures, unusual behavior or more obscure symbolic means. The savior in the suicide's so-called "rescue fantasy" is usually someone close to the suicidal person and the message is, in effect, "If you love me you will save me."

A relatively well-structured individual will make his appeal clear enough so that rescue is virtually assured. However, the message of a severely disturbed or regressed individual may be so obscure that it will be missed by the appointed rescuer. In the latter instances, chosen rescuers have even been persons casually encountered in public with no previous relationship with the victim. Unfortunately, the would-be suicide sometimes miscalculates in assuming that the rescuer has sufficient strength or empathy to respond. If a rescuer feels hostile to the suicidal person because of his excessive demands, or he lacks the emotional strength to respond, he may unconsciously fail to register the message.

Counselors at suicide and crisis prevention agencies need to be particularly alert to pick up these appeals and hope a phone-caller will be sufficiently coherent about his whereabouts and plans so that rescue can be effected. A counselor receiving such a desperate call should induce the caller to talk about himself, to describe his feelings, tell why he feels hopeless, and what alternatives he has considered. The purpose of talking is to help him engage the more rational part of himself by verbalizing, as well as to delay action, and in doing so to obtain enough information about him so that he can be located and protective measures initiated. One should try to elicit a promise that he will agree to wait and think it over, if even for an hour, or if he is sufficiently rational, to come in and talk to the counselor in person or at least give the counselor his phone number and address. The protracted talking itself may be sufficient for him to gain some perspective and control. What seemed an inevitable solution to him in his distraught thoughts may sound less convincing to him as he puts these thoughts into words to a rational and concerned listener. The very fact that he has found a human being who does care may be decisive.

Depressive Reactions to Counseling

The reason for devoting so much space to the subject of depression and stressing its reaction to loss is not only to help counselors understand, diagnose and treat depressed clients, but because depression will be evidenced to some degree by clients in counseling, whatever their diagnosis. As they search for more rewarding modes of behavior they, too, must give up something in exchange. Cherished fantasies (and an unconscious hope for their fulfillment in counseling) must be renounced as clients are confronted with reality. Old and familiar behavior patterns, no matter how destructive, are not easily or willingly relinquished. As clients endeavor to recognize and overcome their problems, and establish new and more mature ways of relating to others, they will nearly always complain of transitory feelings of depression at some time during treatment. The depressions are usually of brief duration, but may be quite intense, as clients work through their disappointments in giving up their childhood and its illusions and fantasies.

EVALUATION TECHNIQUES

So far we have been looking at two aspects of depression, that experienced primarily as a result of current external loss and the more ominous depression resulting from early internal deprivation in infancy. Few persons fit totally in either category, so the counselor will usually see some admixture of both types in depressed clients, representing a range in personality structure from fairly healthy to severely pathological. The danger of suicide will be greater in the individual who had suffered damaging early trauma and is thus less well equipped to master life's disappointments. For this reason it is particularly important to obtain an early history of a depressed client.

Since depression is manifested in a variety of different complaints, the counselor should listen carefully to how a given client describes his symptoms and the feelings he is experiencing in order to assess his particular modes of reaction to loss and the degree of his incapacity. Extremes may range all the way from dejection and decreased productivity at work to the utter paralysis of an individual who has spent days in his room literally unable to make a move.

The onset of the depression should be explored, to learn as much as possible about the origin of the client's suffering. Can he tell you what he thinks caused the depression? How and when did it begin? Was there any recent loss or failure to account for it? Has he been depressed in the past? If the client was depressed on previous occasions, learning how he coped with it will yield information about his strengths and recuperative powers.

ASSESSING SUICIDE POTENTIAL

If a client admits to suicidal fantasies, it is important to ask him about them. How long has he felt so desperate? Has he gone so far as to think how he might harm himself? Has he had suicidal thoughts in the past?

If he has considered concrete methods of suicide, one will want to know what he has imagined doing. Does he have means available, i.e., pills, drugs, etc.? It is never in order to ask, "How do you plan to do it?" because this suggests the counselor's concurrence and alliance with his impulses, but asking what he has thought of implies that you and he can talk it over together. The method of suicide will tell something about the client's personality. Pills to induce sleep may suggest a passive, peaceful impulse to return to an infantile state of bliss, i.e., reunion with the lost object. Fantasies of violent acts such as wrecking one's car or use of a gun give a clue to the degree of the client's self-aggression and anger.

When a client has had suicidal impulses at various times in the past but has not made any overt attempts, one may cautiously inquire just what prevented him from carrying them out. Caution is advised, because the question should not be put so the client hears, "Why don't you do it?" A more supportive phrasing of the question might be, "You have had these thoughts of hurting yourself in the past and I wonder what in you prevented it?'' This suggests your perception of strength in the client. It will be reassuring to the counselor if the client comes up with a strong reason why he could never really take his life. It might be because of his religious beliefs or because he could not hurt his parents. One very narcissistic client once told the writer that he could never disfigure himself or bear to be seen in disarray in a coffin after death.

If a client has a well thought out plan for suicide, means for carrying it out, and no clear preventive defenses, emergency measures should be considered. Of course, there should be a supervisor or other authority person available for consultation. Among alternatives are hospitalization for immediate protection, where further evaluation of the client's condition can take place. If the client is married, notification of his spouse to take charge may be necessary. In the case of a minor or young adult living at home, the family may be called on to protect the client. Be careful, however, not to turn for support of the client to the very persons or environment which creates the desperate situation in the first place.

> In the following case the writer recalls asking parents to come to a college campus to pick up a very depressed young woman student because it was not felt that she should drive herself home in view of her thoughts of wrecking her car on the expressway. The parents demurred, but on urging came reluctantly to take her home and were warned to keep her under observation until she could see the counselor on the following day.
>
> When the client did fortunately turn up the next morning, it was learned that as soon as she got home she was allowed to take the family car to ''drive around''

> with no special destination. We also found out belatedly that previous suicide threats to parents had fallen on deaf ears.

A useful technique in testing for suicidal danger is to inquire about the client's plans for the evening and the following day. If there are concrete plans, such as attending a class, meeting someone or other activity, this will be reassuring. However, if there are vague replies or no plans, especially if the client lives alone, this is a grave indication and some protective measures should be considered.

It is always advisable to make an appointment to see a depressed client the following day, or if he is first seen late on Friday, to make an appointment the first available hour on Monday. His reaction to the offer of the next appointment will be instructive. If he gives clear assurance or a promise that he will be there, it is a hopeful sign. The counselor's reiteration, "I'll see you Monday at 9 o'clock," helps to bind the agreement. If, however, the client is vague or shows doubt about keeping the appointment, this should be a warning and calls for intervention.

Adolescents often tend to dramatize their feelings and may give the impression they are in the depths of despair. In one such case when an adolescent client declared her "life was over," the counselor was seriously concerned, considered calling in her family and suggesting hospitalization. But when she inquired about the young person's plans for the next day, the surprised reply was, "Why, I'll be in the library studying for exams . . . I'm really hoping for two A's," completely contradicting the desperate sounding statements of a few minutes ago.

The principal focus initially should be directed toward the client's verbalization of his feelings in order to arrive at an assessment of the extent and severity of his breakdown. If it is established that he is not suicidal and is functioning at least minimally (going to work, carrying out family responsibilities), a more complete history can be taken, especially with reference to significant relationships and the family emotional climate, past and present.

A Caution About Referral

The decision whether to see a depressed client in short-term counseling or to refer him for more intensive treatment will depend on the counselor's assessment of the client's level of functioning and the apparent intactness of his ego, as well as on the availability of treatment without a long waiting period. If a waiting period cannot be avoided, it may be advisable to continue to see the client supportively in the interim.

If a referral is planned, consider carefully how this is to be communicated and how the client may interpret it. Since he may already feel he is worthless and a burden to others, he is apt to react to referral by inferring that the counselor shares this opinion of him and will be relieved to shift him to someone else. It will be supportive to suggest the referral positively by assuring the client that the counselor wants him to have the best help available. Do not neglect to allow the client to ventilate his feelings about the referral. Asking how he feels about it will allow him to express the anger or disappointment he may experience and help to minimize any sense of rejection.

COUNSELING TECHNIQUES

Short-term counseling may be undertaken in cases of transitory depression attributed to a current and external loss. The precipitant may be some event representing a severe blow to an individual's status and self-esteem; loss of job, health, cherished fantasies or illusions, disappointment in or death of a loved one. If there is no readily identifiable loss, a client may complain of disappointment in himself, a sense of disillusionment or realization that fantasies or aspirations cannot be fulfilled.

Exploring Feelings

Depressed clients should be encouraged to talk about their feelings of despair and to mourn in the case of a death. If a client says he is depressed, ask him just how it feels to him, how he is experiencing it. Putting his feelings into words will bring his healthy ego to bear on the problem because talking is an organized function that will help him structure and bind his anxiety or unmanageable affect.

Counselors need not hesitate to explore a dejected client's feelings on the theory that it will further depress him. It may depress the counselor, but it will help the client if he is allowed to verbalize his feelings. Buried feelings and memories will remain inside and continue to plague him if they are ignored and suppressed.

Examining a client's black inner world can be likened to a child's venturing into a dark forest filled with menacing shapes and imaginary demons. If a counselor shows a disinclination to enter this inner world, it implies to the client that he is scared too. However, if the counselor encourages the client to go into the forest, he is saying, "I am not afraid. I will hold your hand and go in with you." Just as a child finds the demons were only imagined, so the depressed client may find that his fears were not so black when he could share them by putting them into words.

This does not mean that dwelling on feelings and understanding their source should be the exclusive focus in counseling. Ego building, which is the ultimate aim, can be encouraged by seeking alternative gratifications in the present. Communicating that solutions are available and that the client can gain some control of his life will elicit the healthy part of his ego to search for replacements for lost objects and to find meaning in his life.

Dealing With Aggression

It has been noted that depressed individuals have turned aggression on themselves in the form of self-contempt and feelings of worthlessness and failure. The question arises in counseling as to whether one should help depressed clients discharge their internalized anger and redirect it against those in the past or present who disappointed them.

It would be an error early in counseling to provoke a client to externalize his aggression by ventilating anger toward someone who failed him, until he has found some substitute gratification. The effect would be to destroy the old object and leave the client empty, with no replacement to turn to. Counselors should first focus on reinforcing a client's self-esteem so that he acquires a good and reliable object in himself. The following example illustrates the importance for a client of finding self-satisfaction before she could relinquish a relationship which was highly unsatisfactory but represented her only source of emotional supply.

> A dependent woman of 28 was pleasing in manner and considerate of others, but never felt herself to be worthy of love or believed she had rights to self-fulfillment. Other's needs and demands always came first. She began counseling because she was depressed. She had a dull, poor paying job and was unhappy in a relationship with a man with whom she had lived for three years. He was insensitive, unloving, her inferior in education and social background, with crude manners, and hostile and critical of their few mutual friends. He withdrew in silence when she attempted to communicate with him about feelings or about their relationship.
>
> In counseling whenever the client would touch on the possibility of leaving him, she would recall some kindness of his in the past or a small recent gesture of affection. She was so pleased by the thought that someone might care for her that she quickly dismissed or rationalized all her objections to him.
>
> Without encouraging her to express the anger under the surface or to air her criticisms of him, the counselor instead supported her aspirations to seek more rewarding work. She overcame her self-doubts, found a job in line with her superior qualifications, and was gratified to learn that she could handle it capably. After several months she enrolled in an evening course in her field and took a vacation by herself to visit and renew acquaintances with old school friends. She continued to vacillate about the relationship, but her depression lifted and she was often elated by her accomplishments. Fi-

nally, as she gained confidence, began to trust her feelings and become more assertive, she mustered the courage to contemplate living alone for the first time in her life and began to look for an apartment. Her lover either ignored or didn't take seriously her occasional hints about leaving him until she was eventually able to announce definitely that she was moving.

It was only when she found strength in herself and self-worth that she could give up the old, unsatisfying object and experience her anger. Had she been abetted in destructive outpourings of aggression against her mate and been encouraged to leave him before she had a compensating replacement, she would have felt abandoned, alone and helpless, and perhaps become more deeply depressed.

As a temporary expedient for a client who seems to be immobilized by his depression, advising a program of physical exercise, long walks, for instance, often works well. It is not a cure but may serve to get him moving in the early stage of counseling and provide an outlet for the anger that underlies depression. In general, however, advice-giving and oversolicitousness by the counselor should be avoided as they tend to infantilize an already depressed client and accentuate his feelings of helplessness and dependence.

The counselor's attitude in working with depressed clients should be warm, empathic and concerned. He should be hopeful, implying that there are alternatives or solutions to be explored. This will suggest to a client that there *is* a future and that he may not always be so miserable.

RECOMMENDED READING

Anthony, A. & Benedek, T., Ed. (1975), *Depression and Human Existence*. Boston: Little, Brown.

This is a comprehensive study of depression in children, adolescents and adults from genetic, cultural and psychoanalytic perspectives.

Freud, S. (1917), Mourning and melancholia. *Standard Edition*. 14:237–258. London: Hogarth Press, 1957.

This paper presents Freud's first observations on the distinction between depression originating from external losses and internal conflict.

Jensen, V. & Petty, T. (1958), The fantasy of being rescued in suicide. *Psychoanal. Quart.*, 27:327–339.

This article is of interest to all clinicians, especially crisis intervention counselors.

CHAPTER 9

Counseling Adolescents

Because of their sudden and urgent emotional crises, adolescents constitute a high proportion of clientele in crisis intervention agencies and mental health clinics. The fluidity and instability of their personality structures and the rapid changes they undergo account for their frequent unhappiness, emotional storms and behavior excesses.

Counseling adolescents is rewarding because, unlike adult clients, they are labile, open to change and often insightful, particularly in the later phase of adolescence. Since they are in a transitional period of development, and personality structure is still in the formative stage, they have not acquired the rigidities of character of adults, allowing them greater latitude for change and growth. For this reason they can often be helped to resolve what may look like severely troubling conflicts in a very brief period of counseling. As few as two or three interviews will sometimes suffice to overcome a temporary block in the ongoing developmental process so that normal growth can be resumed.

Adolescents' pressing problems and the enormous range of symptoms and behavior they display may often resemble pathological conditions. One needs to be on guard in assessing their complaints not to jump to hasty conclusions as to their severity. Often what might look like deviant behavior in any other age group will be within the normal range at a given phase of adolescence. It sometimes comes as a surprise to a counselor to learn that what appeared to be an alarming symptom one day may have cleared up the next. Therefore, discrimination between normality and pathology in an adolescent is often difficult even for an experienced clinician. For this reason, and to be on firm ground in counseling adolescents, a thorough familiarity with the psychodynamics of normal adolescence is essential. An abbreviated review of the theory of the adolescent developmental process will provide a foundation on which to base a discussion of counseling techniques.

NORMAL ADOLESCENT DEVELOPMENT

Adolescence can be loosely defined as the transitional period between childhood and adulthood. The main thrust—the task to be accomplished—is emotional separation from parents and the establishment of sexual identity, independence and self-esteem.

Volumes have been written about this highly complex dynamic process, but this review will focus on the fundamental issue, the parent-child relationship. The child's pattern of relating to others is established in his earliest attachment to his parents in infancy, when he is wholly dependent on their love and care; the resolution, or renunciation, of this attachment in adolescence is crucial to his attainment of healthy adulthood and ability to love self and others. It thus becomes the principal accomplishment of the adolescent years. Two aspects of the early relationship, dependence and ambivalence, must be resolved, freeing the adolescent to experience a more mature mutuality in love relationships in both sexual and nonsexual modes.

Adolescence encompasses several phases—prepuberty, puberty, early adolescence, the middle years, and the final stages of personality consolidation and integration. Although these phases are separate in theory and marked by characteristic behavior patterns and conflicts, in reality they merge or overlap with one another, and their course of development is never smooth or clearly delineated. One may see strides made in one direction alternated with regression to earlier modes of behavior, often to the bewilderment of parents and the adolescent himself.

Looking at the process as a continuum from puberty to the closing phases, one sees a profound personality reorganization occurring. The relative structural stability the child acquired during the latency years—in general from the age of six to the onset of puberty—appears almost to disintegrate during the next two or three years, followed by a gradual consolidation of structure in the final stages.

Striving for Independence

During this upheaval the child has been struggling with the profound demands made on him, on the one hand, by the new surge of sexual drives, his search for a self-image and his strivings for independence and self-assertion, and on the other hand, by his love for and dependence on his parents and his need for their protection. Torn by the conflict, he often vacillates between rebelliousness and overassertion of his self-confidence, and feelings of despair, depression and self-abasement. These excesses are the outward manifestations of the dynamic process taking place. The child who is excessively critical and angry at parents may be compensating for his own shaky self-confidence. He has to "hate" his parents in order to deny his dependence on them and gain emotional distance from them. If he had continued to be the compliant child of the past, the growth process would have failed and he would be unable to establish healthy esteem and a sense of autonomy as an adult.

Although the repudiation of childlike attachment to parents is a necessary step in growth, it is not without painful consequences. The adolescent still very much needs parents to maintain controls, to reassure him of their love, and to protect and support him through the stormy times. He may long in a regressive way for the security of his early years and must defend against these strivings. He is often guilty and contrite, even though he is irritable, impatient, and oversensitive. Depression can be acute at times. He experiences confusion and apathy as well as bursts of energy. He often feels neither at home nor in tune with his own body, his family or his peers.

Loss of Idealized Parent

A further problem for the adolescent is his sense of bereavement at the loss of the idealized parent image of his childhood. This is manifested in the frequent depressions of adolescence. What the adolescent can no longer ignore or deny to himself is his new perception of his parents as ordinary human beings with problems, flaws, self-doubts and fears. Since the adolescent must give up his fantasy of the powerful, all-wise and all-knowing parent of his early years, this adds fuel to his reproaches and resentment of his parents who he feels have let him down and betrayed him. His self-image is also diminished by no longer identifying with the powerful parent image, with a consequent loss of his own "specialness."

Incestuous Impulses

The emergence of the sexual drive in puberty tends to revive early love and erotic impulses toward parents, which the adolescent must defend against. Attachment to the parent of the same sex arouses ambivalent feelings because it implies dependence, and thus helplessness, while strivings directed toward the parent of the opposite sex are taboo because of their incestuous nature. In the adolescent's struggle against these drives he may turn to premature sexual acting out as a denial or may suppress all sexual feelings and become ascetic for a time. Often there are swings from one pole to the other.

Sexual choices in adolescence are often determined by attraction to the early parental figures; for example, a girl or boy may choose someone *like* the parent of the opposite sex, or someone entirely *different* in order to deny the strong parental attraction. This is one reason early love affairs are so intense, and also why they are transient and do not work. They really belong to old love objects rather than to the real persons involved.

By the time of late adolescence we can observe some calming of the storms. There is a gradual subsiding of the intense activity, the wild enthusiasms, the unaccountable depressions, the excessive idealism, and the irritability and self-doubt of the earlier years. By the closing of adolescence the young person has begun to reassemble, as it were, the personality structure that seemed almost threatened to fall apart earlier. He experiences more stability in his self-esteem, more self-trust and confidence in his sexual identity as a male or female, and a firmer sense of self-worth. He can begin to envision future goals.

For those who go on to college, the college years provide a period of moratorium when perception of self can be further defined, career goals formulated, and more mature sexual relationships established. Career, marriage and a future appear to be more real and attainable.

COUNSELING TECHNIQUES

The extremes of behavior commonly observed during the emotional upheavals of adolescence can and often do appear to the adolescent and his family as crises. Indeed, at times the adolescent's precarious control can lead to dangerous excesses that will require intervention. The distinction between a real crisis and a transient outburst is not always easy to evaluate and takes careful appraisal.

Assessment of ego functions will give some indications of how successfully an adolescent client has been able to maintain controls in the past, his ability to restore equilibrium, and the quality and stability of his relationships. Often talking over his feelings with a concerned adult will in itself be effective in helping him to gain perspective so he will feel less desperate. By pointing out that his behavior may be harmful and eliciting his cooperation in curbing it until his problems can be explored further, a counselor may engage the more rational part of his ego to help him reinstate controls.

Only if it is determined by a counselor that an emergency exists and real danger threatens is further intervention advisable. Any question of alerting parents should be discussed with an adolescent client; he will otherwise feel it is a violation of his confidence and will not be able to establish a trusting relationship with the counselor. If he gives permission to contact his parents or seems to be seeking the counselor's protection, this may be a helpful step and the counselor will be intervening as an ally. Of course, there will be no question of the need to inform parents if there is peril of suicide or other serious danger to the client.

Counselor As Expert, Not Peer

Because of adolescents' struggles for independence and their frequent rebelliousness, they will not ordinarily seek out counseling until other measures have failed. They have undoubtedly already talked to friends by the time they apply for help and are looking for an expert—a stable, objective, and concerned adult—with whom to share and examine their troubled feelings. Realizing this, the counselor should behave like an expert, maintaining some professional distance, rather than taking on the role of a peer. The disturbed adolescent does not need a friend as much as someone who knows more than he does. Naturally, the counselor should relate warmly, with interest and understanding, and seek to establish a trusting and nonjudgmental relationship, always conveying that he is on the adolescent's side. He should be prepared to be tested regarding his attitudes and impartiality before the teenage client will wholly commit himself to reveal feelings and engage in counseling.

Adolescents should be seen by counselors of the same sex, especially if they are in puberty or the early stages of adolescence. Counselors of the opposite sex are likely to be experienced as seductive and may arouse erotic fantasies in young persons who are already in a state of turbulence about their emerging sexuality and still involved with old attachments to parents of the opposite sex. Youngsters in early adolescence are in the process of establishing sexual identity, which is a further reason for working with a counselor of the same sex with whom they can identify.

> A young boy of 14 sought help at a crisis center because he was having a conflict with a competitive, critical and overstriving father, had no friends, and felt lost and alienated. Working with a stable male counselor offered him a model of a man who was comfortable in his own masculinity and a more benign father figure who could accept and understand his feelings. This was crucial for this boy at this particular time in his life when he was struggling with becoming a man.

A girl of 13 came to the same agency, very troubled and confused because of her mother's unwarranted suspicions and continual warnings about pregnancy. Effective help was offered by a female counselor who could talk to her rationally about her sexual questions and was secure in her own femininity. The counselor here provided a corrective experience for this young girl by offering herself as an emotionally healthy substitute for the mother the client needed but could not communicate with. In both cases a counselor of the opposite sex would have been inappropriate.

Case Illustrations

Very brief counseling is often sufficient to help adolescents through one of the frequent storms so typical of this age group. Although the slightest frustration or disappointment can be experienced as a crisis at the moment, the problem can often be resolved as quickly as it erupted. The three following cases illustrate the effectiveness of brief counseling in restoring equilibrium.

Donna, a rebellious girl of 14, was so indignant at the injustice and unfairness of her mother's curfews and especially her refusal to allow Donna to go to a party at a boy's house on the coming weekend, that she was threatening to run away from home in protest. It was learned that the boy's parents were not expected to be at home to chaperone the party. The counselor sympathized with Donna's disappointment and resentment at being treated like a child, then asked her what she considered to be reasonable restrictions for a girl of her age. At first Donna declared that she should be allowed to set her own hours and go where she pleased. When

> asked what curfew she would set for herself, she was thoughtful for a moment, then decided that it generally agreed with her mother's rules. When further questioned if she felt it was appropriate to go to a boy's house when his parents were absent, Donna still viewed her mother's reasoning as "out of the Ark" but was less vociferous in her protest. She returned for a second interview to report that after talking it over reasonably with her mother, they decided together to invite a group of boys and girls to Donna's house instead.

The storm had blown over and her good relations with her mother were restored for the time being. In this case the counselor had appealed to the girl's rational ego, which had briefly been overwhelmed by her strivings for independence.

> A break-up with a girl friend, Diane, was so distressing to Mike, aged 15, that he told a counselor his life was not worth living and he might as well end it all. Diane had meant everything to him; he could not bear to lose her or see any future without her. Apparently Diane had been less involved in their love affair than Mike was and had started to date another boy the week before. She told Mike she did not want to be tied down and was tired of his possessiveness. In exploring why Diane was so important to him and what her special qualities were, Mike could only express at first his sense of despair and how lost he felt without her. In a second interview he was unhappy but somewhat more resigned, was willing to look more objectively at Diane's qualities and to admit that he may have idealized her. Mike returned for a third interview to report that he had been talking a lot to Judy; she seemed to understand him, and he thought he might begin dating her.

While a teenager's despair because of a rejection is not always so readily reversible, this case is a good example of the lability of young adolescents and the ease with which they can shift from one object to another almost overnight. The counselor did not directly suggest that Diane may have been less than the ideal Mike had visualized, but did turn his attention to looking at her with more objectivity.

A female college freshman of 19 was determined, over her parents' objection, to drive to Florida for the Easter holiday with her boyfriend. By seeking the help of a counselor, it was obvious that she was not entirely sure of her decision and was in conflict between her own desires and her allegiance to her parents. In two interviews the counselor reviewed with her the meaning and importance of the trip to her, discussed her readiness for independence, and how she might handle it with her parents if she went in spite of their protests.

The counselor, as a reasonable parent surrogate, listened as the client weighed and reflected on her maturity and good judgment, her conviction that she was able to assume the responsibility to deal with the consequences, even though she regretted incurring her parents' disapproval. In the end she did decide to go, but made the decision only after reviewing and considering both sides and the significance of the trip to her, so that it was an independent decision rather than an act of defiance. The counselor's neutrality allowed the needed opportunity for this young woman to examine her decision rationally and helped her to confirm her self-trust.

EARLY ADOLESCENTS

Because of the instability of personality structure in the early phase of adolescence, counseling should usually be short-term and focused on the immediate problem. Youngsters in this age group are neither motivated nor able to face much self-examination; in any case, it is inadvisable to interfere with the normal growth process while it is still in a state of flux and disorganization. Youngsters between 12 and 16 are having enough difficulty just maintaining equilibrium without undergoing treatment that might upset the precarious balance. Intensive therapy is rarely recommended for very young adolescents unless there are grave symptoms. By the time they have reached the final stages of adolescence they are much more responsive and better able to sustain treatment, so any treatment involving internalized conflicts should be delayed if possible.

Counselor As Parent Substitute

Often a young adolescent will find it steadying just to talk to an adult other than a parent. In such a case he uses a counselor as a somewhat removed parent substitute, when talking to the real parent directly might be a threat to his drive for separation and independence.

> Connie, a 15-year-old girl, talked to a counselor weekly for three months without any more specific presenting problem than some impatience with her mother's rather mild curfew restrictions and the confusion at home with five siblings vying for attention. Mainly she seemed to need someone to listen to her as she talked about being in and out of love with half a dozen boys, her girl friends, incidents at school, the typical day-to-day crises in the social life of an adolescent, and her despair that she would have to wait an endless three months for her driver's license. Occasionally Connie reflected on her

> parents' relationship, her feelings about her father and some annoyance at her mother and younger siblings. The counselor made almost no comments or suggestions during this period but, surprisingly, at the end of three months Connie said she felt better and that she did not need to continue any longer. In the last few interviews she spoke of a savings account she had started to buy a car when she graduated and the job training she was contemplating. She also remarked that she and her mother seldom had arguments any more.

In this case the counselor provided a sounding board as Connie moved into a new phase of her adolescence. No particular problems were focused on, no goals were set, and no interpretations made.

Counselor As Ally

Adolescents are apt to be somewhat alienated from the adult world and be wary about trusting a counselor. It will facilitate establishing a relationship if the counselor can demonstrate that he is an ally. This may sometimes be accomplished by interceding with school authorities, for example, if it seems to be appropriate. Even an offer to do so may be sufficient to gain the adolescent client's trust and prove the counselor is on his side.

When an adolescent complains about a parent's strictness or unreasonable demands, intercession with parents may be considered. One should first find out just what rules the client feels are unfair, and what restrictions he might impose if he were allowed to set his own rules. This will open the way to discussion of just how much responsibility he feels he is able to assume, and of the reasons for parental control and protection. Often after such a review, an adolescent will take a more accepting view of his parents' expectations and endorse most of their rules.

If parents do indeed seem too strict, one might first suggest that the client talk it over with his parents, rationally rather than in anger, and explain his point of view, with an offer from the counselor to intercede with his parents if his own efforts are not successful. The fact that the offer was made will demonstrate the counselor's allegiance with him, even though the client may be able to convince parents himself of his growing maturity.

When a counselor does agree to intercede with parents on his behalf, the client should be assured beforehand that the counselor will not reveal any of his confidences and the subjects to be discussed should be mutually agreed upon. The client should be given a report of what transpired at the meeting. This will obviate any suspicion of betrayal by the counselor.

Sometimes one has to point out to a teenager that it sounds from his communications as if he acts like a child at home so it is not surprising that his parents treat him like a child. It might be suggested that if he can prove by more grown-up behavior that he is able to take responsibility, his parents may revise their attitudes. This works well in such areas as battles over household tasks, for instance. An adolescent who balks at being told what to do and is sulky and uncooperative about sharing work at home might be asked to consider what contributions to the household he feels are reasonable, and to offer voluntarily to take responsibility for specific tasks. If he can carry these out without parental reminders it will eliminate a source of friction at home, as well as giving the client the satisfaction of making an independent contribution and alerting parents to the fact that he is growing up and to be trusted. As a result the adolescent gains in taking a step toward maturity and parents are often more willing to relax controls in recognition of his more responsible behavior.

LATE ADOLESCENTS

Adolescents in the final stages of personality integration are more stable, often insightful and eager to understand their feelings and conflicts, so are excellent candidates for counseling. They are motivated and still open enough to change so that counseling on deeper levels can be contemplated without interfering with the normal developmental process. Though separation problems are not the only disturbances of this age group, they are apt to be at the root of most conflicts even if not initially identified as such.

While separation from parental ties have been gradually taking place all during adolescence, anxiety about separation may be particularly acute at a time when separation and independence are nearer actual accomplishment. Since the development of a firm sense of self—of an identity apart from parents—is the major goal of adolescence, its achievement entails rebellion and self-assertion, sometimes in defiance of parental authority. Feelings of guilt and some degree of hostility to parents are normal by-products of rebellion. When emotional separation has failed to take place or has only been partially completed, a broad range of symptomatology may result. Frequently the troubled adolescent is not even aware of the association between his symptoms and his ambivalence over separation.

In the writer's experience in treating college students, the commonest problems encountered were related in one way or another to conflict over separation. The symptoms were manifested in school failures, inability to study and concentrate, unsatisfying sexual relationships, conflicts with parents, inability to choose a major, and affects of depression and anxiety. Frequent cases of intense graduation anxiety, or failure to graduate just on the verge of accomplishment, were indicative of fears of facing the future and assuming adult responsibilities, all arising from difficulties in relinquishing the child-parent (alma mater-parent) attachment.

Counseling was focused on identifying the underlying separation problem, then exploring feelings of guilt and loss in renouncing parents, encouraging independence, and giving reassurance that parents would not be hurt if their children grew up and separated from them. The therapist, in effect, gave a kind of "permission" that it was all right to become an adult, that even if clients made some "wrong" decisions this was not a disaster and would be a positive learning experience. The counselor's encouragement and a kind of nudge toward growth was often sufficient to help them in overcoming obstacles.

Separation Anxiety: Case Illustrations

Some typical cases involving separation problems will illustrate the many different guises in which these conflicts are manifested.

An immature-looking and dependent female of 19 sought help because she could not break off with a sadistic boyfriend. He threatened to drop out of school, quit his job, and even to commit suicide if she left him, thus making her responsible for anything that befell him. Each time she tried to free herself from his emotional control over her, he manipulated her with a repetition of his threats. In exploring her history during counseling it was learned that when she was six or seven her mother threatened to kill herself by putting her head in the gas oven, in the presence of the client and an older sister. The girls "saved" their mother, but from then on the client felt responsible for her mother's life and happiness and felt unable to leave her.

Undoubtedly through some unconscious process, she found a boyfriend who acted exactly as her mother had, and she could no more leave him to his fate than she could her mother. Only when it became clear to her that she was reacting to her boyfriend as if he was her mother, and that she was not responsible for the behavior of either, was she able to give him up and to loosen her attachment to her mother. After a few months of treatment, she felt free enough to carry out a long desired plan to enroll in a college in another town and move away from her parents' home.

A depressed female of 20 gave an outward appearance of self-assurance and independence. She had attended an out-of-state university, worked off and on, and been on her own for a couple of years. As she flaunted the details of an abortion a year before and boasted about the many sexual affairs she had had and how much she liked to "screw," she was continually making references to her conservative middle-class parents, how she despised them, and had repudiated them and their standards. Her rebelliousness could be seen as a perverse form of dependency, as all her behavior was dictated by and related to them. She did exactly the opposite of what they had taught her, compulsively and repetitively. In counseling this was eventually demonstrated to her. After a long struggle to recognize her attachment to her parents and her rebellious defense against her dependence, she could eventually free herself to make independent judgments without reference to their values.

This client's failure to resolve her adolescent conflict over separation was expressed in behavior excesses. In the following case the ambivalence took the opposite form—outward conformity and internalized anger—but equally signaling a disturbance in the adolescent developmental process.

A pretty, childlike 18-year-old female presented complaints of depression and attacks of ulcerative colitis. She had a very pleasing manner, said she had always conformed to her parents' wishes and that she did not want to ''hurt'' them. It seemed as if her outward compliance and docility concealed the anger within, which was turned on herself in the form of colitis. She was completely unaware of her ambivalence toward her parents and its relation to her symptoms. All her adolescent strivings had been damned up in consequence of her conflict over separation, especially her fear of her aggressive impulses, so she remained like a child. A great deal of reassurance was required during several months of counseling, which helped her to recognize and accept the underlying angry and rebellious feelings and to understand that her growing up and asserting herself would not hurt her parents.

Leaving Home

Leaving home is a final step for many young persons in the transition from adolescence to adulthood.

For those who go away to college at 18 or 19 it is a natural development, expected and acceptable to both adolescents and parents. A residential college provides a kind of half-way house where the adolescent can experience physical separation from parents while still in a more or less protected environment. Leaving home is more difficult for those who live at home while attending a local college or go to work directly after graduation from high school. There is no built-in time schedule to dictate when to move, and an abrupt change from home and family to apartment life, with its attendant responsibilities, is a bigger hurdle than going away to college. Even when an adolescent desires to move, he may delay because of his own doubts or family resistance, which may reinforce each other. Prolonged dependence, however, is not healthy for either parent or child. It breeds resentment on both sides, prevents or delays parents' natural and necessary adaptation to a new phase in their own lives, and allows a slowing or stagnation of the adolescent growth process.

In counseling older adolescents who complain of restlessness and continual strife at home, it is often apparent that they have emotionally all but outgrown the nest but hesitate on the brink of declaring complete independence, as if they needed a final push. Some will threaten to move out during arguments with parents, but give in to parents' strenuous objections. Others, who are on the fence as it were, will rationalize the economic advantages or material comforts of continuing to remain in their parents' houses. In such cases, exploring with them just what it would mean for them to move away from home, in both emotional and practical terms, where they might live and how support themselves, may be sufficient to engage them in considering realistic plans.

> A young man of 20 who both worked and was attending a local college part-time, requested counseling because of continual arguments at home, complaints of parents' interference with his social life, and his lack of a quiet place to study. He stated that he wanted to move out and be independent but had innumerable excuses why he could not leave: His parents would be upset; what would he do about laundry? he did not know how to shop for groceries; how could he budget his money and pay utilities, bills, etc.? When all these subjects were explored he could see the unreasonableness of his excuses and that he was quite capable of handling these situations. It was then explained to him that moving away did not have to be an impulsive act carried out in anger but could be planned in a responsible way over a period of months. He could establish a savings account sufficient to tide him over emergencies, find a roommate to share expenses, look for and eventually engage an apartment, and finally set a moving date, before informing his parents. With the counselor's encouragement and support, he planned carefully for a move to take place three months later. When he finally announced to his parents that he was moving the following week, and it was evident to them that he had acted responsibly, they raised no objections. The counseling gave him the push he needed to reinforce a healthy growth process.

Adolescents who are restive and frustrated at home, resentful of parents' interference and emotionally about ready to leave, will often hesitate to make a move because they are convinced it will somehow hurt their parents or, as one student told a counselor, "My mother would collapse." The mother had often reminded her children of her devotion and sacrifices for them and declared that they were her whole life. Possessive parents do indeed make remarks like this, inducing guilt, prolonging control over their children, and compounding an adolescent's difficulty in making a final move.

For an adolescent who already has some understandable doubts about his ability to function apart from parents, such parental attitudes may be used as a rationalization to defer a move. Sometimes an adolescent will be almost literally convinced that leaving home will have dire consequences for his parents. Explaining to an adolescent that it is natural for children to leave home, that his parents did so, and that parents do not collapse when their children grow up, will help an adolescent to look at the problem more rationally. It can be pointed out that no matter how much a parent may seem to resist losing his child, he really wants his child to succeed in life and be self-sustaining, and that it is a tribute to parents when their children grow up and take on adult responsibilities. On the contrary, a parent would consider himself a failure if his grown-up offspring were to remain a dependent child.

Before encouraging an adolescent to leave home, a counselor should naturally test his readiness to do so. If he appears after exploration to be too immature to be on his own for the time being, it can be presented as a possibility to consider when he feels more sure of himself. Counseling can then be focused on the obstacles that are interfering with his strivings for independence.

Adolescents will sometimes ask if it is not possible to become truly independent and still go on living at home, citing as a rationale the superior accommodations and conveniences at home and the money that can thus be saved, as if they are pleading to have their cake and eat it too. It is true that adolescents can enhance their self-confidence and readiness for independence by assuming greater responsibility for their financial support, behaving in a more adult way in the relationship with parents and voluntarily sharing household tasks, for example. This may be a necessary step in preparation for further independence and an eventual move from home, as long as it is not viewed as a substitute for attainment of complete independence.

Sexual Provocation: A Special Problem

The common sexual problems of adolescents, and counseling techniques, are discussed in the following chapter. One particularly distressing sexual problem for adolescent girls, however, deserves comment here. It is provocation to act out sexually by parents because of the mother's or father's unresolved sexual conflicts.

Sporadic sexual experimentation during adolescence is not uncommon or necessarily alarming if the adolescent girl institutes reasonable controls and takes precautions against pregnancy. But when the sexual behavior is dictated at the unconscious behest of a parent it can result in serious disturbance. A mother who continually voices suspicion about her daughter's behavior, warns about pregnancy and venereal disease and accuses her daughter of sexual involvement gives a double message. On the conscious level she says, "Don't do it," but on a deeper level she communicates, "Do it for me." The accusation of behavior the daughter may not even have dreamed of, expresses covertly the mother's wish to participate vicariously so the daughter hears both "Do it" and "Don't do it." The daughter's rationale, then, is that since she is accused anyway she might as well do it. Underlying her rationale may be a need to gratify her mother. Or a girl may react defensively to her mother's communications and become sexually inhibited to a pathological degree.

A father, in defending against incestuous impulses toward an adolescent daughter, may likewise voice continual suspicion about her sexual behavior, accuse her of misconduct, become obsessively concerned with her dating and impose overstrict rules. He too may drive her into premature sexual activity in order to escape from what she unconsciously perceives as his sexual enticement. Her acting out serves as a denial of her own incestuous feelings.

Girls who experience such provocation from parents are likely to become pregnant, which serves both to inform their parents of their sexual activity and to punish the parents and get revenge. Adolescent girls buffeted by such conflicting messages from parents may come to counseling confused and bewildered, torn by guilt and anxiety. In counseling it is necessary eventually to interpret to the client the meaning of a parent's double message and to help her understand that this is due to the parent's own sexual conflict. This will help her to separate her impulses from theirs and to curb her own behavior. Such an interpretation should be delayed, of course, until a trusting relationship has been established and the child-parent relationship thoroughly explored, so that the client can gradually become aware of the irrationality of the parent's sexual attitudes and is ready to accept the interpretation.

DEALING WITH PARENTS

In helping an adolescent to separate emotionally from parents, it is neither necessary nor desirable to alienate him from his parents. While it is natural for a counselor to be sympathetic and understanding of a young client's angry and rebellious feelings, and to take his side, this can be accomplished without leading him to repudiate his parents. Without denying or condoning a parent's faults, it can be supportive to examine with the adolescent some of the reasons for his parents' failings. An adolescent will be able to take a more objective view of parents who seemed to lack understanding or to have failed in good parenting, if he becomes aware that they may have had troubling problems of their own to contend with. It is far more comforting to a young person to accept that his parents probably did the best they could, given their own emotional conflicts and incapacity to give all their children needed, than to feel that their parents simply did not love them enough.

When adolescents are encouraged to examine their parents' problems and learn to accept their flaws and weaknesses and forgive them for their humanness, the way is paved for an eventual affectionate and adult relationship with them. The writer has often been told by an adolescent client at the close of treatment, "My parents are not so bad after all." This kind of observation indicates a step in maturity on the part of the adolescent and a more successful resolution of his conflict than if he were left at the close of adolescence with permanent feelings of hostility and alienation.

This leads to some final remarks on behalf of parents of adolescents. We, as counselors of adolescents, tend to see the young person's turmoils from his point of view and even at times to share in his indignation at parents. It should be borne in mind that adolescents are prone to exaggerate, to distort their perceptions of parents' behavior, and are given to self-dramatization. Their statements need to be examined and evaluated before one judges parents or condemns them. It may turn out that these parents are not as unreasonable as they sound. Counselors should also consider the dilemma of parents whose loving, even-tempered and compliant child has almost overnight become contradictory, critical, moody and unruly. The parents are likely to be bewildered and hurt, and may blame themselves. It is difficult in these circumstances for a parent not to become angry at his child, to feel rejected and unappreciated. As a result he may act in a retaliatory manner to the young adolescent. Sometimes a parent will unfortunately reproach his child to induce guilt and make the child feel responsible for his misery.

The healthiest parent, with a stable self-image and some understanding of the pressures of growing up, may find it difficult to keep on an even keel and maintain serenity in the face of adolescent storms. Parents who themselves have conflicts and limited emotional resources will be especially assaulted by their adolescents' rebellions. They may take one of two courses: either penalize the child with overstrict rules in an effort to control him or simply renounce him and fail to set any limits. Both, of course, are devastating for the adolescent. Among the many complaints about parents heard from adolescent girls, the saddest are such statements as, "My mother never set a curfew for me—she didn't care what I did.'' These girls were envious of friends whose parents cared enough, even if they were strict. The girls often ended by becoming in effect their own parents and imposing too rigid controls on themselves.

In evaluating adolescent-parent conflicts it is advisable to be as impartial and objective as possible, to try to understand what parent and child are experiencing and to look at both sides of the picture before making judgments. Even in cases of parents who seem to be truly uncaring, it is more supportive to the adolescent to comment that his parents may be doing the best they can, given their own problems, than agreeing that they are unloving.

Often some counseling for parents to help in bolstering their own self-images and to offer support and understanding of their difficulties in living with their adolescents, will be welcome and appropriate. This will not only be sustaining to parents but may lead them to modify their attitudes and be more tolerant of their adolescents. In order to insure confidentiality for the adolescent client, it is usually preferable for a parent to be seen by a separate counselor, although this need not rule out joint sessions in addition, if the adolescent and his counselor agree that occasional family-counselor meetings will be productive.

RECOMMENDED READING

Aichhorn, A. (1925), *Wayward Youth*. New York: Viking Press, 1948.

Aichhorn's book, reporting his inventive use of psychodynamic theory in working with delinquents in Vienna, is regarded as a classic. It is essential background reading for counselors who undertake treatment of adolescents.

Blos, P. (1967), The second individuation process in adolescence. *The Psychoanalytic Study of the Child*, 22:162–185. New York: International Universities Press.

A leading authority on adolescence presents his theory of the psychic restructuring process that takes place in adolescence, involving alternate ego regression and forward movement as the adolescent struggles to disengage from parental ties.

Esman, A. Ed. (1975), *The Psychology of Adolescence*. New York: International Universities Press.

This well-organized and comprehensive collection of papers on adolescence contains selections from outstanding writers in the field. Sections on normal development, psychopathology and environmental and cultural determinants are followed by an extensive bibliography.

Freud, A. (1958), Adolescence. *The Psychoanalytic Study of the Child*, 13:255–276. New York: International Universities Press.

In this important paper Anna Freud expresses her view that intrapsychic conflict is a necessary prelude to the attainment of adult autonomy. She reviews the defensive maneuvers that adolescents employ to avert the dangers of ego regression and to maintain equilibrium.

CHAPTER 10

Sexual Counseling

While sexual problems are by no means limited to adolescents and young adults, it may be anticipated that the majority of clients with sexual concerns, especially in crisis intervention agencies, will be in this age range. Adolescents seek help in clarifying their sexual values, handling guilt if their sexual conduct is in conflict with parental teaching, and talking over their sexual questions with an accepting parent-surrogate. Their frequent inquiries about contraception, pregnancy and abortion often mask underlying questions and doubts about their sexual behavior to which counselors should be alert. Adults as well as adolescents are often painfully troubled about their sexual adequacy, fears of impotence or frigidity, worries about masturbation, and conflicts about homosexuality.

THE COUNSELOR'S VALUES AND ATTITUDES

The same principles of sound counseling practice apply in helping clients with their sexual problems as in treating any other emotional complaint. However, because the subject of sex can stir profound emotional reactions in counselors as well as in their clients, counselors are sometimes reticent in approaching or exploring sexual conflicts. This will be particularly true if they are not entirely comfortable about their own sexuality or clear about their sexual feelings and values.

Some serious self-examination by the counselor about his own sexual attitudes will enhance his objectivity. It will be helpful to consider what he was taught about sex in his early years and its influence on his current views, and to ask himself if he is at ease in talking about sexual feelings and able to be tolerant in accepting others' values even if they do not coincide with his own. If he is aware of any sexual prejudices and inhibitions in himself, but can still condone the diversity of views and sexual behavior in others, he should be reasonably free to counsel clients openly and without restraint. Any hesitance on his part to examine a client's sexual problems will be quickly communicated to the client, with the result that the client may be embarrassed and withdraw from further exploration of that particular area. This will be especially troubling to a client if the counselor's attitude seems to convey the same message received from a parent who was uncomfortable or embarrassed talking about sex, further suggesting that it is unacceptable or dirty.

Using Correct Terminology

It is essential that counselors acquire a thorough familiarity with sexual vocabulary, male and female sexual anatomy, and sexual functions and practices. They should be informed about pregnancy, contraception and abortion procedures, homosexuality, masturbation, the sexual perversions and venereal diseases.

A counselor can best communicate his objectivity by the use of correct sexual terms. Use of the words penis, vagina, and sexual intercourse, for example, rather than slang terms or euphemisms, will be reassuring to a client who may be unsure of his own vocabulary and will welcome introduction of accepted terminology. The words orgasm, ejaculation, impotence and masturbation, if they come easily from the counselor, will facilitate the client's talking about these subjects without embarrassment. They also tend to remove the subject of sex from the realm of vulgarity or shame to the level of acceptable human feelings.

Focusing on Feelings

The subject of sexual feelings is, unfortunately, the area most neglected in sex education and yet of greatest concern to young clients. They may appear to have had adequate sexual information from the anatomical and biological point of view, but parents and educators have often failed to deal with sex on the feeling level, communicating that sexual desires are normal and that intimacy and sexual love are pleasurable and gratifying. On the contrary, young people have often heard more negative than positive messages in frequent warnings about pregnancy, promiscuity and venereal disease. A counselor who can allow and encourage a client to talk about his sexual feelings in an atmosphere of acceptance will provide him a valuable opportunity to understand more about his sexuality from a new and positive viewpoint.

REQUESTS FOR INFORMATION: WHAT DO THEY MEAN?

Whatever the client's sexual complaint, a counselor should explore with him why he is seeking help at this particular time, what has precipitated the problem, and review with him his current and past sexual experiences in order to understand the underlying problem. It is always advisable to refrain from volunteering information a client requests until it is clear just what the request means to him, as this may close off further communication about a problem he really wanted to talk about.

A woman client may ask at the outset for an abortion referral, for example, but almost always will wish to talk over her feelings about her decision to have an abortion. There will undoubtedly be guilt or anxiety about it and indeed she may have doubts about whether she has made the right decision. If a referral is offered immediately she may feel the counselor is not interested and be discouraged from pursuing the subject further. A male client requesting referral to a physician for a potency problem, in the conviction that it is an organic malfunction, should be led to talk about the circumstances before a referral is proffered. It may well turn out to be a transient psychological difficulty which can be resolved in counseling.

One should be particularly cautious about offering sexual information to adolescents until it is clear just what their questions mean. Of several hundreds of adolescents and young adults seen by the writer in a walk-in sexual counseling service, the vast majority ostensibly requested referral for contraceptives, pregnancy testing or abortion. Since most of these clients were aware that they could go directly to a clinic or physician for the service they wanted, the question arose as to why they applied to a mental health agency? The answer, of course, was that most wanted to talk to an informed and accepting adult about their sexual conflicts, feelings, doubts and fears.

Among young women planning to initiate intercourse for the first time, some were seeking a kind of "permission" from a parent-surrogate. The counselor's neutrality gave them an opportunity to examine and confirm their maturity and readiness for such an important venture. Others of both sexes who had evident doubts and decided to defer intercourse for the time being, were relieved by the counselor's assurance that they did not have to prove their adequacy by being sexually active.

> A typical case was a young woman of 19 who requested a referral for birth control pills. The counselor asked her about her relationship with her boyfriend and their decision to begin intercourse. When it was learned that she still lived at home, the counselor then asked the key question: "Where did she expect to keep the pills?" At this the client began to cry and to talk about her wish that her mother would condone her sexual activity. The implication was that if her mother knew about and sanctioned it, she would be sharing the responsibility. As this became clear to the client, she decided she really was not ready to initiate intercourse and to assume the responsibility herself. She was obviously relieved to have made the decision to wait a while.

In another case a young couple came together asking for contraceptive advice, but it was quite evident both were looking for adult guidance and understanding rather than a referral for contraceptives.

> Both clients were very young-looking, even for 18, and clearly uneasy. They were both virgins, in love, and had been talking about having intercourse. As they discussed their doubts and the problems this would entail, where they would go to be alone since both lived at home, and how they would react if their parents found out, both concluded they were too immature for a sexual relationship. The counselor did not offer advice but helped them to examine their feelings and, in the end, supported their decision.

Giving contraceptive information without exploring the reason behind the request would have been a disservice in the cases of two female clients who, it was learned, did not have boyfriends or any immediate plans for intercourse.

> A 19-year-old college student said she wanted birth control pills "just to be prepared." In exploring this with her it turned out that she was very frightened of sex and the wish to have pills in her possession was a kind of counterphobic measure, to prove to herself that she was not afraid. This was discussed further and became the basis for an extended period of counseling to help her with her longstanding sexual inhibition.

> A young woman said she wanted to take pills for a month and then have intercourse with the first boy available "just to get it over with." Her negative feelings about her sexuality, and both her self-contempt and her hostility to men became evident to both the client and the counselor in the discussion that followed. As she became aware of the immaturity and destructiveness of the gesture that she had contemplated, she accepted an offer of further counseling.

Common Myths and Fantasies

Despite the assumed enlightenment of youth today, it is surprising to learn how many young men and women are ignorant of the basic facts of pregnancy, venereal disease, menstruation and sexual anatomy. For this reason, when they ask seemingly sophisticated questions about sex, it is well to inquire just what they do know, or think they know, before replying to their questions. Otherwise the counselor may not be aware of the hearsay, misconceptions, fantasies and old wives' tales that may be contributing to their anxiety and influencing their behavior. As with responding to questions young children ask, one should first find out why they are asking the particular question and what they think the answer is. Once their ideas are clarified, any corrective educational information should be imparted only as fully as they can absorb and respond to it. This will allow further questions to develop as the discussion continues and clients have pondered on and digested what has already been said.

When a young man or woman talks glibly about "having sex" with a particular partner, a counselor may be led to assume they are having intercourse, which may not necessarily be the case. By inquiring just what they mean by this, he may learn that they are engaged in any number of practices: kissing and fondling of the girl's breasts, genital touching, heavy petting, mutual masturbation or fellatio, for example. If the client's statement is not clarified, counseling may be impaired from the start by mutual misunderstanding.

A not uncommon theory among young women, and a stated reason for not using contraceptives, is that they will remain technically virgins if they have intercourse but the man withdraws before ejaculation. Another reason some women give for refusing contraception is that it implies a deliberate intention to have intercourse, while if they can tell themselves that sex "just happened" they are not responsible, thus not guilty. Incidentally, the pregnancy that may occur in either of these cases will be evidence to the contrary. A frequently asked question about petting is whether ejaculation just outside the vagina can cause pregnancy. The answer, of course, is that this is possible.

Masturbation is surrounded by superstitions and misconceptions which even enlightened young people give credence to: it will cause impotence, insanity, sterility and physical weakness, for instance. Some young men and women express shame about masturbation in the belief that they are unique in practicing it. It can be an enormous relief to young persons who feel guilt, shame, or fear of the consequences of their masturbatory practices, to be told by a counselor that it is quite normal and a usual prelude to full sexuality. In initiating and familiarizing young people with sexual sensations in preparation for heterosexual intimacy, masturbation is harmless and natural unless it becomes obsessive, in which case the problem should be explored in counseling.

Myths about menstruation are less common today, but occasionally one finds female clients who have been told they should not go swimming, take strenuous exercise or even take a bath during menstruation. Missed periods are often a cause of anxiety, leading to fear of some functional disorder, or inadequacy as a woman. Occasional missed periods can be caused by tension, psychological factors, excessive fatigue or physical illness; irregularity of periods is often due to psychological rather than organic causes. Intercourse during menstruation is not harmful, as some women have been led to believe. While pregnancy at this time is unlikely it is possible unless precautions are taken.

SEXUAL PROBLEMS

Complaints of sexual malfunction, such as impotence in men and orgasmic failure in women, can often be treated effectively in short-term counseling. Unless such conditions are due to longstanding and deep-seated inhibitions, support and sexual education can offer welcome relief to clients who are troubled by fears of sexual inadequacy or failure.

The exploitation of sex in the media and the "how to" books and literature on the joys of sex which have proliferated in recent years, have contributed to anxieties about their sexuality in both men and women. While current permissiveness may have promoted a freer expression and enjoyment of sex in some, it also implies that any man or woman who is not always sexually potent and enjoying it fully, is missing something and must be inadequate. The kind of illusion that is promulgated is just that—an illusion—and is misleading. The truth is that normal men are not always sexually potent and normal women not always orgasmic. Few in our culture are without some sexual inhibitions, just as the free expression of aggressiveness is necessarily inhibited. This is simply a human condition in our society. Sexual readiness and enjoyment depends on time, place, physical well-being and psychological factors affecting both partners.

Sexual Fears and Malfunctions in Men

Transient Impotence

It can be devastating to a young man to experience impotence in his first attempt at intercourse. He may turn up at a mental health agency in near panic, convinced there is something radically wrong with him. Reassurance that this is quite common, and that it happens at times to most men, will be most helpful in allaying his anxiety. However, before such support is offered, he should be encouraged to explore the situation in which his failure occurred, his feelings about his sexuality and, of course, his relationship with the girl involved. A number of factors may contribute to impotence: emotional tension and apprehension about his ability to perform; doubts and guilt feelings because of parents' repressive attitudes about sex; fear of pregnancy or being found out by parents, as well as the girl's attitude.

The young man's relationship with his girl friend and her reaction to his failure will be important to understand, not only because it may have a bearing on his impotence but because it may be helpful in determining how best to help him in counseling. If she is loving and understanding and did not criticize or depreciate him, she can help him to overcome his inhibition. If she is herself a virgin and fearful, her uneasiness may be communicated and compound his own anxiety. If such is the case, it will be supportive to suggest that they may need patience and that there is no need for him to prove himself or feel under pressure until the right moment arrives for both. If the girl was belittling in her disappointment and made her partner feel inadequate and humiliated, the relationship is probably not very promising. Some girls express their hostility to men in this way.

Explanation that transient impotence occurs to all men, that physical surroundings, one's state of health, other distracting worries or pressures, as well as psychological inhibitions all affect a man's sexual performance, can offer considerable relief, as the following case illustrates.

> A 20-year-old high school graduate attending a technical school arrived at a crisis agency in acute agitation because of impotence the previous night. He was in love with Ann, who had been on pills for a month in anticipation of their initiating intercourse; they had planned to make love for the first time at her home, knowing her parents would be away. He had had intercourse successfully with several girls in the past three years. He was bewildered by his failure with Ann, especially as this was the first girl he had really cared for so deeply.
>
> In discussing the situation, he said he had been tense with anticipation for days; Ann had had only one brief sexual affair and was virtually inexperienced; both felt guilty about sex in her parents' home. He had been counting on it so much, he told the counselor, and was humiliated and devastated when he was completely unable to perform. He was sure something was wrong with him.
>
> As he and the counselor examined the circumstances and he was able to look at the situation rationally, he could see that he and Ann were probably overtense be-

> cause of the long anticipatory planning, which inhibited their spontaneity. The setting in Ann's house was a further disturbing element; they felt guilty and fearful at the possibility of her parents discovering them, especially as they knew her parents would be disapproving. As the client could accept that these psychological impediments rather than his own inadequacy were probable causes of his impotence, he calmed down and felt reassured. He and the counselor considered how it might be managed more happily another time. He decided there was no hurry, but that soon he and Ann would go to a motel where privacy could be assured, perhaps only to love and hold each other. He agreed it would be better not to attempt intercourse under pressure but wait until it happened naturally and spontaneously. There were, in all, three interviews with the client. At the start of the third interview he reported that he and Ann had spent two nights at a motel during the past ten days. On the second night they had intercourse naturally and lovingly.

In cases of men who complain of chronic sexual inhibition with complete or partial impotence for a prolonged period, brief counseling is likely to be ineffective. A neurotic conflict should be assumed and the client referred for psychotherapy.

Premature Ejaculation

While premature ejaculation is also usually a symptom of neurotic conflict requiring long-term therapy, it may sometimes clear up in counseling, especially if it occurs only sporadically. As with other sexual problems, the history of the complaint must be explored as well as the client's relationship with his sexual partner. A patient and nonthreatening sexual partner, who is sympathetic and willing to cooperate, can be extremely helpful in overcoming the client's insecurity underlying his symptoms. On the other hand, a woman who is deriding or belittling may have exacerbated the problem in the first place.

Sexual Fears and Malfunctions In Women

Orgasmic Failure

Fear of inadequacy aroused by the media portrayal of an idealized sexual response frequently brings women to counseling. Woman who do not experience orgasm are particularly apt to seek help, in the conviction that something must be wrong with them. However, one finds in reviewing their sexual experiences that many women have enjoyed and participated in a satisfying sexual relationship for years without having orgasm, or only occasional orgasm. The pleasures that they give to their partners, the intimacy, closeness and affection, have been sufficiently satisfying and they do not complain of feeling particularly frustrated.

Some women never experience vaginal orgasm; some enjoy clitoral orgasm if their partners are sensitive and loving in helping them to induce it manually; some have occasional spontaneous orgasm. Few are always orgasmic.

Women who seek counseling because they seldom or never experience orgasm will find comfort in learning that their condition is neither unusual nor abnormal. The exploration with a counselor may be the first time they have been able to talk freely about their sexual feelings and experiences, as women are apt to be reticent about revealing their sexual practices. A counselor who is encouraging and comfortable in examining sexual feelings with women clients and able to help them dispel some of the myths about sexual performance can be most reassuring. As the client's self-consciousness is reduced and she is enabled to freely discuss her sexuality, the way is often opened for its fuller enjoyment and acceptance.

For a female client with a long history of complete frigidity, who has avoided sex or merely tolerated it out of a sense of obligation, a referral for long-term psychotherapy should be considered, as this is a neurotic symptom unlikely to yield to short-term counseling.

SEXUAL VARIATIONS

It should be recognized that sexual drive and need vary a great deal among individuals, whether because of constitutional factors or psychological inhibition. Either one or the other partner in a marriage may become concerned because of infrequency of intercourse and feel something is missing, but it will often turn out that neither has been particularly unhappy or frustrated. It should not be surprising to learn that two persons with limited sexual needs have happened to find each other for that very reason. If it is suspected that this is indeed the case with a particular couple in counseling, treatment focused on support and acceptance that occasional intercourse may be sufficiently satisfying for their particular needs, will be more helpful than to arouse hope of some unattainable outcome. This does not suggest that improvement in sexual functioning should not always be the goal in sexual counseling, but that goals must be realistic and in accord with the client's emotional capacities.

> A young woman who had been married for less than two years sought counseling because of her dislike and avoidance of sex and what she felt were her husband's excessive sexual demands. She was raised by a repressive, devoutly Catholic mother who had always given negative messages about sex and was controlling and overprotective. She had had no sexual experience prior to marriage and was still very much under her mother's sway when she married. After marriage her mother continued to make demands on her, insisting on daily phone calls and frequent visits home. After several months of counseling that focused on her ambivalent relationship with her mother, her conflict between her sense of duty and her anger, the client began to stand up to her mother and to gain some emotional separation, gradually shifting her role from child to wife. As a result she became more tolerant of her sexuality and enjoyed intercourse occasionally. It only then became apparent that her husband was satisfied with the infrequent intercourse they practiced, that his demands had never been as excessive as she had imagined, and that they were quite compatible. It seemed unlikely that either would be able to overcome some degree of sexual inhibition, but this was acceptable since they met each other's limited sexual needs. To have attempted to free them from their inhibitions would have required long-term psychotherapy for both, for which neither was motivated.

A wide variety of sexual practices, including perversions, need not be considered damaging if they are mutually satisfying. The goal of counseling should not necessarily be to change what may seem abnormal activities, but to offer reassurance that acts which give pleasure are acceptable as long as partners do not harm one another or others. Sexual fantasies are normal. For men and women to indulge in sexual fantasies during intercourse or to have romantic fantasies involving other persons are not a betrayal of their partners, and are harmless unless carried to obsessive degrees. Clients sometimes feel guilty about their fantasies and passing attractions to others than their mates. In these cases it will be helpful to remind them that these are thoughts not deeds, that they are natural and need not be condemned as disloyalty or infidelity.

Homosexuality

Everyone has male and female components in his personality and some homosexual feelings, even though heterosexual impulses predominate in most persons. All children experience tender feelings toward parents of both sexes and the touching and caressing have led to pleasurable sensations, laying a foundation for both homosexual and heterosexual responses. Heterosexual impulses are reinforced with the powerful sexual awakening in puberty and normally take precedence over homosexual feelings. The latter may be suppressed or sublimated and find expression in nonerotic forms. For instance, men enjoy the kind of backslapping camaraderie of other males and occasional all-male gatherings; women enjoy confiding and affectionate friendships with other women and often greet each other with mild caresses. These are desirable and harmless expressions of their homosexual side.

Homosexual Panic

Emotional problems do arise when the latent homosexual feelings remain eroticized and break through the defenses, or threaten to do so under conditions of excessive stimulation. This can produce great anxiety, especially in men, when their defenses are insufficient to stem the tide of homosexual impulses. Treatment for these men, who may turn up at mental health agencies in panic, should be aimed at helping them to reinstate defenses and reinforce their heterosexuality. The following illustrates successful supportive counseling in such a case.

> A tall, attractive looking young man of 20 was shaken and almost panicky when he came to a clinic declaring he thought he was losing his mind. He had a history of fairly adequate functioning through his adolescence, had dated off and on and had had two sexual affairs with girls. Recently he had been coaching young boys aged 12 to 14 as a volunteer at a recreation center. His contact with these boys had aroused some unacceptable and frightening homosexual feelings and fantasies by which he felt threatened and horrified. He talked about his ambition to become a physical education teacher and was about to choose a major in this field. It appeared that his wishes to work with young boys both gratified his unconscious homosexual drives and at the same time threatened his inadequate defenses.
>
> It was explained that while homosexual feelings are normal, they need not lead to homosexual acts, and his basic heterosexuality was emphasized. As he calmed down after several interviews, with support and some educational information about homosexuality, he was encouraged to talk about his current and previous relationships with girls. This focus on his heterosexuality

and the shoring up of his defenses were the main goals of counseling. Because of his vulnerability to homosexual stimulation, the counselor asked if he had considered the choice of a less threatening occupation than physical education. He reflected on his interest in math and science and was relieved at an eventual decision to change to a science major, a field in which he already had a good basic background.

Counseling Overt Homosexuals: Three Case Studies

Overt homosexuals rarely seek treatment for their homosexuality or have a wish to change their sexual orientation. They have the same kinds of problems and symptoms that heterosexuals present, though often intensified by the pressures inherent in their life styles. Anxiety and depression over unhappy love affairs, conflicts with parents, school failures, career problems, guilt, and lack of self-esteem are among the manifold complaints that homosexual men and women present at mental health agencies. Treatment techniques will be determined by evaluation based on ego assessment, taking into account their particular personality qualities, their strengths and weaknesses, and the impact of their problems on their lives, just as in cases of heterosexual clients.

Homosexuals often suffer a great deal because of the restrictions their homosexuality places on their lives. Even though they may acknowledge that their sexual orientation is irreversible, they pay a high price in renouncing family life, marriage and children, and often, stable relationships. While women are as a rule more likely to find and enjoy enduring relationships with sexual partners, this seems to be rarer among male homosexuals, whose shifting and often acrimonious relationships are likely to incur pain and disappointment.

In the three cases discussed below, presenting problems were: (1) depression over the loss of a lover; (2) a father's death; and (3) school failure. While the clients' homosexuality indirectly played a part in their problems, it was not the reason for their seeking help.

> A young man in his late twenties had been severely depressed for several months before he entered counseling. He had been an overt homosexual since his first affair when he was 19, after sporadically trying and failing to consummate intercourse with women. He was intelligent and manly-looking in a boyish way and did not have effeminate mannerisms. His depression had dated from his rejection by a male lover whom he had idealized and had hoped would become a permanent partner. He said he had been seeking all his life "someone to love me," but his last disappointment convinced him that it was hopeless. He had come to acknowledge to himself that conflict-free and permanent liaisons among homosexual males were rare. Despite the impression of adequacy he gave initially, he was so lacking in self-esteem that he only felt loved and important when he received positive feedback from others. As soon as he failed to get this reinforcement he felt empty and worthless.
>
> His father, who appeared to have been a rather inadequate man, died when he was six. He was attached to his mother, who never remarried, but since his adolescence had an ambivalent relationship with her, resenting his dependence on her and her overprotectiveness. In counseling he complained about his mother's demands on him and her strong resistance when on two

occasions he wanted to take a job in another state. In exploring a series of four or five homosexual relationships, he began to recognize that he had been transferring his dependence from his mother to these mates, expecting them to be both mother and the father he longed for.

A positive breakthrough was accomplished when he was finally able to confront his mother with a sort of declaration of independence, informing her, though with much anxiety, that he was no longer going to accept handouts of money from her or tolerate her interference in his life. During counseling his positive attainments were commented on and supported, i.e., his ability to function successfully in responsible jobs and to make lasting nonsexual friendships. He was well-liked, a witty companion and an adept pianist. As he felt more confidence in himself and relished his freedom from his mother's manipulations, his depression lifted, and he made plans to accept a challenging position out of state. When he was asked near the end of a year of counseling whether he still had fantasies of finding an idealized lover, his reply was, "I don't need to. I already have someone," pointing to himself.

The counseling in this case was focused not on the homosexuality per se, but on his establishment of a more secure identity, the renouncement of his fantasy of finding an unattainable love match, and on increase of self-esteem and independence. He still had to accept the reality of the limitations imposed by his homosexual life style, but was better prepared to deal with it.

His father's terminal illness precipitated a request for counseling by a graduate student in his middle twenties, who was tall, very slender, and almost fragile in appearance. Though he had been intellectually precocious as a child, he complained of doing poorly in his studies, inability to concentrate, depression and continual quarreling with a male sexual partner with whom he shared an apartment. He had never been interested in girls and had been actively homosexual since his late teens. His parents divorced when he was ten and both soon remarried. He was on fairly good terms with his mother and stepfather, but was jealous and resentful of his stepmother and had dreaded the forced weekend visits to his father and stepmother when he was younger.

All of his old ambivalent feelings toward his father were stirred by the news that his father had terminal cancer. His recognition of his attachment to his father, his anger because his father left him, and especially his father's betrayal in marrying the hated stepmother, came out in a flood of recollections and emotions in counseling. His father died a month after he began treatment. He was alternately guilty and resentful in the following months as he worked through his loss and mourning. At the same time he learned that his sexual partner was unfaithful, and even more troubling was the partner's platonic relationship with an older woman who reminded him of his stepmother and of whom he was bitterly jealous.

In counseling sessions he was anguished, often wept, and dwelt on old memories and hurts in his efforts to come to better terms with his conflictual feelings and to give up his childhood attachment to his father.

By the time he felt ready to terminate after nine months of counseling, he left the male partner and moved to an apartment of his own. He also took his first full-time job and dropped out of college. It appeared that sufficient emotional separation from his father had been accomplished to enable him to grow up and assume a more adult identity. His lingering on in college without much scholarly motivation had been a way of prolonging his dependency.

The following case illustrates a common problem encountered in counseling homosexuals, the emotional conflict of a client in accepting a commitment to homosexuality.

> An intelligent and articulate woman of 29 who had been living with a homosexual partner for two years, sought counseling because she was depressed over failure in a professional school, felt unable to achieve and very confused. She had been divorced for several years following a brief unsuccessful marriage entered into impulsively when she was a 19-year-old undergraduate. Following her divorce she became involved with an extreme leftist political group, and drifted into promiscuous homosexuality. As this life became increasingly unsatisfactory, she settled down with her present sexual partner, regained some control over her life and returned to college for a professional degree. Her anxiety and depression became acute soon after she began her studies.
>
> In exploring her feelings about making a commitment to a profession, it seemed linked to also making a commitment to her homosexuality. Several weeks of counseling were devoted to reviewing her past, her unhappy relationships with men, her early conflicts with her mother, and her gradual discovery that homosexuality was gratifying and fulfilling. She had no wish to change or break off with her present partner. The reasons for her repudiation of heterosexuality and the possibilities of a choice were explored, but this only reinforced her conviction of her basic homosexual orientation.
>
> The price she had to pay for her homosexuality, the renunciation of normal family life and motherhood, and the guilt and anger this aroused, became the focus of counseling in following weeks. Entering professional training had forced her to acknowledge the reality of her situation, that she was embarking on a permanent way of life and had to face the inevitability of the compromises involved. As she began to accept that she had made the only possible choice for her, there was sadness, regret, and a sense of loss which she realized she would

probably always experience in some degree; yet her depression began to lift and her academic performance markedly improved. She did not resolve the early conflicts that led to her homosexuality—the ambivalent attachment and intense rivalry with her mother and her jealousy of her brothers. While this might have been an ideal outcome, the strength of her resistance was observed and, as with many homosexuals, motivation was not sufficient to reverse a sexual orientation that had become entrenched.

CHAPTER 11

Marriage Counseling

Marriage counseling is an integral part of the practice of all counselors in mental health agencies. Whether or not clients specifically request help with their marriages, the subject will almost invariably come up in working with married, engaged, living-together, separated and divorced clients.

Although our culture has been traditionally anchored to the institution of marriage, it is undergoing rapid and possibly disquieting changes. Whether one agrees that there is cause for alarm or that it is a healthy development, as many in the mental health profession do, the fact is that more and more married couples are experiencing conflicts in their marriages. Because of the changes in the traditional attitudes toward marriage, it is particularly important that counselors who treat unhappily married clients examine their own cultural indoctrination and prejudices about marriage and family life in order to eliminate bias and be open and objective in exploring marital problems. Sensible and nonjudgmental marriage counseling can be a positive and helpful service of particular value today.

FOUR COMMON MISCONCEPTIONS

Before discussing counseling techniques, some of the misconceptions and mystiques about marriage counseling need to be dispelled. The aims and procedure of marriage counseling are largely misunderstood by the lay public and, to some degree, within the mental health profession as well. Common erroneous assumptions are that (1) marriage counseling is a specific professional discipline; (2) the "marriage" is treated as an entity and focus for counseling; (3) the sole aim in marriage counseling is to salvage a faltering or unhappy marriage; and (4) marriage counseling follows a formula whereby clients participate in a procedure designed by the counselor.

Examination of each of these misconceptions will not only clear up some myths, but help to define and clarify a positive concept of marriage counseling, how it is done, by whom, and what its purposes and values are.

1. *Marriage counseling is not a distinct discipline—it simply focusses on a special problem.* Marriage counseling is not a unique or distinct discipline any more than is counseling persons who have sexual problems or adolescent conflicts or depressions, or who complain of school or job failure. It offers help for troubled individuals with a particular problem—conflict, unhappiness or dissatisfaction with their marriage. As in counseling clients with any other disturbing complaints, counselors explore with married clients the history of their difficulties, the onset of the problems, their views of their marriage, attitudes toward one another, and their goals and options. The counselor's

function is to aid them in understanding their feelings, assessing the value, meaning and prospects of their marriage, as well as searching for acceptable solutions for their difficulties. Of course, during the learning period counselors should have the help of experienced supervisors just as they receive help in working with their other clients. With time and experience they should expect to develop skills and technical ability.

While some colleges and universities in recent years have introduced programs leading to master's degrees in marital and family therapy, marriage counseling is practiced by professionals in all the clinical mental health disciplines, including psychology, psychiatry, social work, guidance counseling and pastoral counseling. Some counselors do specialize in marriage counseling just as there is some specialization in other areas of counseling. These practitioners are usually engaged in private practice or work in private marriage counseling clinics.

Laws in nine states now require that individuals who advertise themselves as marriage counselors and engage in private practice be licensed or certified. Requirements vary according to state standards, but in general demand a specific number of years of experience under supervision by qualified professionals and at least master's degrees in their particular disciplines. The laws were enacted to protect clients from unqualified practitioners without professional credentials who advertise themselves as marriage counselors. States which have licensing laws as of 1984 include California, Florida, Georgia, Michigan, Nevada, New Jersey, North Carolina, Utah and Virginia. Legislation is sought and pending in other states. In states without licensing, clients are warned to check the professional background of marriage counselors before consulting them.

In community mental health clinics, family agencies and crisis centers all counselors do marriage counseling just as they help clients with other personal and emotional problems. Even those who specialize and enter private practice have usually received their training and experience in such agencies. Courses in marriage and family counseling are offered as part of the curricula in most graduate professional programs in social work, psychology and guidance and counseling.

2. *One does not treat the marriage—one treats the individuals within the relationship*. One cannot treat a marriage, but only the individuals who are involved in this particular relationship. The personalities partners have brought into the marriage, their reasons for marrying each other, their expectations of the marriage and the interaction that takes place can all be explored. But a counselor is still working with people, one or both of whom may be unhappily married, not with something as intangible as the marriage itself. It is true that a marriage is greater than the sum of its parts, that the marriage relationship often brings out qualities and behavior that were not apparent in each as individuals prior to marriage. This dynamic interaction created by the intimate relationship of marriage, the ways in which the partners affect each other, must be examined and assessed in counseling. But while exploration of this relationship is an important ingredient in marriage counseling and may lead to a better understanding of one another's feelings, and in some cases to a more harmonious marriage, the relative satisfaction each

partner derives from the marriage should not be lost sight of.

A concept of treating a "marriage," even if this were possible, would imply a value judgment and could lead to a focus on making the marriage work, even though it might be at the expense of one partner's personal growth. A couple who apply for counseling because being married to each other has caused distress are entitled to help in clarifying and understanding their feelings as individuals as well as partners, and with the recognition of the right of each to make an independent choice. Unless each partner feels free to participate wholeheartedly and make the compromises inherent in marriage willingly, it may be stifling for at least one partner and probably in the long run for both. Thus, the partners who are married rather than the "marriage" is the proper focus of treatment in counseling.

3. *The sole aim is not to "save" a marriage—all options are objectively examined.* The conception that the aim of marriage counseling is primarily to "save" a marriage is particularly misleading. This would suggest a prejudgment on the part of the counselor that a marriage should be patched up at all costs, whatever the prospects for the health and well-being of each spouse, and without a preliminary and objective evaluation of the marriage. Any bias toward perpetuating a marriage rather than trying to understand its dynamics would be a reflection of the counselor's own cultural indoctrination and prejudice and could thereby interfere with the clients' opportunity to examine their marriage freely and openly. Primary focus on salvaging a marriage can be harmful to clients by playing on their guilt and limiting them to one point of view rather than

allowing for an honest appraisal of their marriage and other options.

Helping couples to improve and enrich their marriage is one goal of marriage counseling and can unquestionably benefit clients who have a sincere desire to make their marriages work. In such cases, a full and unbiased exploration of the marriage relationship is still necessary in order to provide a foundation of mutual understanding on which to build. If clients and counselor perceive healthy and gratifying aspects to the marriage for both spouses, in spite of current conflicts, then counseling can proceed on a sound basis to examine contributions each spouse can make in helping themselves, their relationship and their marriage to be enriched.

Marriage counseling, however, provides many other services and is not limited to a single goal. In its broadest sense, the purpose of marriage counseling is to review the relative satisfaction marriage has brought, as well as the dissatisfaction, to help the couple evaluate and decide their marital future. This alone may represent a successful outcome of short-term counseling. Further counseling may ensue depending on the couple's decision.

Counselors using a flexible and positive approach can offer valuable help to couples and individuals in such a diversity of situations as the following:

1. If a couple decide that their marriage will not survive, to help them relieve guilt and view their decision not as a failure but as a positive choice.
2. If each spouse expects the counselor to fix the blame on the other, to help them understand that mutual incompatibility may be the difficulty rather than one spouse's "fault."

3. If only one partner appears to be motivated for help, to offer individual counseling to help him accept, alter, or end the marriage.
4. If separation or divorce is decided, to help one or both handle the situation as maturely and as amicably as possible and to minimize destructive aftermaths of separation.
5. If an individual feels miserably trapped in a marriage, to help him prepare for and to gain courage to separate from it.
6. If an individual's marriage has failed, to help him solve emotional conflicts that contributed to it and prepare him for a more satisfactory marriage relationship in the future.
7. If a client is recently divorced, to support him in adjusting to a new life and dealing with both emotional and practical problems.
8. If both partners are basically loving and motivated to build a mutually satisfying marriage, to help them examine means for achieving this.

Some clients come to marriage counseling as a last resort, not to save the marriage but to tell themselves that they "tried everything," and thus assuage guilt or feelings of failure. Others seek confirmation from a counselor that they made the right decision after having determined to separate. Still others seek to place the blame for marriage failure on their spouses in order to justify themselves. Some clients bring their quarrels to a counselor, expecting the counselor to act as a referee and to take sides. Other clients lay their whole problem in the counselor's lap, hoping that counseling will provide formulas and rules to follow which will magically repair unhappy marriages.

In agencies offering short-term counseling, probably a smaller proportion of marriage counseling is actually devoted to helping motivated couples to consolidate their marriages than in many of the other situations mentioned. Quite a large share of marriage counseling involves working with individuals rather than with couples. A husband or wife may seek help because he or she feels responsible for whatever is wrong with the marriage; to decide if he or she wants to stay married; to prepare emotionally for an eventual separation; to have help with feelings of rejection and frequent depressions following the break-up of a marriage; and to understand his or her part in the failure of a marriage in order to insure that the same mistakes won't occur again. Cases such as these all come under the broad category of marriage counseling.

4. *No set procedure is followed—approaches are flexible and varied.* Contrary to the expectations of some married clients that they will be offered some kind of "program," marriage counseling does not rely on any set formula or procedure. It can be seen from the diversity of goals and services discussed above that any preset program would be unproductive and inappropriate. Individuals and couples who seek help for their marriages are entitled to an objective and thoughtful appraisal of their particular situation and for counseling to be adapted to their special needs.

Even the question of whether a couple should be initially interviewed jointly is open to question. If the partner making the appointment expects that the couple will be seen together and his spouse has agreed to this, then a joint consultation should be offered. If, however, it is learned that the spouse is not motivated and would come only under protest to appease his mate, it is best to offer the client a choice of initially being seen alone or with his partner. In some cases, only one partner is ever seen in counseling because of a spouse's refusal to participate; in other cases, both partners may continue to be seen jointly from the start. Sometimes after a joint interview, each may prefer to be offered separate appointments, with a joint interview to follow. After a couple are seen together initially, one partner sometimes decides to drop out, and the counseling continues with the other individually. If after a period of evaluation in joint interviews, both partners conclude that they have personal problems with which they want help, each may be seen individually by different counselors, with the possibility of occasional joint interviews.

This indicates the wide variety of arrangements that are available and the flexibility of marriage counseling approaches. The decision as to how the counseling will be set up should be made by mutual agreement between clients and counselor following the initial evaluation period. While no one approach is advocated or should be adhered to in all cases, the following procedure is frequently used in evaluating a marriage: When both partners request counseling, though they may not be equally motivated, a series of four appointments is arranged. Both partners are initially seen together; each is then given individual appointments; and both come for a joint interview at the fourth meeting. In this last session, the couple's reactions and the counselor's impressions are discussed and further plans made. This may result in a decision to continue to explore the marriage jointly, to have a mix of joint and individual interviews, or for one or the other or both to have individual counseling. Even such plans should be flexible because the situation may change as counseling proceeds.

MARRIAGE EVALUATION

What Makes a Good Marriage?

As a preparation for counseling married couples and helping them to explore and evaluate their marriage, a counselor should have a clear concept of what constitutes a good marriage. Without at least some of the basic ingredients of compatibility, a marriage may be tolerable at best, or a continual battleground at worst. Most would agree on the following criteria of a satisfying marriage: (1) that the partners like each other, as distinguished from loving, (2) that they share at least some interests and have similar backgrounds, (3) that they are considerate of one another, able to listen, communicate freely and fight fairly when they disagree, and (4) that their sexual relationship is mutually satisfying.

Romantic love and sexual attraction and passion, important as they are in a happy union, are unlikely to endure over the years unless the partners genuinely like one another as well. Enjoying each other's company, respecting and appreciating particular qualities in the other, and admiration for each other, while accepting the other's flaws, are at the heart of a good marriage and can enable it to weather many storms. Friendliness also implies trust and confidence in each other.

Sharing at least some interest outside children and home will add zest to their recreational and leisure activities. Equally important is tolerance for one another's divergent interests and freedom to pursue these. If a husband is deeply involved in his business or work, his wife should be interested enough to listen and talk about it with him; if he has a hobby she doesn't share, she can still encourage it and learn enough to discuss it with him. If a wife has an absorbing job or becomes involved in community or political activities, or a hobby, she should expect to talk about and share her experiences with her husband and for him to respond and encourage her. Marriages are enriched to the degree each is free to bring in his own interests and experiences. Too much togetherness without this freedom can be stifling and eventually generate a sense of imprisonment.

Good communication in a marriage does not rule out inevitable disagreement or quarrels, but a willingness to listen to and respect a partner's point of view, complaints and feelings, is essential in establishing and maintaining communication. A partner who refuses to listen or discuss an issue and withdraws or walks away in silent reproach is behaving just as destructively as one who shouts and overrides the other. The worst kind of fighting is bringing up a battery of old grievances that are irrelevant to the issue. This leads the partner to reply in kind and to an endless and pointless bickering, with the reason for the original disagreement lost sight of.

The sexual relationship is another area in which good communication helps to avoid resentments and misunderstanding. Partners should be able to talk freely about their feelings, desires and shared pleasures, seek ways to gratify one another and be tolerant of the other's occasional disinterest or failure to respond. Endearments and talk during sex are valued and can lead to mutual understanding, where silence can often be misinterpreted or felt as rejecting. An active and intense sexual relationship is desirable, of course, but only if both share it and neither feels used or exploited. A wide variation of sexual needs exists among individuals. If those with limited sexual needs are matched in marriage, or those with more active needs are paired, a harmonious and satisfying relationship can be expected. Only when one partner's demands far exceeds the other's is there likely to be frustration, resentment and reproach for both.

It has often been said that marriage is for grown-ups. Immature persons, whatever their ages, are less able to make adjustments and accept the realities, inevitable disappointments and problems that are bound to crop up in a shared life. If partners are expecting some fantasy fulfillment in marriage, to be given to rather than to give, are impatient and intolerant of frustration, inflexible in compromise, belittling of the other's faults, they will be disappointed and end up blaming each other for their failure. Fortunately, some couples develop and mature in marriage together. In less fortunate cases, one partner may outgrow the other to the point where there is real incompatibility and the original attraction no longer exists. When this happens, the frustrations are usually insurmountable and the partners need help to release themselves from the marriage.

Evaluation of the Married Couple

With these thoughts in mind about marriage and what goes into the establishment of a good marriage, a counselor can embark on counseling married couples with a better understanding of what to look for, as clients and counselor evaluate the marriage together.

In an initial meeting with a couple who are troubled about their marriage, the counselor's first step will be to encourage each partner to state his views and complaints about the marriage, noting which one takes the initiative and how attentively each listens to the other. If there are frequent interruptions, the counselor may need to intervene and ask that each hear the other out. If one partner remains silent or passive the counselor should comment on this and try to draw this person out. Probably the most difficult task for the counselor at this stage is to remain impartial and divide his attention equally between the two so that there is no indication that he is taking sides. Since some clients will try to manipulate a counselor to line up with them against their spouses, the counselor must be on guard to avoid falling into the trap.

History of the Relationship

In exploring the couple's complaints more deeply, questions as to how and when the problems began, how they have been handled, and details of specific complaints and incidents should be inquired into. A history of their relationship should be obtained: how they met, their courtship and the early years of marriage. Was there a period of time, for instance, when their marriage was satisfying? The reasons for their decision to marry are important to explore. How did they view each other at the time of their marriage? In reply to this question, one or both may reveal an idealized image of the other or attributed qualities to the other that he or she did not actually possess. It is possible that one may have seen undesirable qualities—"He drank too much" or "She was too attached to her mother," but assumed this would change after marriage.

How Do They Feel About Each Other?

Asking each about the particular qualities in the other that he or she especially likes and the mutually satisfying aspects of the marriage will give some clues to the positive values and strengths in the marriage, which in the heat of marital combat may have been forgotten. A thoughtful and balanced evaluation of a marriage must focus on its assets as well as its flaws.

A question to each, "Do you love your husband?" and "Do you love your wife?" will give pause and the replies will be significant. Will it be a conventional answer, "Of course I do," or "Yes . . . but," or an effort to examine feelings? This should lead up to another important question: Do you like each other?

One will want to inquire about shared interests, how money is handled, who makes the decisions and how they are made. The counselor should feel free to ask specific questions about their sexual relationship and practices, the degree of mutual satisfaction each has experienced as well as any complaints either may voice.

If the counselor is comfortable about exploring their sexual feelings, it will help the couple overcome any hesitance they may feel in discussing the subject. If it turns out they have not been in the habit of talking openly to each other about sex, this will afford them an opportunity to talk about any covert resentment or previously unexpressed feelings and clear up misunderstandings.

What if one partner suspects the other of having an extramarital affair? Sometimes such accusations are made without foundation, but the counselor is not in a position to respond or evaluate it unless he has elicited information on the subject when he talks to the partners individually. Usually clients will be willing to disclose information about affairs if they trust the counselor. While the counselor may justifiably be hesitant to ask a client directly, a question such as, "Is there anything else you would like to tell me?" will often be enough encouragement to a client to confess to an affair. The counselor will naturally not betray this confidence; on the other hand, if the accusation by his spouse is untrue, the accusing partner's suspicion may be profitably aired in joint counseling.

Parental relationships also have an important bearing on marriages, especially with young couples. How much is each still involved with parents—is there parental interference, undue dependence, or resentments of one another's parents brought into their quarrels? Information about the parents' marriages, family relationships before marriage, and the family climate, culture and environment in which each grew up may be pertinent.

Reviewing this material is not so much for the benefit of the counselor making the evaluation, albeit helpful, but to engage the clients in an appraisal of their marriage. Such discussion, continued for several interviews, should be directed toward helping the couple come to a decision about their marriage: Some couples may discover enough positive indications to motivate them to cooperate in joint counseling; others may realize that the marriage is unworkable and make a decision to end it; still others may have doubts, but decide on a trial period to learn if they are able to instill new vigor into their marital relationship. The evaluation process may be accomplished in a few interviews or continue for some time while the couple thinks over their options.

It is not uncommon for some couples to drop out of marriage counseling early in the proceedings because they perceive and fear that really looking at the marriage might lead to its break-up. They would prefer not examining the relationship rather than risk learning of its weaknesses and facing the consequent threat of separation, divorce or disruption no matter how unhappy they have been together.

The neutrality of the counselor should be maintained during the evaluation so a couple does not feel influenced either to end the marriage or to endure it for conventional reasons, "for the children's sake," or because divorce would be painful. Bias on the part of the counselor can be subtly conveyed and make it more difficult for clients to make an honest appraisal of their own needs.

What is There to Build on?

A couple who cannot recall any period in the past when they felt they had a thoroughly satisfying marriage will have little to build on. If, however, there was a length of time when the marriage was stable and relatively free of conflict, this realization may give a couple confidence that the earlier relationship can be restored or at least used as a stepping stone to a happier marriage under present circumstances.

> It was quickly apparent to one young couple who came for counseling that there was nothing viable in their marriage. Neither could recall any reason for marrying except that they enjoyed dating and both wanted to get away from home. They had given no thought to the kind of marriage they wished to build, and each had developed increasingly diverse interests since marriage. The wife had returned to college; her husband had a rather menial job, no particular ambition and spent his spare time modifying and racing motorcycles. It was only pressure from both sets of parents and their outspoken prejudice against divorce that kept them together, though they were both unhappy. After exploring this and realizing that they had a right to make an independent judgment, their decision to divorce came as a great relief. Counseling helped them to view this as a healthy and positive move for both rather than as a failure in marriage. Thus, it was a maturing rather than a destructive experience.

In commenting on this case, it should be noted that the transfer of dependence on parents to spouses is commonly encountered in failed marriages of young couples. Moving directly from one nuclear family to another without first achieving personal autonomy may be a means of avoiding the transition to adulthood by merely substituting one dependent situation for another.

With marriages of longer duration, a decision to preserve a marriage is frequently made for the wrong reasons: because divorce is unthinkable, or separation would be an admission of failure, or grown children would be critical, or one should endure one's mistakes, etc. Sometimes counseling can be helpful to couples with truly miserable marriages in enabling them to examine such attitudes and allow themselves to end a mutually disagreeable alliance.

In other cases of middle-aged marriages, where a couple have gradually drifted apart, counseling may alert them to positive values in their marriages and the possibility of a new and viable relationship after their child-rearing years.

> After 24 years of marriage, one couple who came for counseling were at odds, had little to say to each other, felt that there was no mutual concern for one another and that their marriage was a mere form. They had drifted apart during the child-rearing years, the wife occupied with her family and her husband involved in his work, immersing himself in TV and sports when he was home. They had had a satisfying marriage in the earlier years and recalled a genuine liking and respect for each other.
>
> With these positives as a foundation they were encouraged to talk about the past, their current feelings of alienation, to listen to one another and to search for ways to develop a closer companionship in their loneliness. As each began to show interest and respond to the other's feelings, they were able to envision a satisfying future together. They spoke of renewing some of the activities of their courtship and early marriage, making "dates" for dinner and planning weekend trips as well as resuming their sexual relationship which had lapsed because of the resentments they had been experiencing. They decided early in counseling that their marriage was worth invigorating, and both worked toward this goal in counseling.

Is Divorce an Option?

The subject of divorce may be raised during evaluation by one or both partners, either as a realistically considered option, or as a threat one partner uses to induce the other to change or submit. In either case the subject should be explored, once introduced. What would it mean to the partner suggesting it? How does he or she envision living alone? What are the advantages and drawbacks? Would it be a relief? In accepting it as a possible solution, the counselor will induce both to review the option thoughtfully. It will soon become apparent if this was a frequently used "threat" by one partner, or a serious possibility to be weighed.

> The wife of a couple who had been married 20 years wept as she cited her grievances and recriminations against her unfeeling husband, then blurted out that she would divorce him rather than put up with his cruelty. When the counselor asked what she thought her life would be like as a single woman and inquired about possible living arrangements, financial support and social life, there was a quick about-face. Both husband and wife were obviously alarmed, her reproaches and his counterattacks subsided, and they began to discuss their problems more reasonably. In this case, by calling the wife's bluff, the counselor got the discussion back to a more adult level and made both aware that divorce was not an answer for either of them.

If, on the other hand, divorce is a seriously considered alternative, it can be thoroughly investigated with all its implications for both. The discussion then will provide a new dimension for assessing the marriage, helping the couple to recognize that there are choices and solidifying their commitment to whichever decisions they make.

The counselor's activity in the evaluation process is directed to the involvement of both partners' talking and exploring details of their interaction and, by raising questions and clarifying at times, to stimulate communication with the goal of helping them to understand and assess their marriage. As a rule, the counselor should withhold advice or direct suggestions and instead encourage the clients to search for answers.

COUNSELING COUPLES

For a couple who have decided to engage in joint counseling, the preceding evaluation process was the beginning of treatment. They gained some recognition of their conflicts and made a commitment to each other to work on their marriage. They experienced what counseling is like, the searching questions it involves, and the demands it makes on both for honest answers and self-examination. Counseling thus is a continuation of the evaluation, going more deeply into the details of their interaction and exploring means of reducing friction and giving and gaining mutual satisfaction.

In general, young couples whose marriages haven't settled into rigid patterns are more amenable and able to change, more open to new approaches to one another, and more flexible in making adjustments than those who have been married for a number of years. The latter have acquired so many ingrained and habitual ways of dealing with one another that it is both more difficult for them to recognize these behaviors and to overcome resistance to change. The outcome will depend on their capacity for insight and a genuine underlying caring for one another.

Examining Trivial Incidents

The larger problems in a marriage are most often illuminated by examination of trivial incidents. Quarrels and misunderstandings that couples bring up should be examined thoroughly, as if under a microscope. If one complains about some slight oversight on the part of the other, for example, questions as to how it came about, how each reacted and the outcome should be asked. In going into one incident thoroughly, the core of the marriage problem may be revealed. While the incident itself may seem unimportant, it is often an enactment in miniature of underlying hurts, unmet needs, the hostilities they breed and the kind of retaliations that are employed. Once a couple have examined how they reacted in such a situation and understood its significance, they are ready to take a next step to consider how they might deal with the situation differently.

In this context the counselor might point out, for the couple's consideration, a variety of ways each might have handled the situation. As counseling proceeds, continued exploration of minor incidents and the couple's reports of experiments in handling them differently will begin to build a foundation for change and mutual understanding. This should lead to further enlightenment about the larger issues which underlie the petty quarrels. Often the important conflicts have been so covered over that it is only by looking at the trivial incidents in which they are manifested that a couple are able to become aware of the feelings at the root of their problems.

Handling of marital quarrels in counseling sessions can pose a problem for an inexperienced counselor. It may be helpful to observe the quarrels that flare up in understanding a couple's interaction, but the counselor should not permit endless arguments and be put in the position of a referee. He can intervene, tell the couple that they cannot use the counseling session as a battleground, but that their feelings can be explored calmly and that each can have a hearing.

Learning to Fight Fairly

The above brings up the subject of helping a couple to fight fairly. The first rule the counselor should impose is that each not only listen, but actually hear and try to understand what the other says. Mutual shouting matches or withdrawal of one in mute resistance and silence are equally nonproductive. A second rule is to stick to the issue at hand.

> The wife of a middle-aged couple immediately shifted to enumeration of old wounds and grievances, going back ten years in response to her husband's explanations of why he could not always arrive home for dinner at exactly six o'clock. The mutual recriminations that followed became entirely irrelevant. Only when the counselor interrupted and asked them to review could the discussion get back to the original point. Many repetitions of the same behavior occurred during counseling before the wife was able to realize how unfair her tactics were and how she habitually attacked this way instead

of hearing and responding to her husband's remarks. In his frustration he had also unfairly retaliated by attacking her with cutting personal comments.

In other instances of unfair fighting, one partner may refuse to respond to the other's anger and take refuge in a prolonged and rebuking silence, or depart from the scene entirely, leaving the other to fume with his unexpressed feelings and no way to clear the air. The seemingly passive partner who refuses to fight is expressing hostility and, in a way, becomes the victor by frustrating his partner who wants to have it out. Through repetitions of such scenes, as reported to the counselor, the silent partner should be encouraged to face issues instead of running away. It may be that he or she fears and is uncomfortable with quarreling and has always run away from it without realizing that he too is expressing anger and punishing his partner in a covert way by refusing to fight. Exploring the origin of his problem with anger will be fruitful in such cases.

Difficulties in the handling of money often surface in counseling. While this may be a major source of friction, a manifestation of a deeper struggle for power, it can sometimes be rationally resolved if the couple are willing to delegate money management to the partner who is more efficient and practical. Whichever one, husband or wife, undertakes the responsibility, there should be an agreement that any major expenditures or decisions will be discussed and mutually acceptable.

EXPLORING THE ROLE OF CHILDREN

Attitudes toward child raising, especially if the parents have widely divergent views, may need to be explored in counseling. Complaints of one partner that the other does not back him up are common. When this happens the children are confused, tend to play one parent against the other, and can become the center of marital quarrels. It's not so important whether the parents are relatively strict or permissive as whether they tend to stand together on issues. Adolescent children can be particularly disruptive to a marriage, even one that has been relatively harmonious in earlier years. If either parent identifies with the rebelliousness of a child and fails to intervene in his attacks on the other parent, the result can be harmful to the adolescent and cause intense marital strife. This is exemplified in the following case:

> A couple who had a fairly satisfactory marriage for 22 years, even though both had many unresolved problems, came to counseling in complete discord. Quarrels immediately erupted with many accusations and recriminations against each other; old grievances were brought up leading to personal attacks on each other's characters. They had to be asked to halt the quarreling several times in the first interview so that the complaints could be sorted out.
>
> The wife accused her husband of having no respect for her or appreciation of her performance as wife or mother. She felt abused and depreciated. He accused her of constantly talking disparagingly to her mother and sister about him. She counterattacked by accusing him of being rude to her family. He had had a mild heart attack several months previously, and an argument ensued over whether this had been brought on by his playing golf against medical advice and whether she should have prevented him from doing so. The implication was that she didn't care about saving his life.
>
> Though the sniping at one another continued, with

frequent bouts of reproachful tears on the part of the wife, it was clear after several interviews that the couple did need each other and valued their marriage. They had not talked much about their children, an 18-year-old son and a 21-year-old daughter, except to agree that the son was stable and gave them no problems, but that the daughter was often critical and refused to contribute to any household tasks.

As they calmed down to some degree, the counselor began to focus on the daughter, why she was living at home and how her behavior affected them. It then became evident that she was the core of the problem. She was intensely hostile and rebellious toward her mother, had returned home after two years away at a junior college, and kept deferring a move to an apartment although she had a good job. It appeared as if she were perversely enjoying her role in stirring up marital strife. She continually criticized her mother, demanded waiting on, and refused to pick up her own room or even fix herself a meal. The mother had been playing the part of a long-suffering martyr and the father withdrew and took no part in the scenes.

As they were questioned about this, the wife was able to express her feelings of rejection and anger. Because her husband had not come to her protection, she interpreted this as his acquiescing in and abetting the daughter's attacks on her. While advice is not often advocated in marriage counseling, at this point the counselor took a firm stand, telling the parents that their grown daughter's living at home was imperiling their marriage, was upsetting their son, and furthermore, that it was not in the best interests of their daughter to permit her continued dependence on them. It was proposed that with the father as spokesman, the parents should present a united front in telling her that she must move out by a given date; meanwhile, the father should make it a point to intervene when she made hostile comments to her mother.

The parents talked over their reaction to this sug-

> gestion for two more interviews, during which tensions had remarkably subsided. It was difficult for the rather passive father to summon up the courage to take the initiative in asking his daughter to leave, but with support he was able to do so. In two subsequent interviews, after the daughter found a roommate and moved (with relief, it appeared), the parents spoke of each other positively and fondly.

Reviewing Sex Roles

Women's growing consciousness and insistence on rights for equality are increasingly reflected in cases of marital strife. Working wives are especially vociferous in demanding that their husbands share in household and child-rearing responsibilities. With younger couples who are more attuned to current trends, cooperative plans can usually be worked out in counseling, since these husbands are more apt to accept their wives' expectations that they participate fully in family management. Many find that they enjoy it and that playing a larger role in the home is more rewarding than being relegated to wage-earner and excluded from the full interplay of family life. Husbands reared by traditional mothers who waited on them and assumed all the household tasks are often more resistant and resentful when their wives ask them to share in what these men consider menial work.

Joint counseling provides a forum in which couples can examine their attitudes and biases, explore what is fair and reasonable in two-wage-earner marriages and hope to come to a reasonable agreement in sharing housework and child care. Arrangements will vary with the couple's interests and skills: Some men find that they enjoy cooking and will take over this responsibility; others may contribute by caring for the children while their wives reign in the kitchen. There have been successful marriages in which the wife is the principle wage-earner in a demanding job while her husband takes over the main responsibility for household management. Conversely, many nonworking wives do find real gratification and creativity in child-rearing and domestic duties, contrary to the views of some women's libbers.

Making Environmental Changes

Often a simple environmental change will restore communication and help get a troubled marriage back on the track, as in the following case:

> A young couple married four years had been basically content with their marriage until several months before they came for counseling. Though somewhat immature and inarticulate in expressing feelings, they had no particular complaints before the husband accepted a promotion that meant working from 8 p.m. to 4 a.m. His wife worked part-time days and was gone when he woke up shortly after noon. They had almost no time together as he worked the majority of weekend evenings. She had little social life and felt abandoned and rejected as she sat home evenings. Their sexual relationship suffered because of her increasing resentment, and he in turn felt rejected. Neither had been able to talk to each other about their feelings. They no longer saw the friends they used to meet on weekends, and he began to spend Sundays drinking, was silent and depressed.

Gradually, with encouragement from the counselor, the wife began to talk about her loneliness, some childhood fantasies about abandonment at five years old when her mother went back to work, and her fear that her husband no longer loved her. He in turn began to talk haltingly about his own feelings of depression, missing the good times they used to have together, and his affection for his wife. He decided after a few sessions to take a new job working days, as he was not entirely satisfied with the employment that had contributed to his depression and withdrawal. They terminated counseling shortly after this, both expressing more understanding of themselves and each other, and both agreeing that they must express their feelings more openly and talk about it when either felt aggrieved.

Alternating Individual and Joint Sessions

Couple counseling may be as brief as a few interviews to help them through a current misunderstanding or interruption of communication, or they may continue for several months, often with individual interviews interspersed with the joint sessions. In individual interviews, either or both may focus on old conflicts they brought into the marriage. One partner may have had individual counseling at the beginning and only after gaining some insight will recognize his or her part in marital disharmony and propose that the partner join in counseling. The following case is an illustration.

A young wife began counseling because of depression. She had a long history of a troubling and ambivalent relationship with her mother, which was explored in counseling. As she became aware that she had transferred onto her husband some of the hostility and disappointment she had felt toward her mother and that they had not been getting along well because of this, she suggested that her husband participate in counseling. He was receptive, and both gained a better understanding of their feelings through examination of her behavior toward him and his hurt and retaliation. In this case marriage counseling would not have been productive until the wife recognized and resolved the prior conflict with her mother.

THERAPY FOR NEUROTIC INTERACTION

Successful counseling of couples can be accomplished in many cases by helping them iron out the kinds of difficulties discussed above. Some couples, however, have developed such deeply seated animosities or have used the marriage as a battleground for unresolved early life conflicts that short-term counseling is usually ineffective.

When spouses choose each other to fulfill childhood needs rather than for their real qualities, the result is what is termed "neurotic interaction." A husband may cast his wife either in the fantasied role of the all-giving mother or as his disappointing and rejecting mother. A wife may see her husband as the remembered punitive father, the overindulgent father, or a wished-for loving mother. Whatever the combination, there is a complementarity in these choices. Each partner seems to "psych" out some qualities in the other that reminds him of the early parent figure even though each may have seemed on the surface to be very different from the parent they have come to represent.

Some of these marriages may be workable as long as each is able to fulfill his role, but if one partner fails to do so, the marriage will break down in mutual reproaches and disappointment. For instance, if a man wants his wife to be his nurturing mother, and she wants in him a strong and dominating father, and each is able to fulfill this need for the other, the marriage may be satisfying. Conversely, a passive man may be the nurturing partner and his wife the strong figure he needs, and this too, may provide satisfaction as long as the roles are maintained. All the old ambivalence once felt toward the real parent will surface, however, if either fails to provide for the other's needs. The revenge each takes then becomes excruciating.

Occasionally marriage counseling may help to restore a previously satisfying pattern if the neurotic marriage was based on needs that were possible to fulfill. This is true, for example, when one partner is dominant and the other is passive or dependent and both are loving enough to enjoy meeting the other's needs. If the marriage has been temporarily derailed, the partners may be helped to get back on the track by exploring happier times together, airing their current complaints, and gaining understanding of each other's feelings.

A common neurotic pattern is that of two dependent individuals who marry, each expecting the other to take care of him. Since neither is capable of this, both will be disappointed and reproachful and feel cheated. In counseling each is likely to demand that the other change, and the counseling will end in a stalemate.

The most painful neurotic marriages are the unions in which one partner is sadistic and the other masochistic. Because of one partner's early identification with a torturing parent and the other's with a victimized parent, each may seek to perpetuate the old situation in marriage. Either the original torturer and victim roles will be maintained or at times will be reversed so the victim becomes the torturer. The torturing may not be manifested openly or in physical actions but in a subtle psychological undermining that is continually destructive and insidious. Painful as such marriages may be, they provide enough perverse gratification so that the undercover battle may go on for years. One often sees such a marriage persist to the bewilderment of children and friends unable to understand how a couple who hate each other continue to stay together. In these cases it is the bond of hatred that sustains the marriage. It has been observed that when such a marriage has been dissolved after one partner has undergone treatment, the other partner often regresses and is unable to adjust without the prop, or defense, that the embattled marriage provided.

The above are only a few samples of the many combinations of neurotic interactions that may occur in marriage, but they illustrate the tenacious and repetitive behavior patterns that may result when two neurotic persons marry. The only effective treatment for severely neurotic marriages is long-term individual psychotherapy for one or both participants who are motivated. Psychotherapy may not patch up the marriage, but will free the partner or partners from a miserable life. In some instances when both partners are successfully treated, their marriage has been sustained. Even when unhappy partners in a neurotic marriage divorce, each is likely to repeat a similar marriage by finding another partner like the first, unless he or she has undergone psychotherapy and resolved his conflicts. The following is such a case.

A young woman of 24 had been married for three years to a weak, unloving and cruel man her own age who was almost a carbon copy of her father and a brother. The marriage repeated the pattern of her childhood when she felt unworthy, inadequate and despised as a female, but had always behaved in a pleasing and appeasing manner. She put up with her husband's taunts, constant criticism and hostile dependence on her until it became intolerable. When she sought counseling, however, she had already met another man, a friend of her husband's, who appeared attentive and loving. Only because of his interest in her could she contemplate separation from her husband and the bond of mutual dependency and hostility.

In supportive counseling over several months she gained enough self-esteem and strength to mobilize herself to leave her husband, but the separation was so threatening to her that she became increasingly attached to the other man and moved in with him. It appeared that he was somewhat more adequate than her husband but had the same underlying qualities. Fearful of examining this relationship, she abruptly terminated counseling to follow him to another state where he had taken a new job. She seemed to perceive that if she continued counseling and became healthier it would have led to another separation which she was not strong enough to tolerate.

INDIVIDUAL MARRIAGE COUNSELING

Often only one partner is seen in marriage counseling. Among the reasons are that the other has refused to participate; a separation or divorce has already taken place; only when the client comes to counseling for personal problems does the marriage unexpectedly becomes the focus of treatment, or a client feels that his or her personal problems are contributing to marriage conflicts.

Some may object that this is not marriage counseling, strictly speaking, but the marriage is usually the catalyst that brings the individual to counseling or has a direct bearing on his problems. Helping these individuals may result in improving the marriage, or for others, in gaining strength to end a marriage, in building self-esteem following a divorce, or in preparing for a more satisfying marriage in the future.

> A woman in her mid-forties came to counseling because of despair about her marriage but never made any real effort to involve her husband because she felt he was too indifferent and resistant to accept counseling. She was attractive looking, always meticulously dressed and groomed, and her efficiency and intelligence were attested to by her excellent management of the family finances and the household. She was poorly educated and had worked only a short time before an early marriage. Her husband had been a skilled factory worker for many years and was nearing a 55-year-old retirement option. He was passive, inadequate and inarticulate and almost never talked to his wife. His only interest was camping and fishing in a Northern wilderness area where he grew up. In the past year or two he had been going North alone during his frequent lay-offs, often for a week or two at a time. He never asked his wife to accompany him or even told her where he stayed.
>
> Their two sons had left home and their teenage daughter was in high school. The client felt her marriage had been fairly tolerable during early years as her husband had been more interested in the family when their sons were home. At the time the client started counseling her husband had made frequent threats to move up North when he retired and she feared he meant to leave her, though this was never openly stated.

The client had grown up with a rejecting mother and a punitive stepfather and four brothers who were often brutal and contemptuous of her as a female. She completely lacked self-esteem and felt worthless, even when she pointed out her many accomplishments as a mother and household manager. She was extremely dependent and fearful of being left and having to cope without her husband's support. Anger was always close to the surface and erupted at times against her husband, her mother and brothers, and at the counselor whenever she feared becoming too attached. Being close to anyone meant a threat of rejection.

During several months of counseling she vacillated between rationalizing that her marriage wasn't too bad and railing about her husband and his continual silence and indifference. He refused to respond to any of her questions about his plans or his feelings about the marriage and evaded all issues. She would not consider divorce, felt too inadequate to support herself and protested that it was ''unfair'' for her to be asked to give up the satisfaction of her home and domestic life. In fact, the word ''unfair'' came up often in her protests about her situation.

Counseling focused on her old feelings of worthlessness and review of her traumatic early life experiences, with the aim of helping her to gain a more positive view of herself as a woman. As she felt stronger she eventually gained enough self-confidence to investigate job training through a government agency and pending this took a part-time job. She had more or less accepted that the marriage was over by the time her husband indicated, mostly through hints, that he was planning to retire and leave the family in a few months. Because of the preparation for this in counseling, she was able to view his leaving without panic and with some relief. She could see the possibility of working full-time, retaining their home until her daughter finished school, and even felt she could attract and enjoy other men. The ten months of counseling were highly successful in helping this client to develop inner strengths leading to more independence and a more positive view of herself.

A basically good marriage that had begun to deteriorate was restored and enriched for another client after individual counseling helped her resolve personal problems which predated the marriage:

After four years of marriage during which a young couple had been attending college (she as an undergraduate and he in a professional program), irrational arguments began to flare up, he started drinking, they weren't communicating as they had in the past, and both felt unhappy and discouraged.

The couple were originally seen together in a joint interview. While discussing the marital relationship the wife made a seemingly irrelevant remark about seeing a dead dog beside the expressway several months before. She had a strong impulse to go back and pick it up. Although she didn't do so, she had been haunted by the thought ever since that it might only have been wounded and she had failed to save it. Because of this and her apparent depression, the counselor asked her to return for an individual interview.

The following story came out: When she was eight years old, her father was killed in an accident while driving a car in which she, her mother and younger sister were passengers. Her mother was seriously injured and hospitalized for several weeks, the sister had a broken arm, and the client was the only one who was not hurt. She had managed to repress her guilt and terror over the accident and functioned well for many years until the experience of seeing the dead animal while driving to school recently. This incident reactivated the old memories and feelings and had so affected her functioning that she was irritable, anxious and depressed and unable to respond to her husband. He in turn had started drinking and sniping at her because of what he experienced as rejection by her.

In several months of individual counseling, the wife worked through the traumatic experience of the accident, her relationship with her mother toward whom she had felt a covert resentment since the accident, and the client's own guilt as a survivor. No further difficulties in the marriage were reported after she began counseling, and at termination nine months later both felt the marriage was more satisfying than it had ever been. The husband had been seen individually for three interviews for help in understanding his wife's problems, and was generally supportive during her treatment.

Separation and divorce is extremely painful for a dependent and rejected partner who does not want to give up his marriage but is forced to when his spouse makes an independent decision to end the marriage. Men and women in this situation often come to counseling in a panic, unable to cope with their loneliness and depression.

A man in his early thirties who had moved to an apartment at his wife's insistence when she instituted divorce proceedings, sought counseling in the hope that he could change and therefore persuade his wife to reconsider. She complained that he was cold, never expressed affection or talked about feelings. She also accused him of lack of warmth for their three sons aged eight, six and three. She was adamant in her decision to divorce him.

He was depressed, very lonely, and had no outlet but work and occasional golf and racquet ball. The sports seemed to offer him some expression for his aggression. He was a passive, dependent individual who was submissive to his superiors at work and in general to his wife.

He was the only child of strict Catholic parents, born when his mother was in her late thirties and his father over forty. His parents never talked about feelings or showed open affection, and he never felt permitted to express his own feelings. He was not allowed to bring friends home, and his parents had no social life. When he was asked how he felt in his loneliness and isolation as a child, he was at first unaware that he had experienced any particular feelings. He had been taught to respect his parents and been a dutiful son, just as he was a dutiful (but emotionally frozen) husband. He was surprised to realize, as he was encouraged to talk about his early life, how much anger and despair he had suppressed. He once remarked to the counselor, "I've never talked so much about myself in my life."

He was genuinely fond of his sons and visited them several times a week as well as spending weekends taking them on outings to ballgames, picnics and zoos, and sometimes keeping them overnight. After some weeks of counseling, he said he had never previously been able to show so much affection to the boys as he was now expressing openly in words and embraces. While his wife continued to refuse any possibility of reconciliation, he did speak up to her for the first time and take a stand about her excessive demands for support in the divorce settlement. He also spoke up in his defense at work on several occasions, and to his surprise found he thereby gained respect rather than rejection.

While he had been dreading the divorce hearings and the finality of divorce, when the time came he was able to cope with it emotionally. He continued to see his sons regularly, gave his wife a generous but reasonable settlement, and had gained the courage to ask two women he had met at work for dates.

In some cases of a broken marriage, where a partner has all but made a decision to divorce, he or she may come to counseling for reinforcement, to talk about and confirm that the decision was right.

A wife in her late twenties, living apart from her husband of five years and dating several men, used four counseling sessions to review her marriage and to assure herself that the divorce she contemplated was a positive move for her. There were no children, she had a good job, she enjoyed her present independence, and as she talked her conviction grew that she could manage on her own. Her marriage had never been very satisfying for either; they had little in common, and although her husband would have preferred reconciliation she did not feel especially guilty at leaving him. The counselor merely listened while the client weighed the pros and cons, observing that the client mostly needed a neutral listener while she reviewed and confirmed her decision. She felt comfortable at termination in deciding to go ahead with the divorce rather than prolonging the separation.

CHILDREN AND DIVORCE

While the problem of children in marriage and divorce has not been addressed, much has been written about the effects on children of unhappy marriages and divorces. In general, it seems to be the consensus of most studies that children are more adversely affected in two-parent families where there is an atmosphere of hostility, tension and disharmony between parents than by divorce of the parents. Children often express relief that the fighting is over and usually adapt if the parent they live with is loving and adequate. If parents who divorce can be helped in counseling to come to reasonable and mutual agreements about visiting and support, this can be of enormous benefit to children and parents. Parents can also be helped in counseling in explaining about divorce to their children and in answering their questions truthfully without placing all the blame on the other parent. It is particularly damaging to a child for one parent to enlist a child on his side and to alienate the child from the other parent.

Counselors who can be understanding and helpful to parents in coping with these problems are making just as valuable a contribution to marriage counseling as when they work with a couple to restore or consolidate a marriage.

RECOMMENDED READING

Gettleman, S. & Markowitz, J. (1974), *The Courage to Divorce*. New York: Simon & Schuster.

The authors present a fresh and stimulating view of marriage counseling and a thoughtful critique of traditional practices.

INDEX